Mixed Messages

As always, for Patricia and for our daughters Louise, Sarah and Amanda but now for our grandchildren Teddy, Jojo, Barney and Emily too.

Peter Vacher

Mixed Messages:

American Jazz Stories

www.fiveleaves.co.uk

Mixed Messages by Peter Vacher
Published in 2012 by Five Leaves Publications
PO Box 8786, Nottingham NG1 9AW
www.fiveleaves.co.uk

ISBN: 978 1 907869 48 8

Copyright © Peter Vacher, 2012
Photographs copyright © Peter Vacher unless stated

Five Leaves acknowledges
financial support from
Arts Council England

Designed and typeset by
Four Sheets Design and Print

Contents

Introduction	7
Louis Nelson	10
Norman 'Dewey' Keenan	19
Gerald Wilson	31
Fip Ricard	45
Ruby Braff	56
George 'Buster' Cooper	78
Bill Berry	89
Benny Powell	107
Plas Johnson Jr.	126
Carl 'Ace' Carter	137
Herman Riley	144
Lanny Morgan	155
Ellis Marsalis	174
Houston Person Jr.	184
Tom Artin	194
John Eckert	212
Rufus Reid	225
John Stubblefield IV	234
Judy Carmichael	264
Tardo Hammer	279
Byron Stripling	290
Acknowledgements	306
Index	308

Too many good and interesting people go to the grave without being given the chance to tell us about themselves, so that when their lives are chronicled in obituaries it appears extraordinary that we knew so little of them when they were alive.

Ian Jack,
Guardian, 1 January 2011

Introduction

Why 'Mixed Messages'? Well, it's a play on words obviously, but what it suggests to me at least is that the career commentaries of these 21 musicians are sufficiently varied, their entry points into the music diverse enough, their racial experiences so vivid that they fully justify the title. I hope you agree.

I started interviewing American jazz musicians in the late 1950s. At first, it was largely a matter of chance. We (that's my photographer friend Ian Powell and I) would turn up at a London hotel on a Sunday morning with a tape recorder and camera hoping to find a musician who might be willing to spend some time with us. This was back in the days when the Ellington and Basie bands or the Jazz at the Philharmonic troupe would take over a central London hotel as a base for their latest tour before setting off for dates in the Midlands or further north. We usually targeted the lesser-known players, sensing that they might be prepared to talk. We were seldom turned down. Some of those early 'as-told-to' interviews are included here; others appeared in my previous collection *Soloists and Sidemen: American Jazz Stories* (Northway Publications, 2004).

These informal encounters were usually cordial and often revealed telling information about the wider jazz scene. The musicians who gave us their time seemed pleased to relate their stories – some were even flattered to be asked. They appeared happy to overlook our limited knowledge and obvious lack of professionalism and forgave various mishaps with tape recorders. I think they were amused by our enthusiasm.

As a then novice jazz writer, my main intention was to document the career stories of these fascinating people. In my innocence, I thought of these endeavours as research. I didn't know how to write a feature or 'colour' piece then – I just wanted the facts, man! Along the way, we did manage to elicit some useful data and even to clarify certain aspects of the music's development in America. A case of assembling tiny pieces of the great jigsaw of US jazz history. And yes, it was the Stateside scene that consumed our interest – in more recent years the balance has shifted and now I am just as likely to be interviewing British players, veteran or contemporary.

This collection continues the focus of the earlier compilation by concentrating exclusively on American jazz musicians – some caught in conversation in London, others in the US itself or while they enjoyed short residencies at one of the many European festivals that have become so important to them. Looking back, the opportunities to spend extended time with visiting musicians in London were so much more plentiful then than they are now. Where a band like the Mingus Big Band would spend two weeks or more in Ronnie Scott's, allowing plenty of opportunities to sit down and talk with a band member who had nothing else better to do, the tendency now is for far shorter visits and for agents and managers to act as intermediaries. In and out in a matter of days, so to speak, with little time to relax so that an interview is by definition hurried and usually tied to something specific like an upcoming concert or a new album.

The other change – and an even less welcome one for a writer seeking to present career stories – is the continuing demise of specialist jazz magazines willing to take extended profiles like those included here. Of the magazines from whose back numbers I've culled these pieces, only *Jazz Journal* in the UK has survived; the much-lamented *Coda* in Canada, always a supportive outlet for my kind of work, succumbed in 2008 while even the specialist *Double Bassist* magazine has been subsumed into another title. Of the remainder, *Jazz Monthly*, *Jazz and Blues*, *Jazz FM*, and *Jazz the Magazine* all disappeared decades ago. Indeed, it could fairly be argued that I have been in at the death of more jazz periodicals than is wholly decent!

More seriously, it is now virtually impossible to find outlets (or editors) who will print lengthy pieces like those devoted to Ruby Braff, John Stubblefield or Lanny Morgan. All the more reason, then, to preserve them in a collection like this. I make no excuse for including these extended pieces – each of these players had valuable insights to offer and I'm glad to have captured as much from them as I have. Some of the musicians depicted here are journeymen, the bit players of jazz if you like, others again are prominent soloists with many albums to their names.

It has always been my contention that jazz musicians are good at spotting pretentiousness and often keen to deflate powerful egos. In other words, they 'tell it like it is' and I applaud them for that as I hope readers will as they work their way through these pieces. I have tried to retain the authentic flavour of these conversations by presenting each speaker's thoughts and comments exactly as they were offered to me. The language on the page may lack the tone and emphasis given it by the interviewee in person but rest assured the actual words are theirs. I make no apology for the fact that some of these reminiscences seem to move from topic to topic without always conforming to the exact trajectory of an individual's career. After all, how many of us can remember the precise details of our working lives, job by job, year by year?

By and large, these pieces are reproduced here in much the same form as they appeared when first published, although in some cases I have reinserted sections of my original manuscript that were excised by editors and I've tweaked the text where appropriate to allow for the passage of time. I've also added a short introduction to each article to provide some context or to update the subject's activities since these interviews were conducted. I should also emphasise that these profiles are not critical studies – you'll need to look elsewhere for detailed evaluations of these players' performances and stylistic foibles. Even so, I can confirm that each of these jazz musicians is or was a player of genuine worth.

Readers may care to note that this selection only goes some way to scooping up my published interview articles and indeed, there are far more untranscribed taped interviews in my filing cabinet than you might imagine. Why not publish more? Well, we're back to editorial willingness and sometimes one has to recognise that an interview is simply too dull to print or that it is so imbued with a play-safe attitude that it is worthless. Indeed, I recall setting out to talk to a very friendly veteran New Orleans saxophonist in Ascona, as arranged, only to find that his responses to my questions about his early days invariably resulted in a dismissive "you don't want to know about all that old stuff" (which, of course, was exactly what I did want to know) and his assessments of various famous employers veered from "fantastic" to "he was the greatest, man". The interview was quickly curtailed: an opportunity lost. Oh well.

Certain celebrated players had a standard interview that they gave everyone. This was the situation when the *Melody Maker* asked me to interview the modernist hero Art Blakey, track-suited and relaxed after he had come back from his daily run around Hyde Park. It was only when I queried his time with the Fletcher Henderson band and other formative experiences that Blakey switched off the autopilot and we began to get somewhere. Fortunately, the musicians whose stories we present here were more than willing to 'tell like it is' and to open up rewardingly about their musical aspirations and career experiences.

Peter Vacher
Pinner
May 2012

Louis Nelson

Louis Nelson (1902–1990), Preservation Hall Jazz Band, New Orleans, 1980s. Courtesy Chris Lee.

Louis Nelson the New Orleans trombonist was in London in 1975 performing with the Legends of Jazz. Then aged 72 and still very much an active musician he was happy to tour as a single or as a member of this lively band of veterans. Highly regarded by his peers, his playing with the Legends had earned him these appreciative words from the late Canadian writer John Norris: "A trombonist who has never succumbed to the huff and puff limitations of tailgate trombone. He is a versatile, lyrical player…"

Nelson revisited Britain as a soloist a number of times and often led his own bands in New Orleans until his death in April 1990. Severely injured in a hit-and-run car accident that month, he collapsed and died ten days later. He was 87.

I had been warned that he might be quite taciturn and uncooperative. In the event, he seemed content to talk about his life during a break in the tour, inviting me into his rather seedy hotel room and showing me the array of medicines he had to take. What follows is his story as he told it to me.

"My mother was a graduate from the Boston Conservatory of Music and played piano and my father, well, he could play a little organ – he used to play that in the church. My sister, she fiddled around with the piano also (she was a graduate nurse), while my brother George used to play clarinet and saxophone with a band out of Baton Rouge by the name of Tuts (or Toots) Johnson. My father was a medical doctor, and when I was born we left New Orleans and moved to a town, Napoleonville, 80 miles west of New Orleans. I stayed out there 25 years.

"First I played the alto horn, one of the peck horns they use in a brass band, and when I got started on trombone at about 14 or 15 I just picked it up myself. I heard a very fine, talented trombone player named Lawrence Hall and I say 'One day I'm going to play like that man.' He was leaving Napoleonville to go to Lake Charles, Louisiana. Never heard any more from him.

"I started playing with a band out of Thibodeaux, Louisiana, led by Joe Gabriel. He played the same kind of music Sidney Desvigne did, a full reading band. He had myself, trumpet, bass, guitar, piano, drums, saxophone, clarinet. Gabriel, he played violin; Adam Adams played guitar – they called him 'Shiny Goldmine', he had his mouth all full of gold. That was late in the twenties.

"Then around when my (first) wife died, in the early thirties, I was with Kid Harris. One of the trumpet players out of Desvigne's band passed by the house when we was having a rehearsal and he told Sidney that he was going to introduce me to him. So we met at the Bulls one night, that's a dance hall they had there in New Orleans where Sidney was playing, and he told me to come to the rehearsal out on the steamer *Capitol* and that's when I got the job. It was a swing band. Just like Basie and them. We played on the *Capitol* for about five years. We used to run from New Orleans all the way up the river to St. Paul, Minnesota. That was every summer. You see Fate Marable played on the boat every winter and when the summertime come he'd go back to St. Louis and we'd take it from New Orleans and that's why we didn't do no other travelling. We was working every night.

Sidney Desvigne's S.S. *Capitol* Orchestra, on board, New Orleans, 1931. *L-r:* Louis Nelson (tb); Eugene Porter (reeds); Eugene Ware (t); Emanuel Sayles (bjo); Adolphe Duconge (p); Sidney Desvigne (t, ldr); Marcellus Wilson (voc?); Ransom Knowling (b, tu); Adolphe 'Tats' Alexander Jr. (reeds); Theodore 'Wiggles' Purnell (reeds); Ward 'Bucket' Crosby (d).

"It was two nights for coloured. Every Monday we was on at the Pythian Temple, they call it the Roof Garden, and every Tuesday at the Bulls Aid and Pleasure Club, and the rest of the week was for white. We played at all the leading hotels, all the leading restaurants, all the country clubs and the yacht club. Around New Orleans. Well, New Orleans always was a hot town – a very popular and lively town. You always had fun and plenty pleasure down there. Still going on.

"We was playing mostly dances. Like the Roof Garden, that was a pay affair, you bring your lady company who want to dance. At least 600 people were up there. At the Bulls they had a yard and we played on one side and in the middle, that was Kid René. There was three divisions and Papa Celestin was on this other side. When he finish up playing his numbers, maybe four or five, then we play four or five numbers then go to René. That going to work from eight to two in the morning.

"We used stock numbers except when the banjo player, Emanuel Sayles and Eugene Ware, the trumpet player, would write and do the arrangements. You had to read to be in there because they had nothing but music. We didn't play no head numbers at all. The trumpet player would take jazz solos and I'd take one every now and then, you know, mix them in. And then some of the solos would be written out. You had to play what the other fellow wrote. With this Dixieland music you play what comes in your mind not what comes in his mind. We had three reeds, three brass, that's six and four, big four rhythm, that's ten. And the entertainer. Sidney Desvigne, trumpet, was the leader; Eugene Ware was trumpet, myself on trombone, Louis Barbarin on drum, Ransom Knowling on bass horn and bass violin. Emanuel Sayles on banjo, Adolphe Alexander on alto, Theodore Purnell (Alton's brother) on the other alto, second alto and you had Louis Cottrell who was playing tenor saxophone and Professor Osceola Blanchard, a schoolteacher, on piano. Eventually he added in other men, you know, as others left. One time our tenor took sick and Earl Bostic replaced him.

"The steamer *Capitol* used to leave New Orleans, then its first stop would be Donaldsville, that's coming upstream. We'd play a dance there from eight to 12 and then we'd move up to Baton Rouge, play a dance there, on to the next town, eight to 12. Then continuously until it got to St. Paul. When we was in St. Paul they had excursions, day excursions, from ten in the morning 'til five in the evening. We used to go down to Hastings Locks, go through the Locks and come back and dock at five. Then go play the night dance from eight to 12. We did that for about five weeks. Then go back vice-versa down the river, stopping, same thing going back down to New Orleans. We had our sleeping quarters, maid service, three meals a day. In those days $25 a week was plenty money. We hit all segregated towns through Mississippi, Arkansas, Tennessee; they was all segregated. Only when we got to St. Paul, where it wasn't segregated, black and white could go on. It's all changing now – took a long time.

"When the boat land you can go out and walk in town, come back. No time to hear other bands – you see, that Mississippi River, there's a terrible current and that old back-wheel boat, you got to pull right out after the dance in order to get to the next town. It was very slow. We didn't do nothing 'til that night. Just rehearsal every Tuesday. About five years playing on it. That was very good. I used to like it. Get away from New Orleans, get a rest.

"I used to like Tommy Dorsey but I never did copy him. I didn't copy from anyone. What I play is my own music – it's a gift. They didn't have too many trombone players in New Orleans in those days. We had Bill Matthews, well, he played a rough style, vamping style. Jim Robinson, he wasn't thought of until George Lewis took him to New York. I could've had that job but I was working with Desvigne every night. Bunk Johnson wanted me but I stayed right there with Sidney. After, Sidney put in another trombone by the name of Eddie Pierson. I was first chair man and he played second. We had a trumpet player there, used to play valve trombone and trumpet, and we made three-part harmony. I was the top man.

"Other bands? Well Papa Celestin's band was very good, all reading too. Along with Sidney that was about the two largest coloured bands in the city. Sam Morgan, he had something similar, about ten pieces. Later I worked with Herbert Leary; he had the same kind of band Sidney had, big swing band. I took Bill Matthews's place, that was just before the war. We did dances, waltzes and different things. Leary had a trumpet player who used to play hot. Sometimes he'd put in what we call head numbers, you understand, played without the music. I know we had Jeanette Kimball on piano, Willie Humphrey on clarinet, Gilbert Young, he's dead now, on trumpet. I just can't remember the others.

"I worked a couple of jobs with Victor Spencer, he's a left-hand trumpet player. Wonderful trumpet man. He had a small band. He just vanished out the picture. Like Steve Lewis, used to play piano, don't hear too much talk of him and he was a wonderful player. He used to play in A.J. Piron's band. Piron had a wonderful band, one of the best around the city. Henry Hardin, he was a tenor player. He had a large band. Fact is in those days they had mostly large, all-reading bands because we played mostly for dances and when they went later to them little Jitney dances, well, that's when the smaller group came in, five or six pieces continuously playing. I didn't bother with that; Sidney kept me going every night.

"The only small group I played with (regularly) was Kid Harris. Buddy Petit and Kid René had small combinations and they played that Dixieland. Petit, he was a wonderful trumpet player. If he'd been a living man today, he'd have been another Louis Armstrong. Little slim fellow: you ever seen George Lewis? About the same size as George, but he could play. He wasn't no high-note man, he'd play all his variations down in the staff. Very seldom he'd go up and make them high notes. Kid René, same thing, no high-note man either – I played with him sometimes.

"Kid Howard, he was very good. Small-group man. I played with him on dances and played with him on marching bands – in the Carnival parades. He wasn't too high but a little more fluent that Petit. When he was with George Lewis he played very good. Just before he died he started drinking so much and he got real sick. He got better and then he started drinking again.

"During the war with Japan I joined up in the Navy. All the other fellows went. I didn't have to go, I was over age but I volunteered. They was making up a band and I put up 27 months in it. Came out Musician First Class. I was stationed in Millington, Tennessee, that's about 17 miles north of Memphis. That's a big air base where they train cadets going to be pilots. We played for colours in the morning and play for those cadets, marching them and then go to the recreation hall and play between 12 and one and that's it. We gave concerts, play out of town at the USOs and different places. I played with some very good musicians there like George Dixon, used to play trumpet with Earl Hines, Skeeter Best, the guitarist did all the arranging and we had Earl Austin out of St. Louis, used to play with Fate Marable on the boat.

"After the war I got with Kid Thomas. I learnt that Dixieland style after Sidney left New Orleans. He broke his band up, him and his wife went to California. He died out there. I been with Thomas since 1945, right after the war, although like now I'm with Barry Martyn, he's my agent. I be in New Orleans such a little time that the man I put in my place in Thomas's band, I told him 'Just stay there.' They call him 'Showboy' but his name is Worthia Thomas. He plays all right. Well there's nothing 'round New Orleans now. I'm only working at Preservation Hall two nights a week – paid $35 a night for four hours. That's what put me out and made me travel. Out on the road you can make that hundred and some a night.

Preservation Hall Jazz Band, Preservation Hall, 726 St. Peter St., New Orleans, 1966. *L-r:* George Lewis (cl); De De Pierce (cnt); Billie Pierce (p); Josiah 'Cie' Frazier (d); Louis Nelson (tb); Narvin Kimball (bjo); Chester Zardis (b). Preservation Hall series. Courtesy Terry Dash.

"Then George Lewis, they wanted him to come to Japan. He made up a group to go over there, he took me. I stayed with him all the while. I helped him when the poor man was sick. I got stuck with the man. If he'd come out of his grave he'd tell you. I helped him. Fanned him, toted his grips – many nights I didn't sleep. Poor man, gasping for breath. Emphysema they call it; the same as asthma. Terrible. He said the most he ever weighed in his life was 100 pounds. I went over to Japan with him three years, '63, '64 and '65 and then I went back three years myself, one year with Thomas, two years with a group I made up. I've played to over 300,000 Japanese people. I've been there more times – get me straight – than any musician from New Orleans. When I was with Kid Thomas on that George Wein package with Dizzy Gillespie I went to Poland, Romania and Yugoslavia. And then Australia, Malaysia, Dakar, Hong Kong – I've been almost around the world. All since '63.

The Legends of Jazz, unknown US location, possibly Los Angeles CA, c.1974. l-r: Ed Garland (b); Joe Darensbourg (cl); Andy Blakeney (t); Louis Nelson (tb); Barry Martyn (d, ldr); Alton Purnell (p, *obscured*). Photo by Julius Adelman.

"I used to work for the Post Office, drive a truck, haul the mail from the trains to the office where they sort it out. My brother George, he's retired from the Post Office too. He plays golf now, that's all. He had trouble with his mouth and put the horn down. That was years back, in the thirties.

"I have two children: my son was born in 1925, my daughter in 1927 and I have seven grandchildren and about 14 great-grandchildren. No musicians – my son, he's a painter and a roofer and my daughter, she puts the roll edge on those coats in a suit factory. My daddy always told me to let your children do what they want to do and they come out better.

"I live over in Algiers. Before, I was living where I was born, 1492 Touro but I met this lady and I moved over to Algiers. She has her own home so I just sit back and rest. Take my medicine – got to take penicillin every day of my life to keep my lungs open. The doctor told me to give up that smoking so as not to go into asthma and I give up drinking about ten years ago. I just ride around in my car – take my wife out in my big Chrysler when I'm home, go visiting and see the grandchildren before I go back to the Coast and meet the Legends again.

Barry Martyn and the Legends of Jazz, Los Angeles CA 1975–78. *L-r:* standing: Louis Nelson (tb); Barry Martyn (d); Dolph Morris (b); Alton Purnell (p). Seated: Andy Blakeney (t); Joe 'Brother Cornbread' Thomas (cl). Promo from Westerberg Associates, Los Angeles CA.

"As to music, we was taught the melodic style, all phrases, reading, loud, soft, we regarded all signs. If it was staccato, we hit 'em; soft, we'd try to play it like it was written, with more feeling. That's how I try to play now so people can sing it and know what I'm playing. But I can turn it off and rough it up. Gutbucket they call it. I'd rather play the smooth style – I'm not much of a hot man, but the smooth I think I do pretty good."

First published as
'Louis Nelson and, the New Orleans Navy' in
Jazz Journal, October 1977

Louis Nelson (tb), JazzAscona, Switzerland, 1986. Photo by Romy Steinegger. Courtesy Terry Dash.

Norman 'Dewey' Keenan

Norman Keenan (1916–1980), bassist, Count Basie Orchestra, London, May 1970. Photo by Ian Powell. Courtesy Ian Powell.

I first caught up with bassist Norman Keenan at a London hotel in May 1970. Like most of Count Basie's musicians, he was cordial and had a good story to tell. It follows in the 'as-told-to' style as we taped it that day. I came to know Norman fairly well, spending time with him whenever the Basie band returned to the UK and can recall him preparing to go to work, carefully placing two 'jugs' in their brown paper bags among the rest of his travel essentials. His old boss, Eddie 'Cleanhead' Vinson, was featured with the Count on the 1972 UK tour and the Keenan-Vinson reunion was pretty exhausting to watch. I lost touch with him after Basie's next visit but I know he was excited when we published his story, complete with these rare photographs from his scrapbook.

The father of eight children, Norman husbanded his investments well and owned a number of apartments in Brooklyn. Born in the small town of Union, South Carolina, on 23 November 1916, he died on 12 February 1980 and is buried in the Veterans' cemetery at Riverhead, Long Island. A month after his death, his music friends gathered at Sonny's Place in Seaford, New York, to pay tribute to him. He had been house bassist at the club from 1974, when he left Basie, until his final illness. An avowed admirer of Jimmy Blanton, Norman took few solos, concentrating instead on laying down a propulsive bass line. His skills are evident on many of the recordings he made with Cootie Williams and Basie.

"My mother was a church singer in the choir at the African Methodist Episcopal church. My father was an old ragtime piano player and he used to play for all the dances at the Oddfellows Hall in Union. When my parents went to the dances the children went too; I was four or five years old. They'd have square dances, that was the thing at the time. At home we had records, mostly blues by Mamie Smith and things like that. We also had one of those old pedal organs in the house so I started picking up little things that I'd heard.

"Now we weren't allowed to play blues on Sunday. I was very fond of *St. Louis Blues*. I just picked it out on piano and began playing it one Sunday. This was sacrilegious as far as my mother was concerned and she gave me a good beating. I think this made me want to play even more than anything else. So at about eight they sent me to a piano teacher, Mrs. Ruth McKissick in Union and I studied under her for a couple of years.

"When I was 13, we went to New York with my grandmother. My mother and father had already migrated there to get work and left us with my maternal grandmother. When it was time to return after the vacation, for school, I just told them I didn't want to go back home. I'd adopted Brooklyn at that point. Anyway, they permitted us to stay so right away we went to look for larger apartments which were pretty easy to find during the Depression. Soon I was carrying ice, I was an ice-boy; they had no electric refrigerators at the time. I had to do this because my father's tailoring business had failed and my mother had to take work as a domestic.

"I took more piano lessons. One of my best friends, Herbie Thomas, was a good piano player so we used to have little cutting sessions. Our music was what we would call gospel-rock now. I'd listened to that music a lot in South Carolina, as far back as I can remember. I found out that I wasn't a very good piano player. We started a little neighbourhood band and there was no place for me; there were too many other guys that could play better than I could. By this time I was 15, and going to High School. Every day I'd go into the music room between classes and sit down and play the piano. The assistant dean in charge of music said I seemed to be musically inclined and asked me what I'd like to play. All of a sudden I said 'bull fiddle'. I picked myself one out from the locker room and changed all my study periods to music. Along about Christmas I was able to take a bass home on a holiday and I kept it three or four months and after that I just came out playing.

Joe Allston and His Famous Orchestra, New York, early 1930s. *L-r:* Joe Allston (reeds, ldr); Herbie Thomas (p); Cecil Edwards (t); Jimmy Simmons (tb); Jock Tuborg (g); Norman Keenan (b); Al Allston (d); Jimmy Brown (ts). Courtesy Norman Keenan.

"I joined a little group we had around in the neighbourhood. Our friend Joe Allston was the leader of the group and we started with about six or seven of us. The band was the Joe Allston Orchestra and we played club dates, dances, parties, on the East Side of New York and around Brooklyn. I was still carrying ice in the mornings and after school to pay for my music lessons and to buy my clothes. Apart from Joe and his brother Albert, who became professionals like me, we had Herbie Thomas, a wonderful tenor player, Jimmy Brown, and Cecil Edwards, a trumpeter who was also very good; they took jobs out of music later on.

"After graduation I studied under Professor Yerbury and he helped me along quite a bit. Having the piano background gave me the foundation. I play mostly chords that are basic and in this band (Count Basie) it works very good because that's the way Basie plays the piano, so there's a little marriage there between us. We have a kind of rapport.

Joe Allston and His Famous Orchestra, Brooklyn, New York, c.1933. *L-r:* Joe Allston (ldr); Herbie Thomas (p); Cecil Edwards (t); Jimmy Simmons (tb); Jock Tuborg (g); Al Allston (d); Norman Keenan (b); Mathew 'Mattie' Day, Tubs Taylor (t); Jimmy Brown (ts); Charlie Fowlkes (reeds). Personal management of Dave Popick. Photo by Kenby Studio, Brooklyn. Courtesy Norman Keenan.

"I was lucky enough to get into Long Island University for a year but jazz kinda had me by then. I quit school to join the Tiny Bradshaw Orchestra. It was our old band with Joe still the leader and Tiny just fronting. We had had a summer season out at a place called the Haufbrau in Long Island and ran into a lot of professional talent. An old comedian, Crackshot Hackley, and his former wife Doris Rubottom had given us some tips on how to play shows. Tiny had gotten word of the band somehow and he came over and quick-talked us and took over. We got all the music and enlarged the band up to 13 pieces so we were really a big band and became quite adept at copying all the other bands like Lunceford and Ellington. I was 18 or 19 at this time.

"Our trumpets were Cecil Edwards, Mathew Day, Tubs Taylor; trombones, Jim Simmonds, Mathew Vaughan; saxes, Joe Allston, Jimmy Brown, Charlie Fowlkes; Herbie Thomas, piano; Dutchie Tabard, guitar; myself, bass and Albert Allston, drums. We were a bunch of very young men on the road. We went down South, playing the old dance places, the old tobacco barns. We had a few bad days when the promoters ran away with the money. We were playing almost exclusively for the coloured community; on occasion we'd do a broadcast or we'd play some of the white clubs in the different towns. Sometimes we'd play two dates, one white date, one coloured date. Even the whites were not allowed to mix in most of the states we played in; there would be a roped-off area. But they could still come and listen.

"I left in 1939. They acted funny with the money so I cut out. By this time we'd made several changes. Henderson Chambers was a member of the band and different fellows were dropping out. Mathew Day, our lead trumpet was a bit older and he couldn't afford to be out on the road when there would be no pay-days sometimes. He and Jimmy Brown and Mathew Vaughan were all family men. They were constantly being replaced by regular professional players. Charlie Shavers and his friend Carl 'Bama' Warwick helped us out during that time. They were inseparable and both good trumpet players. Later on 'Bama' had his problems with his lip, blew it out with so many high notes. He became Music Director out at a prison on Long Island.

"Tiny Bradshaw's thing was what they used to call jive, or scat singing. He was a better drummer than he was a singer; very adept at playing shows. He'd gotten his early training from places like the Cotton Club in New York City. With his band we used to have Battles of Jazz. From time to time we played against Andy Kirk, and the Sunset Royals wiped us out a lot of times. We were the small fry of the business but every now and then we were pitted against the bigger names. We ran into Milt Larkin in Texas, a great band with Illinois Jacquet, Arnett Cobb and Cleanhead Vinson; we used to get together with them on little sessions when we came into town. We went everywhere but especially east of the Mississippi; out as far as Chicago, Omaha, and back through Kentucky, Illinois, Minnesota, Ohio, then all the Southern states, mostly into Texas, meeting all the bands, like Snookums Russell, Hartley Toots from Florida, the old McKinney Cotton Pickers etc.

Tiny Bradshaw. Tiny Bradshaw and His Famous Orchestra, Brooklyn, NY, late 1930s. Paramount Orchestra Bureau promo. Courtesy Norman Keenan.

"I joined Lucky Millinder in September 1939 for a few months, working at the Apollo and the Savoy Ballroom and out to Pittsburgh, Harrisburg and Boston. Then Henry Wells, the trombone player that was with Lunceford, started a band and about six or seven of us from the Bradshaw band joined him in late 1939 or spring 1940. Henry was singing all those pretty tunes like 'Trees' and 'Garden in the Rain'. He didn't write the roaring style, he wrote softly. Places he'd have five trombones and it was all very good. But the money wasn't there once again, and I was married by this time. So I had to leave and I was offered a job with Earl Bostic at Small's Paradise in June 1940 and stayed until the latter part of 1941. Although Earl wasn't formally trained he insisted on having a good band so we had p enty of rehearsals. He was very good at modulating and changing keys; he played several instruments very well himself. It was like going to school. We had Roger Jones, trumpet (from Don Redman's band), Ruby Thrower, alto and baritone, Herbie Goodman on piano and Eddie McCarney, drums.

"We played for shows and dances; it was a six-hour job, ten to four in the morning. Every night after work we'd go to Monroe's Uptown House which was diagonally on the corner across the street from Small's and stay until four in the afternoon, jamming and playing. Yardbird Parker was coming along at this time and he began to make a reputation around NYC as *the* player. I'd met Parker and the guys from McShann's band when I was with Bradshaw; we used to meet up in Kansas City for sessions. Parker was the main one and I was not really impressed when I first heard him. We thought he was like crazy at that time; he was above the conventional playing. We were getting ourselves together at Monroe's. Dizzy was there, little Tinney[1] playing piano, Monk, Joe Guy, Charlie Christian, one of our favourite ones, just about everybody. The harmonies were basically still the same for the bass player but there was only one player during these times that was really up to playing the fast things. That was Jimmy Blanton. New York was wide open for jammin' in clubs. One night Art Tatum would be in a place and I'd go sit in with him. We did this many times. You could even go down on 52nd Street which was beginning to come into its own. Fellows would come on my job sometimes and sit in and we'd go to after-hours joints like Max Maddocks. It was al just playing.

"Earl Bostic was enlarging his band from 14 pieces for the Apollo Theatre. But then at the end of 1941 Small's decided that they had to cut down on one of the players to save that money and that was me. Let the bass player go! I was out two weeks, then just before Christmas, Small's asked me to put the first band into the new Blue Room upstairs. I had seven or eight pieces, fellows like Floyd 'Horsecollar' Williams, Freddy Williams, tenors, and a drummer named Alston (not Albert), kinda cock-eyed guy. They were all eccentric kind of fellows, the only guys that were available at the time. It was a nice little band, playing swing and the regular jump things, all the rice tunes.

Cootie Williams and His Orchestra, debut engagement, Grand Terrace, Chicago IL, 20 February 1942. L-r: Kenny Kersey (p); Norman Keenan (b); Cootie Williams (t); George 'Butch' Ballard (d); Robert Horton, Jonas Walker, Sandy Williams (tb); Rostelle Reese, Joe Guy, Louis Bacon (t); Don Stovall (bs); Greely Walton (ts); Eddie 'Cleanhead' Vinson, Charlie Holmes (as); Bob Dorsey (ts). Courtesy Norman Keenan.

"But then I heard that Cootie Williams was starting his band. One of my friends, R.H. Horton, trombone player, was going to be in the nucleus of the band so he said 'Come on, go with Cootie.' I was kinda bored with the other guys at Small's anyway; some times they wanted to play, some times they didn't, and I wanted to play. So I gave them the library of arrangements by Robert Hicks and left them the band. In February 1942 I went with Cootie. Our first date was in the Grand Terrace in Chicago and we stayed a month. Then we started doing one-nighters. Some of the original members were Joe Guy, Louis Bacon, trumpets, Horton, Ed Burke, trombones, Eddie Vinson on alto, Ed DeVerteuil, who became one of the great baritone players, and Kenny Kersey, a great, underrated pianist and a good trumpet player.

"We started going into the Savoy and Apollo and then on the whole Keith circuit, playing all the big cities. It was in 1943 that they started making packages up and we worked with the Ink Spots, Ella Fitzgerald, Moke and Poke, and Ralph Brown. We made records and by this time Bud Powell had been in the band and another piano player, Fletcher Smith, also worked with us.

"I was drafted for Army duty in 1944. I spent my time in the South Pacific near Dutch New Guinea as a personnel clerk, on mopping-up operations. I was in an anti-aircraft unit and then a foot battalion. Later on we went to Manila and then Japan

Cootie Williams and His Orchestra, Savoy Ballroom, New York, c.1946. L-r: Fletcher Smith (p); Norman Keenan (b); Sam 'The Man' Taylor (ts); Cootie Williams (t); Eddie 'Cleanhead' Vinson (as); George 'Butch' Ballard (d). Gale Agency promo. Courtesy Norman Keenan.

where I was discharged on 10 January 1946. I rejoined Cootie's band on 20 January 1946. The band had kept going but with a lot of changes. Cleanhead Vinson had left to start his own big band and in September 1947, when he was down to nine men I joined him and stayed through part of 1949. He had Lee Pope, a very good tenor player from Monroe, LA, his cousin from Texas playing trumpet, Percy Brice, a good drummer, and Fletcher Smith for a while. We were based in NYC, booked by Universal Attractions, same people that had Dinah Washington. Eddie's singing and playing was hot. He was really good and as far as I am concerned he's the next player to Bird. We used to have things jumping, had the pots on. But later Cleanhead got kind of lazy: he had just gotten carried away with his little success. He got so he wouldn't make the jobs properly and I couldn't stand that. So eventually I left and joined a group called the Harlemaires.

"Chester Slater was the piano player and we had Carl Lynch, a wonderful guitar player, and the girl in the group that used to sing and play cocktail drums was Etta Jones. We became a tight little group. We sang together and this was my first experience at singing; what happened was that I had to sing the bass notes but sometimes I had to sing half a tone off. They were written like that by Chester. We played cocktail lounges and we did the Arthur Godfrey show and other early TV shows. We finally broke up and Carl and I went to the Village Vanguard in December 1949 with

Clarence Williams, a very fine pianist and accompanist. I stayed there with Carl and Clarence until June 1957. We played for a lot of people and became pretty sharp during that time. In the meantime I did a lot of records; all the groups with bird names like the Cardinals, the Orioles and the Ravens. Along about 1954 Harry Belafonte was getting pretty warm and I started doing all of his sessions. By now folk music was kinda catching on and I did all the first records with the Weavers, Pete Seeger and Rod McLary. We were backing all these different people at the Vanguard; later on we used to double at the Blue Angel, also owned by Max Gordon at the time.

"In 1957 the Vanguard changed its policy on Saturday nights to regular jazz groups and straight after that Belafonte asked me to go with him. I stayed until July 1962 and I enjoyed the whole experience. He had a nucleus of musicians with him; in the beginning, Bob DeCormier was director, with Millard Thomas, guitarist, Danny Barrajanos, conga drummer, and for a while, George Giordanio was playing straight drums. Clarence

Count Basie Orchestra, unknown US club, c.1971–72. *L-r*: Harold Jones (d); Norman Keenan (b); Pete Minger (t); Freddie Green (g); Al Grey (tb); possibly Paul Cohen (t, *obscured*); Sonny Cohn (t); Mel Wanzo (tb); Waymon Reed (t); Eric Dixon (ts); John Watson or Frank Hooks (tb); Curtis Peagler (as); Bill Hughes (b-tb); Bobby Plater (as).

Williams was the piano player and Franc Williams from the old Chick Webb band was on lead trumpet. We came to Europe with this group and played all the great halls in the big cities, including Kilburn in London. I left Belafonte as I'd just met a pretty little blonde girl that was also trying to get ahead at that time. I went straight into Basin Street East with Nancy Ames and through some friends of hers I was asked to join the Hootenanny TV show in NYC. I did two seasons and in fact I always like to think of myself as being the first Negro on a sustaining or regular weekly TV show.

Count Basie Orchestra, London, early 1970s. Count Basie (p, ldr); Norman Keenan (b).
Photo by Brian Foskett. Courtesy Brian Foskett.

"We used to go around all the different colleges and play their clambakes. It was a great show and I met all the people on the folk scene like Johnny Cash, Eddy Arnold, the Carter family, Buck and Owens, the Limeliters, just everybody. After that, Bob Decombier started with the Community Artists Association and I stayed with him for a couple of seasons. We had a choir of 18–20 singers and three or four musicians under Myron Weiss. We played up in Canada in a lot of small towns; all community things, sometimes with audiences of 20–30,000 people. We played real classical music, Bartók, all of that.

"Then I came back to New York to do club dates in the latter part of 1964. Eddie 'Lockjaw' Davis, who had been in the Cootie Williams band with me, knew of me. At the time he was Basie's straw boss and when they needed a bass they called me. I joined the band in March 1965. It's a great band to play with. Fellows can be kinda indifferent at times but I haven't found any band I'd rather play with other than Basie.

"For the future I don't think that I'd prefer to do much heavy travelling any more. After this band I guess that'll be just about it. Things for bands are not too good right now. Most of my life has been in accompaniment anyway. There's been very few solo spots for me."

First published as
'Musicians Talking: Norman Keenan to Peter Vacher' in
Jazz & Blues, April 1971

---

[1] The pianist Al Tinney was a harmonically advanced player who worked with all the leading beboppers as leader of the house band at Monroe's Uptown House in New York from 1939 to 1943. In later years he concentrated on commercial music and died in Buffalo, NY in December 2002.

Gerald Wilson

Gerald Wilson, trumpeter, bandleader and composer, Los Angeles CA, 2000. Courtesy MAMA Records.

Gerald Wilson is a phenomenon and a true jazz hero. He has been a trumpeter, bandleader, arranger, composer, orchestral innovator, educator, broadcaster and historian. Still active at 93, he seems to have levels of energy and of creativity that defy definition or analysis. He'd been up half the night when we talked at his hotel, flanked by his daughter and his wife Josefinas yet kept up a flow of reminiscences that left me open-mouthed. If anyone was wilting, it was me as we came to the end of the interview. Gerald sent me photographs to go with the piece and since the interview has gone on to make a number of significant new orchestral recordings on the Mack Avenue label, including a six-part suite devoted to Detroit, premiered at the city's International Jazz Festival in September 2009, and another dedicated to Chicago.

I'm conscious that our interview covered only a minute part of his career story but I'm glad that he gave me what he did. Fortunately he recorded his reminiscences at greater length for the Central Avenue Sounds project under the auspices of UCLA's Oral History Program. "I've had a very fulfilling career. I've reached all my goals. I've played and written for all the greatest jazz orchestras. I've written for movies and television, I've written for concert orchestras and I've maintained my own band for many decades. Jazz is the language I speak and it's my music," he said in 2011.

Observing Gerald Wilson in action was a treat. He carried himself like a dancer, slim, narrow-hipped and lithe. In front of an orchestra he moved with a balletic grace, darting this way and that, as he cued sections and controlled dynamics.

We talked in Gerald's hotel on the November morning following his triumphant concert in the Queen Elizabeth Hall when he conducted the BBC Big Band in a programme of his own compositions and arrangements, as part of the prestigious London Jazz Festival in November 2005. In conversation, he was as animated as he had been on the bandstand, leaning forward conspiratorially when he confided an opinion, eyes glinting, teeth gleaming in a brilliant smile as he recalled past triumphs and formative experiences. It was only the shock of white hair that haloed his expressive face that gave a clue to his age. Gerald Wilson may have been 87 at the time but I don't think he knew it.

As is the way of these things, each reminiscence sparked off another, and it soon became clear that the Los Angeles-based Wilson had an ability to summon up memories and vital detail that was of a high order. Here was a man whose regular jazz classes at UCLA commanded audiences of 400 and more. What's more, his personal history had taken him from a Mississippi Delta boyhood (born there in 1918) to a high-level career as a working trumpeter and bandleader, and on to his present eminence as an educator and composer whose work is heard on concert stages in America and around the world. It is rare – a privilege to be cherished, in fact – to meet someone whose musical experience has encompassed so much. And for so long! Gerald Wilson has played, and orchestrated or composed for just about anyone who's anyone in this business, including Duke Ellington, Count Basie, Nancy Wilson and Ray Charles, while maintaining a series of distinctive big bands of his own, all staffed by sidemen of the highest quality. His recorded legacy is substantial, to say the least, and growing, all of it bearing evidence of a distinctive stylistic signature.

Gerald Wilson Orchestra, North Sea Jazz Festival, The Hague, Holland, July 1990. Randall Willis (solo alto); Gerald Wilson conducting; Louis van Taylor (ts, left). Photo by Brian Foskett. Courtesy Brian Foskett.

Wilson always knew he wanted to be a musician. "At five, I could already read music, actually read the notes and play them on the piano," he explained. "My mother was a piano player, she taught music in the school, and she played in the Baptist church. She taught there until she retired, when it was a segregated school, and she taught there after it was integrated. My father, he fooled around with the mandolin, and he had a little trombone around the house and a clarinet, but he was really a master blacksmith, the king of it around in that area. He'd be in there shoeing the horses and fixing the metal rims on the wooden wagon wheels."

Still 91 per cent African-American today, "Shelby was only 250 miles from New Orleans, on the direct highway, so they (travelling musicians) all had to come through my home town on their way to Chicago. They'd come in cars and stop in Shelby, and get on a wagon with the mules pulling it. They'd just get in the wagon and start playing, and drive around the little town and come back and play a dance that night, and then continue on to where they were going. All black guys, but I can't remember them now," he said, shaking his head. "My grandmother owned the store in a little town four miles north of Shelby called Hushpuckena, that's an Indian name, and we had a gas pump and many of them had to stop to get gasoline. I was a kid, I used to pump gas, and I'd see these musicians going through."

Wilson's elder brother played a significant part in his younger sibling's musical education. "My brother and Teddy Wilson graduated in the same class at Tuskegee in Alabama. He played piano and he used to sub for Teddy. He's the one who really influenced me to be a musician because he'd come home during the off-season and he would play all these jazz records, and we'd listen to them together. We'd stay up all night listening to the bands coming from New York, like Earl Hines or Duke Ellington, on the radio. Not only the black bands, we'd listen to all the white bands as well," he added.

When I asked Gerald how his mother had viewed his later musical prowess, his reply startled me: "My mother didn't like jazz at all, never came to see me play in person. She was very serious with her (Baptist) religion. My mother wouldn't go in a nightclub, no, not at all, yet my father owned the building in Shelby where they had the dances. I remember bands coming from Eldorado, Arkansas, they had a great saxophone player, Spirey Wadley, he played all the saxophones. Good bands kept coming through there. My mother did see me on television later when I was the Music Director on the Redd Foxx show on ABC TV. She liked looking at the show. Wouldn't miss it."

When Wilson was 14, his family moved to Detroit, setting in train a sequence of events that proved crucial to the aspiring musician. "My parents divorced when I was eight. I went to Memphis for three years, studied at Manassas High School where Jimmie Lunceford used to teach. I had good teachers there then I got to Detroit. The school that I went to, Cass Tech, you can't go there to learn *how* to play; you (already) have to be able to play. You have to read music good. When you get there, they give you a test. One year my mother went to another school in Laurel, Mississippi. That school started at the sixth grade. My mother just passed me from the fourth grade to the sixth grade. So when I got to Detroit, they put me back to the ninth grade. That was like a blessing. I got five years of study at Cass. Music all day. Harmony and orchestration. Rudy Rutherford (Count Basie saxophonist), Wardell Gray, Bobby Byrne, trombone player, these were my classmates. Bobby's father, Clarence Byrne, was head of the music department. His boys could play every instrument in the orchestra. I'm not kidding. Saxophone, trumpet, trombone, I mean, they could *play*. The father was a trumpet player. He was teaching his trumpet players, of which I was one, and we could all play, like, double B-flats. Later on I had some problems with a mouthpiece, and it kinda messed me up for a while but I got back to a fairly good range. You gotta have range to be a trumpet player."

Asked to comment on his first influences, Wilson recalled that, "I came up when Louis Armstrong was the king of the trumpet. He was the greatest at that time. Until he played, jazz was a very rigid thing. The guys were playing like, horizontal, but here was this guy playing all over the instrument and it was loose, and it had that feeling. He could play all of Papa Joe's stuff but the stuff that he played, Papa Joe (Oliver) couldn't play. That tells you how great Louis was. In my second year in Detroit I got to see Louis Armstrong with his band. His valet would put, like, an attaché case on the piano and I'm wondering 'What's in that case?' Louis's up there blowing, I mean, he can blow! You know what's in that case? It's full of neatly laundered and pressed handkerchiefs. Now what did he do with that? He would take those handkerchiefs out and he would hold them as he played his trumpet.

"He played what is called a 'skeet' system and the side of your mouth opens up, so saliva comes out and the handkerchiefs were to keep the audience from seeing that. He could do that when he wanted to go up high. I learned how to do that too, by the way. Louis hit about 50 high Cs and people would count: one, two, three, four… they just keep counting and he just keeps hitting 'em. He could play like that all his life." Wilson was clearly in awe of Armstrong, as most trumpeters of his generation were. "I had just joined Jimmie Lunceford in Chicago, playing the Regal Theatre, and Willie Smith and Trummy Young says, 'Hey, Gerald, we gonna take you down to meet Louis Armstrong tonight'. That was one of the greatest things that ever happened to me. Later, I got to know him well. Oh yeah. I used to have a radio show in Los Angeles and I interviewed Louis not too long before he died."

I also wanted to know more about Wilson's drive to write and arrange. How had this developed? "It was first hearing Duke Ellington on his early records, like 'Creole Love Call', 'Black and Tan Fantasy'. I knew then I wanted to learn to write. Well, in Detroit, I got started with a band called Bob Perkins, fine saxophone player, but I was just a beginner. It was like a school for me and I learned a lot with Bob. Those numbers I'm talking about, he would take them off the record and orchestrate them. Never got anything from him about it, but I joined another band after that called Hal Green. He had a fine band, they played good, and there was a trombone player named Joe Wilson. You never heard of him, no, but Joe could score, he had his scoring paper, everything was transposed, and his arrangements were good. 'King Porter Stomp' that Benny Goodman played that Fletcher (Henderson) made, he could take all that off the record. Joe would help me and show me things. Milt Buckner also wrote for this band. He was a fine writer. We would play his arrangements and I learned a lot from listening to them.

"Then I joined Gloster Current's band. He was a brilliant young musician, played sax, played clarinet, he was a writer too. He could score an album. His was the top young band in Detroit. We played the Graystone Ballroom, we played Edgewater Park, that's one of the big parks there; he had all the dance things sewn up. Gloster took his band to West Virginia State College and started a music department at that college, but I didn't go. Later on, Gloster became the Executive Secretary of the National Association for the Advancement of Colored People where he remained until just three or four years ago. He was a *big* man. Very brilliant guy. That's when I joined saxophonist Cecil Lee's band. Those were professional guys," Wilson emphasised. "They'd all played with McKinney (Cotton Pickers). I was just a kid, like, seventeen. Karl George, great trumpet player, played later with Count Basie and Stan Kenton, he was in the band. I loved him. Did you ever hear of a guy named Buddy Lee? Now he could play double B-flats too, I mean he could *play* them. He was a fine writer, never did leave Detroit. He finally came in the band with Cecil Lee, so I was in the band with him too, after Karl left. He's the guy who wrote the arrangement of 'I'm Falling for You' for Billy Eckstine.

Cecil Lee Orchestra, unknown location, Detroit MI, 1939. *L-r:* Harold Wallace (ts, arr); Leonard Morrison (b); Kelly Martin (d); Jake Wiley (tb); Cecil Lee (as, ldr); Gerald Wilson (t); Todd Rhodes (p); (Howard Thompson and Karl George (t) absent from photo). Courtesy Jim Gallert.

"There was a guy in Lee's band, his name was Harold Wallace, who played tenor sax and he was a helluva writer. Milt wrote for Cecil too. You know how Milton Buckner wrote? First trumpet, so and so; second trumpet, so and so; these are the parts, no score! He'd just start writing out the parts. Harold Wallace, the same way. I can't do it, and I don't know many guys that do. Harold was a very nice guy to me. I used to pester him because he'd write arrangements all the time. He says, 'Look, Gerald, you learn the three diminished chords and then go from there. Now, this number that we played last night (with the BBC Big Band) called 'The Diminished Triangle', I had to teach the guy (BBC pianist James Watson) here chords he'd never known before. Eight-part harmony. That's my legacy. I'm the first one to use it. Duke Ellington, he'd never heard it before. He called it the double diminished.

"Here's what it does. Let's take Count Basie's band, they're playing their ensemble. The four trumpets are playing four notes, the trombones are playing the same four notes, the four saxes are playing the same notes, so they're only playing four notes! I

Gerald Wilson with his guitarist son Anthony Wilson, Newport Beach Jazz Party, Newport Beach CA, 16 April 2004. Photo by Gordon Sapsed. Courtesy Gordon Sapsed.

don't care how loud you play it, it isn't going to get any bigger than four notes. I write whole ensembles with *eight* notes. When that brass hits down on those eight notes, they're gonna blow anybody away! The trumpets are playing four notes, but the trombones are playing four different notes and then you voice your saxophones in between there. It opens up a whole new scope of orchestrating," he emphasised.

Wilson's signature harmonic concept is at its most effective on the many Pacific Jazz albums recorded by his big band and reissued on Mosaic, and on more recent albums on MAMA and Mack Avenue. He went on to tell me more about his other (playing and writing) associations, first with Duke Ellington and then with Count Basie. "I wrote fourteen numbers that Duke recorded. I didn't get credit! They were 'Smile', 'If I Give My Heart to You', 'Isle of Capri', they were on Capitol in 1954, and his own numbers, 'You're Just an Old Anti-Disestablishmentarianist' and 'You Gotta Crawl Before You Walk'. I had started writing for him in 1947, on Columbia Records. He didn't put my name on there either, but in the Ellington Capitol big box (Mosaic) the guys put everything in there that I did for him and gave me credit.

"I joined Basie's band in '48. He was getting ready to go into Carnegie Hall to do his first concert there. I lived in his house for nine weeks. He was also getting a big show ready to go into theatres with chorus girls and vaudeville acts, so that was my first job, to write the music for the show. He commissioned me to write an eight-part suite for the concert. He loved to play poker, all the little games you play with cards, he'd do that in the bus so that's why I called it 'The Royal Suite'. The concert was a huge success. We had five trumpets, we had Clark Terry, we had Jimmy Nottingham, we had Sweets (Edison). For a while I was with almost the original band, with Dicky Wells, Walter Page, Freddie Green, Earle Warren, Jack Washington, Buddy Tate, they were all still there. I'll tell you what Basie taught me by being in that band – he taught me how to swing! I did a bunch of numbers for Basie. He put a vocal group together: CQ (Price), Earle Warren, Clark Terry, me, Little Willie (Martin), that played tenor sax in the band after Buddy was gone. I did this number with the (vocal) quintet, we recorded it, 'St Louis Baby' (July 1949) and for Rushing, I did 'She's a Wine-O' (June 1949).

It's clear that Wilson's call to join Jimmie Lunceford's orchestra in August 1939 was hugely significant for the young trumpeter. "I'd gone with Chic Carter's band – only played four jobs with them. We're battling Erskine Hawkins, this is in Dayton OH, and I get a telegram from Jimmie Lunceford saying if I wanted to join the band to call this number." Disinclined to leave Carter's outfit – "we had a good band" – Wilson was astonished to hear from Sammy Lowe, Hawkins's trumpet star that Carter was to disband after the gig. "He says, 'Go and ask Ray Perry if you don't believe me.' I went over and said, 'Ray, what they talking about, the band breaking up tonight?.' He says, 'Yeah, Gerald, I'm getting ready to go home to Boston in the morning'. I went directly to the telephone and called Jimmie Lunceford. He was home and I told him I'd like to

Jimmie Lunceford Orchestra, Fiesta Danceteria, 42nd & Broadway, New York, 1940. *Rear, L-r:* Russell Bowles, Trummy Young, Elmer Crumbley (tb); Jimmy Crawford (d); Al Norris (g); Moses Allen (b); Eddie Wilcox (p). *Front:* Paul Webster, Snooky Young, Gerald Wilson (t); Dan Grissom (as); Willie Smith, Ted Buckner (cl, as); Jimmie Lunceford (ldr); Joe Thomas (ts); Jock Carruthers (bs). Courtesy mr.jazz photo files (Theo Zwicky).

join the band. He said to go down to the railroad station in the morning, told me the station to go to, said there'll be some money for you there, and there'll be a ticket to New York City. Now you can't beat that!" Wilson said, beaming.

"When I joined Lunceford, it was Duke and Jimmie first, Cab (Calloway) was next. You can look at it like this, if you're playing in the Savoy Ballroom six nights a week you're making $37 a week but Snooky Young and I, we're making eleven dollars a night with Jimmie, and when we played the Savoy Ballroom we're still making eleven dollars a night. Our band was so popular, we could out-draw Duke, we could outdraw Count. We played the Paramount in New York and all the big theatres, we'd do sometimes seven shows a day, and we'd change (uniforms) seven times, from head to foot. We had trunks to hold them, four different kinds of music stands, our own curtain when we'd go to the theatres. They take down the theatre curtain, put ours up. This was class. Plus we'd got hit records, we'd got Dan Grissom, who was a helluva singer, he also played sax so it gave the Lunceford band five saxes.

Jimmie Lunceford Orchestra, Fiesta Danceteria, 42nd & Broadway, New York, 1940. *Rear: L-r:* Gerald Wilson, Snooky Young, Paul Webster (t). *Front:* Willie Smith, Ted Buckner (as); Joe Thomas (ts); Dan Grissom (as); Jock Carruthers (bs); Jimmie Lunceford (ldr). Courtesy mr.jazz photo files (Theo Zwicky).

"I replaced Sy Oliver, so I sang in the trio, I sang in the quartet. You've heard 'For Dancers Only', well, in one part, all of a sudden after the trumpets make a certain passage, you threw the horn way up, spinning, snatch it with your left hand and continue playing. Can you imagine what the people said when you see these three trumpets thrown up in the air like that? My opinion of Lunceford? A beautiful man. A man that got respect from you without him asking. We didn't even curse in front of him. He didn't drink, he didn't smoke, he didn't curse. He played flute, he played sax, he played the guitar, he could write. He and Glenn Miller had studied with Wilberforce Whiteman, that's Paul Whiteman's father, he taught them harmony. He was a great teacher in Denver, Colorado.

"In those days there were not many black hotels, we had to live in people's homes. Jimmie had college friends in all of these places, and we'd be (staying) in doctors' homes, in lawyers' homes, see what I mean? That's the kind of guy he was. He treated all of his guys well, paid them well. When Snooky (Young) and I were making $11 a night, that's because we were new; the other guys, all the big stars like Trummy, Joe Thomas, Edwin Wilcox, were making, like, $15, $16. Wilcox, who taught me a lot, was a great writer. You know how great he was? He wrote all of his scores in *ink*. He knew it was right. And one of the greatest sax chorus writers you ever heard. You listen to the early numbers – his sax choruses were fabulous. Very difficult. Wilcox knew that I wanted to write. I'd go to him with any trouble I'm in, and he'd help me."

Wilson achieved success with Lunceford and then relocated to Los Angeles in 1942, seduced by the sunshine, performing with Phil Moore, Les Hite and Benny Carter, before enlisting in an all-black Navy Band where his colleagues included Clark Terry and Lunceford colleague Willie Smith. He organised his first big band in 1944, staffing it with many younger, more progressive musicians. "My dream was always to be a bandleader," he said. He was already into bebop, having befriended Dizzy Gillespie as early as 1937 and was present at Billy Berg's when Gillespie and Charlie Parker made their West Coast debut. "I had just recorded 'Groovin' High', I had the acetate with me. After they got off that night, Charlie and Dizzy and Norman Granz, we all went to a friend's home and played my new record. When you play it now you can see how far ahead we were. I knew Dizzy's stuff for years. See, he came to Detroit for about 12 weeks with Edgar Hayes's band. We both wanted to write so we'd get together and fool with the piano. We became great friends then and we remained so until his death.

Gerald Wilson Orchestra, debut engagement, Shepp's Playhouse, First & San Pedro St., Little Tokyo, Los Angeles CA, November 1944. *Rear:* Henry 'Tucker' Green (d); Robert Rudd (b); Hobart Dotson, unk, James Anderson (t). *Middle:* Jimmy Bunn (p); Isaac 'Zeke' Livingstone, Melba Liston, Robert Huerta (tb). *Front:* Vernon Slater (ts); Leo Trammel (as, cl); Gerald Wilson (t, ldr); Floyd Turnham Jr. (as); Eddie Davis (ts); Maurice Simon (bs).

I did a number he called 'Dizzier and Dizzier', and another, 'Out of This World', that he liked to play."

I was interested to know when Wilson last played trumpet. "I tell you, the last time was when I came to the North Sea Festival (Holland) with my band in 1990. I was still playin' then, I would play things with the brass, it was after that I returned home, and this is a funny story, I was eating my breakfast, some Kellogg's Bran Flakes, and I'm chewing and all of a sudden, I thought I bit on a rock. I laughed and commented to my wife, 'You know what, I'm gonna sue Kellogg's, there's a rock in this cereal,' just kidding, you know, and that rock was my front tooth. It had broken off, and that was the end of my career. In a single moment! It wrecked me for a while."

Gerald Wilson Orchestra, San Francisco CA, 1953–54. L-r: Cedric Heywood (p) (out of picture); Curtis Lowe (bs); Teddy Edwards (ts); Addison Farmer (b); Jerome Richardson (ts); Jerry Dodgion (as, *concealed*); Gerald Wilson (t. dir); unk (ts); Atlee Chapman (tb); Allen Smith (t); unk (tb); Elmon Wright (t); unk (tb); Ike Bell (tb). Courtesy Gerald Wilson.

A chance reference to trumpeter Art Farmer brought us finally to a little-known period of activity in San Francisco when Wilson chose to live there in the early 1950s. "In Los Angeles in 1951, I was the MD on the (weekly) Joe Adams Show (on KTTV) and Art was in the band," he said, in his slow Southern drawl. "His (twin) brother Addison played bass with me all during the time I was in San Francisco. I lived there for three years. I'd always loved San Francisco. To me, it was more like New York. First I played trumpet with Teddy Edwards's quintet at a place called the Champagne Supper Club for a few months. The guy that owned it, Don Barksdale, he was a basketball player, the first black to play in the NBA, with the Celtics. After a year, with the kind of money he made, which was nothing like they make now, we put a big band together, and he helped us," he recalled.

"There was a young fellow there named Pat Henry who was a radio announcer (he later owned KJAZZ) and he was our manager. Jerry Dodgion was in the band, Teddy Edwards played in it, Curtis Lowe, we had a fabulous band. So we had good success there, we played two or three times a week in the clubs. I took that band to Los Angeles; we played at the Oasis, that's the nightclub where all the big bands played. We made a record date there in 1954, on Federal Records. I had a fine young piano player in the band, he was from Texas, his name was Cedric Haywood. He could arrange, and everything. I had heard him with Milton Larkin's band, they were a fine band. They had (saxophonists) Arnett Cobb and Eddie Vinson. Illinois Jacquet had been in there too but I didn't meet Jacquet until he came to Los Angeles to join Lionel Hampton in 1942. I worked with Jacquet later on, that would be about 1950. I was with Dizzy Gillespie's big band in the fifties, I was with him when he disbanded. At the same time, Illinois was

Gerald Wilson, bandleader, composer, arranger, Los Angeles, 2003. Mack Avenue Records.

getting ready to do a short theatre tour and he had to enlarge his band, so I wrote the numbers for the opening with the big band, and the middle and then the finale for him, and played trumpet in the band. Ella Fitzgerald was on one of the shows with us. Illinois was a tough tenor player. He was young then and he was full of fire. He had top billing over Ella and he was always looking for top billing wherever he was. See, he had hit records. A powerful ego, sure, and not only that, he was smart, a very smart businessman," he smiled.

When I asked about future plans, Gerald smiled, and said simply, "I want to continue. I enjoy what I'm doing. I want to play my music and I plan to write some more, to do things that I can do now that I haven't done before."

First published as
'Gerald Wilson: Soundtrack to a Life' in
Coda, November–December 2006

Fip Ricard

Fip Ricard (1923–1996), trumpeter, Count Basie Orchestra, London, September 1963. Photo by Val Wilmer. Courtesy Val Wilmer.

> We turned up at Flemings Hotel in London, the headquarters for the Count Basie band during their 1963 UK tour on a September Sunday morning lugging the heavy reel-to-reel tape recorder that we used then and happened on trumpeter Fip Ricard. An engaging and friendly interviewee, Ricard had quite a story to tell. Later the same day we hung out with the band backstage at the Hammersmith Odeon as they readied themselves for their concert performance. Ian Powell's photograph of Ricard dates from this encounter.
>
> Once home, I found that the tape we had used had jammed irrevocably and wrote up the interview from memory. Years later Ricard said it was pretty accurate, which was a relief. He was absent from the Basie band when they returned to Britain in 1965. He later told me the band's 'straw boss' Sonny Cohn had somehow engineered his removal in spring 1964. After a period back home in Chicago, Ricard hooked up with his long-time friend, the pianist George Rhodes, who was Musical Director for the entertainer Sammy Davis and he eventually spent 23 years touring as Davis's lead trumpeter.
>
> After Rhodes died suddenly on Christmas Day 1985, Ricard stayed on and continued to travel the world with Davis, rehearsing the musicians and conducting when required. The drummer Rick Porello who was with Davis in the early 1980s said, "I was friends with Fip who kept me in line and out of trouble musically and personally." After Davis himself passed away in 1990, Ricard looked for work in Los Angeles but told me he was disappointed that few calls came. By the time we met again in 1995, he had ceased playing the trumpet and was recovering from colon cancer. He died in Los Angeles in the Daniel Freeman Hospital in 1996, following a heart attack. He was 72.

Search the jazz discographies and you'll come across the names of Paul Ricardo, F.P. Ricard and Flip Fortuna but they are one and the same – trumpet man Fip Ricard, seen in this country with the Count Basie Orchestra in September 1963 on a tour where the band shared performance time with Sarah Vaughan. His full name, Fortunatus Paul Ricard tended to lead to inaccuracies and variations, hence the opening to this paragraph; he preferred to be called 'Fip'. "As kids in Chicago we had our own baseball team and we decided to have some jackets made with our nicknames on the back. I was normally known by my initials 'F.P.' but my jacket came back marked 'Fip'. The name stuck from there."

Fip was born in Chicago in 1923, raised on the South Side and educated at Wendell Phillips High School. He was the first of his family, originally Creoles from New Orleans, to be born in the Windy City. "When I was in New Orleans one time they took me to see my grandfather's grave. His name was the same as mine and it was funny to see it written out on the stone. He had died in 1941 and they tell me he was a pretty good violin player, in the legitimate style, although I didn't know of this until long after I took up trumpet."

His parents had little or no interest in music although his grandmother played piano occasionally and Ricard was not involved with music in any way until he was about 15 years old, always preferring baseball. An accident provided a stimulus to consider music as a pastime. "We were out cycling one day when a car hit us. I can remember being thrown into the air and realising as I fell that I had been propelled to a height where I could look into second-storey windows of the buildings around. All I got were scratches on my knuckles – no broken bones! My friends were injured and my bike was completely wrecked. The car driver wanted to compensate me for the bike but I wasn't interested in a replacement. I suggested that he buy me a trumpet – not that I was really sure about music or anything, it just seemed like a good idea."

After a year or so Fip found himself a member of the school band but the music teacher, a German, heard him playing a few swing riffs, and lacking a feeling for good American music, made sure that Fip left the band immediately. From there, he got together with friends to play in small combos, entertaining the local youngsters. These small groups gradually gelled into a 14-piece swing band that played arrangements taken down from records. The band played at school dances and each musician made a little money, often only a few cents, but enough to satisfy schoolboy requirements. The superb trombonist Bennie Green, also a schoolboy then, was in the band.

"I was at school with Bennie at Wendell Phillips. He's a wonderful musician and he was extremely advanced musically even when young. He was the first person to teach me anything about chords. He's still terribly underrated even today[1]. He's one of the few modern trombones that isn't influenced by Jay Jay. I saw him before this tour and he was telling me that Jay Jay had asked him to work in a two-trombone group, before Kai Winding and 'Jay and Kai', but Bennie had his own group doing well with some strong records, and turned the job down." In 1941 Ricard and Green joined the big band led by King Fleming, a pianist well known in Chicago, but not often seen out of that city. This band served as a stopping-off point for nearly all the young Chicago talent, including fellow Basie trumpeter George 'Sonny' Cohn, tenorist Johnny Thompson and trumpet men Melvin Moore and Jesse Miller. Moore, in Ricard's opinion a most original stylist, was an influence and stimulating to work with, both as trumpeter and violinist. "The band played Basie arrangements, taken from the records as they came out. We used to listen to Basie all the time. For me, Harry Edison was the man. Whatever he played on record I played. I knew all his solos by heart. I couldn't read at that time, but I've always had a good ear so I was able to pick up the solos and play them. Strangely enough I didn't hear Roy Eldridge until years later."

Fleming's band played for dances every Saturday and Sunday night, the musicians sharing a percentage of the gate and often making three or four dollars for each date. Ricard was drafted into the Army in 1943 along with many other young musicians including his constant associate Bennie Green. Their first camp was only 50 miles from Chicago and as a beginner Fip was put into the reserve band. At this point music was still a hobby. Ricard could not read and was not interested enough to study, preferring to solo and continue playing by ear. He played later in the camp marching band, then moved, again with Green, to another camp, somewhat further away, but still in Illinois, some six to seven hours by train from Chicago. Here the first band was under the

Horace Henderson (p, arr, ldr), Horace Henderson Quartet, on tour, December 1974. Personal promo.

direction of the famous pianist and arranger Horace Henderson, and was ratified as an approved band, the 343rd AAF Band. Ricard graduated to the first band as he improved and thus came under the experienced Henderson. Green was always at hand, helping Ricard and continuing to amaze all with his musical ability, playing baritone horn parts to increase his command of the trombone.

"One day the dance band was playing a Harry James arrangement and I had the trumpet solo. Horace asked me why I wasn't playing the solo as written and I told him that I knew the solo anyway. He then said, 'I order you to play that solo from the music' and I couldn't. I knew then that I had to learn to read. I've never been so near the horn as I was in the Army. We got up at five to do formations, then played reveille. In the morning the marching band rehearsed, then we played for the men in the afternoon, then retreat. In the evenings we either played dances for the officers' club or played special shows in the area, often getting back to camp in the early hours."

After the European War was over the 343rd Band moved to Oakland, California, all concerned anticipating a Far East posting. Instead they took over Henry Ford's yacht moored out in Oakland Bay and played off all the many troops destined for the Pacific Area. While stationed in Oakland Fip enjoyed every opportunity to jam with the best musicians. "I used to jam all the time – there was a club in Oakland where jazz musicians used to gather and there'd be sessions there every night. Bennie Green, Jerome Richardson (who always swore he'd never leave the coast – he lives in New York now), and so many others. That's where I first heard Roy Eldridge in person – he used to have a pocket cornet that he kept in a bag in his coat pocket, specially for jam sessions. These experiences plus the Army training did everything for me; I really came out of the Army a professional musician."

In 1946 Fip returned home to Chicago and jobbed around before joining the Andy Kirk Orchestra for six months. With Kirk were, among others, Clarence Trice, a trumpeter who particularly impressed Fip with his ability to sing a phrase and then play it straight off on the horn, altoist Reuben Phillips, later leader of the house band at the Apollo, New York City, and Ben Thigpen, drummer with the band for many years and father of Ed Thigpen, Oscar Peterson's drummer. The Kirk band broke up and Fip joined the Earl Hines Orchestra, another short-lived organisation because Earl reduced to sextet size after a few months. Fip remembered John Ewing, Bennie Green, Clifton Smalls, trombones, Gus Johnson, drummer some of the time, and tenorists Budd Johnson and Johnny Thompson, an old friend from the days with King Fleming. "Johnny died in Chicago in February. He had been a close friend of mine for years."

Seemingly fated to join bands shortly before they broke up, Fip played three weeks with Gerald Wilson's big band at a club in St. Louis, alongside Snooky Young in the trumpet section. While there he heard Clark Terry and Jimmy Forrest for the first time, with the George Hudson Orchestra. Returning to Chicago Ricard received a call

Earl Hines Orchestra, brass section, unknown US location, 1947. *Rear: L-r:* Willie Cook, Marion Hazel, Fip Ricard, Palmer 'Fats' Davis (t). *Front:* Gordon Alston, Walter 'Woogie' Harris, Bennie Green, Cliff Smalls (tb). Courtesy Jean-François Villetard.

from Horace Henderson. "Horace wanted me to join his quartet. You can imagine that I was surprised to hear from Horace after those Army experiences. Still I was very pleased to work for him – it seemed like real acceptance! We toured mainly the Middle West, Montana and so on, for a year. I was the only horn and once again this was excellent experience for me. We had Chick Booth, a drummer who later worked with both Count Basie and Duke Ellington."

Tiring of the road Fip joined the famous Red Saunders Orchestra, resident at Club DeLisa in Chicago, working alongside his old friend Sonny Cohn, and replacing Nick Cooper. "Nick was a superb trumpet player and arranger but he was also a lawyer and was very busy all the time. I was sitting in his old chair when the news that he'd died came through. In all I stayed with Red six years and eight months. Sonny was with him 13 years right until he joined Basie. The tenor man Leon Washington has been with him for 20 years and the baritone player McKinley Easton has been there for 15 years. I must also mention Porter Kilbert, a superb alto man who was with Red for some years. He had been Musical Director for the Benny Carter band out on the coast and in style he was

Red Saunders Orchestra, Chicago IL, c.1948. *Rear*: unk (b); Porter Kilbert (as); unk (ts); unk; poss. Fip Ricard; unk (t). *Front*: Leon Washington (ts); unk (as); Red Saunders (d, ldr); poss. Harlan Floyd; unk (tb). Courtesy Robert L. Campbell.

a cross between Benny and Charlie Parker. His musical ideas were very advanced; I tried to play along with Porter's ideas before I could really take them.

"Red was a fantastic show drummer as Sonny will tell you; he could actually play a show in his sleep. We used to do a lot of breakfast dances, eight o'clock in the morning, after finishing the show at the club. Red would be there, sitting at the drums, fast asleep, a comedian would come on and Red would enter right on cue with his drum break."

After leaving Saunders, Ricard worked with Porter Kilbert's own band, taking over leadership when Kilbert left the band. From there he freelanced in Chicago, finding that work was plentiful. In 1957 he joined Eddie Chamblee's Band accompanying singer Dinah Washington. "I had grown up with both Eddie and Dinah at Wendell Phillips High School and I knew them very well. They were married then and having hassles all the time. Each would appeal to me, I was in the middle and I knew them both so what could I say? I had to leave after six months. Before I left we made an album for Emarcy. The band had Julian Priester, trombone, Charles Davis, baritone, Jack Wilson, piano, Robert Wilson, bass, and James Slaughter, drums.

Later in 1957 Fip moved to New York at the instigation of pianist George Rhodes, the musical director for Sammy Davis Jr. "George is really my greatest friend, musically or any other way. When I got to New York he and his wife put me up and George did everything for me. He steered me; he found jobs for me, getting me into record session work and once he even arranged a solo date for me, with strings. My knees were knocking so hard and I was so nervous that I was glad that they never released the record. I went out to work with George at a club called the Rip Tide on Coney Island. Seldon Powell the tenor player was in that band also. One night Eddie Barefield came by to sit-in and a few weeks later he offered me a job with a band under his direction, backing Cab Calloway at the Copper Door in New York. There were Herbie Jones, Francis Williams and myself, trumpets; Keg Johnson (he'd just bought his bass trombone at that time), Eddie, Willard Brown, Bill Crump, Bobby Greene, saxes; Cyril Haynes, piano, Harold Jackson, bass and Solomon Hall, drums.

"The job lasted six weeks and I was sorry to see it finish. After that I went to Bermuda for eight days with Erskine Hawkins. Jonesy (Reunald Jones) was also playing trumpet and he was very helpful. In fact he phoned me the week before I joined Basie to wish me luck and tell me that I'd do all right. As nervous as I was I appreciated that."

While in New York Fip was employed by the City Welfare Department for three months, doing youth work. He had studied sociology at university in Chicago for three years and needed to complete one more year for his bachelor degree. Married in 1950, with a son, Ricard looked upon his work in the youth welfare field as an insurance against the time when music might become a less rewarding profession.

"My boy was listening to me practise recently and I asked him if he wanted to play a horn. He said, 'No, you practise too long,' but he and Sonny Payne have a scheme where Sonny selects him a special drum kit and I pay for it. Only I'm not supposed to know about this. My wife and I have a real understanding. Being a musician's wife needs special strength; she knows that I have to go out on the road and we've talked it all over very carefully. I call her on the phone when I'm away and when I'm home it's wonderful; the kid gets home from school about three and we play baseball all the time. I've missed the last two Christmases with them but I hope to be home this time. At the moment I'm apartment hunting in New York and that way we'll be together much more."

In February 1960 Fip received a call from Red Saunders again, this time to take the place of Sonny Cohn, his fellow section man of former years but then about to join the Count Basie Band. He moved back to Chicago and stayed with the drummer until he himself joined the Basie Band in May 1962. "All through the years, whenever I was in Chicago I had been having lessons from Charlie Allen, a wonderful trumpet player who came up through all the Chicago bands and who was associated with Wendell Phillips High School for many years. He has taught many fine musicians including Sonny Cohn. These days Charlie works weekends, designs mouthpieces and teaches during the week. In fact, all the present Basie trumpet section use his Charlie Allen Special mouthpieces. For him the Basie Band has always been the epitome; he'd been preparing me for Basie for years. Each time one of the trumpets would leave he'd tell me that my turn was coming and that Basie would call me anytime now. These days I always go and see him when I'm in Chicago as does Sonny, and he puffs out his chest as he tells all the guys that two of his boys are with Basie!

Count Basie Orchestra Finsbury Park Astoria, London, September 1963. *L-r:* Eric Dixon (ts); Sonny Payne (d); Freddie Green (g); Don Rader (t); Frank Wess (as); Fip Ricard (t); Henry Coker (tb); Marshal Royal (as); Sonny Cohn (t); Grover Mitchell (tb); Al Aarons (t); Frank Foster (ts); Bill Hughes (tb); Charlie Fowlkes (bs). Photo by Brian Foskett. Courtesy Brian Foskett.

"Basie called me a few times but I was always out on the road, but this time my wife phoned me with a forwarding number, so I phoned him and he said, 'That you, Fip? You wanna join the band? Come on over.' And that was it. I had played a few times for Count when Thad Jones was having his teeth fixed and another time when Snooky was away. I joined the band when Snooky left; I don't say I took his place because nobody could take his place. He's fantastic and I'm glad to say he's doing very well right now.

"I play the second trumpet book and usually the lead alternates between Sonny and myself. Playing lead is very demanding, but I aim to do the best job I can. Don Rader and Al Aarons take the solos; I don't have any features. On record sessions Snooky Young is often added as fifth trumpet.

"There are over three hundred numbers in the book. Frank Foster writes his arrangements in the bus, and Charlie Fowlkes copies them. Each tune has a set intro

Fip Ricard (t), Count Basie Orchestra, Gaumont, Hammersmith, London, 15 September 1963. Photo by Ian Powell. Courtesy Ian Powell. (PV present).

by Basie so we don't really need to know the title. There are very few head arrangements in the book, although I do remember us putting one together between St. Louis and Denver, Colorado, one time.

"I think back to some of the trumpet players I have heard – first of all, Harry Edison; one time in Chicago when I was freelancing I played lead trumpet with a big band in a show with Gloria Lynne, Joe Williams and Harry. He helped me; he stayed backstage listening and then came and talked to me in the dressing room, encouraging me and giving me hints.

"I heard Orville Minor with Jay McShann one time – he was always buzzing on the horn. This seemed like a good idea to me so I did it all the time, until some guy asked me if my horn was leaking. I never did it again. I remember when I first heard Dizzy Gillespie – I didn't know how anybody could play so much trumpet, I felt I wanted to give up. Someone told me to take heart, after all Dizzy couldn't play all the jobs!

"Just before I joined Basie I made an album in Chicago for Riverside – September 1961 – Junie Cobb's New Home Town Band. The guy that was supposed to make the date, Bill Martin, had to go out on the road at the last minute so they called me. Red

Saunders was drumming and most of the men were also members of his band. Leon Washington, tenor, Harlan 'Booby' Floyd, trombone and Walter 'Chippy' Cole on bass. I said to Junie, 'I don't know much about playing Dixieland so you'll have to put me right.' All we had were some outlines, then solos and an out chorus. Ikey Robinson was on banjo – he's quite a character. Still everything seemed to go OK.

"Walter Cole, the bassist in the Red Saunders Band, joined Basie at the same time as me. He wasted his opportunity – he's a good rhythm man and a good reader but he had a terrible instrument. He never took care of it, used to leave it on the stand, let anybody play it. He couldn't record with it when he was with Basie – it used to sound horrible. We warned him. He's with the Trenier Twins now."

First published in February 1964 in
Jazz Monthly as 'Fip Ricard Talks to J.M.
in an Interview with Peter Vacher'

---

[1] Trombonist Bennie Green died in San Diego, California, on 23 March 1977. He was 53.
Before he joined Davis in 1967, Ricard performed with George Hunter's Moonlighters at the reopened Club DeLisa in Chicago supporting vocalist Arthur Prysock. The band included Ricard, Billy Broomfield (t); Harlan 'Booby' Floyd, Steve Galloway (tb); Donald Myrick, Earl Crosley, Hunter (reeds); Prince Shell (p, arr); Wayne Bennett (g); Louis Satterfield (b); Jimmy Duncan (d). Both Floyd and Galloway went on to work with Count Basie.

Ruby Braff

Ruby Braff (1927–2003), US, 1970s. Courtesy Chris Lee.

The cornetist Ruby Braff died on Sunday, 9 February 2003, in Liberty Commons Rehabilitation Center in North Chatham, Massachusetts, from complications due to asthma and emphysema. When we spoke a number of times on the telephone, it was obvious that this was not the Ruby of old – no strong opinions, no surrealistic statements or affectionate remembrances, for that matter, just the sound of a frail individual barely able to cope. In our last, brief chat a month before he died, Ruby told me that he would never play again. Sadly, his words turned out to be only too true.

Some of the obituaries in the national press here and in the US commented on his abrasive turn of phrase and cantankerous nature. In a considerable number of encounters extending over thirty years or more, I was fortunate enough to experience Ruby at his relaxed and expansive best, while observing that others, notably Dave Bennett who organised his UK tours, were more tested by his demands. As far as we were concerned, he wrote often, telephoned at unusual hours and kept his promises. He usually liked what I wrote about him. To say I loved his recordings and looked forward to his visits – he started coming to Britain in the 1960s – is a considerable understatement.

It was at Dave Bennett's instigation that we conducted the (videoed) interview whose transcribed text follows. Ruby was appearing at the Brecon jazz festival in Wales in August 1999 and we used up a pleasant afternoon sitting in his hotel lounge and letting him air his opinions and talk about his life. The results were spread over three issues of Jazz Journal. Short in stature and famously pugnacious, Reuben (Ruby) was a true Bostonian, born there on 16 March 1927.

Childhood

"I remember being a year old or so and I remember the effect that sound of any kind had on me. I could hear my mother humming to herself, and it had an effect on me. I knew that much. People say to me, what made you choose music? I never chose music, nature, genes and God, whatever, music was chosen for me. The proof of it is how I reacted to sounds and responded. By then radio had come in and when I heard a song being played on the air it did something to me that it didn't do to the little kid next door. That much I know, because it did it from then on."

Radio

"Radio was the college I went to and radio is still my friend. It's the most intimate source of communication to me. Everything happened on radio, it was the joy of my life to hear the radio. I had a little Zenith next to my bed, and that's how I learned to play music softly, because next to my ear I could hear the broadcasts from 11 o'clock onwards, 15 minutes apiece. They came in from all over the country, it would be: 'And now from Chicago, Stuff Smith', how the hell could I go to bed? Then: 'Now we go to New York for Art Tatum'. It just never ended until two or three o'clock in the morning. Who the hell was interested in school after this? Earlier in the evening on the main channels there would be things like the Camel Show with Benny Goodman. Then there was the Bell Telephone Hour for symphony things. Radio got us through the Depression, radio got us through everything."

Early Learning (i)
"Most of the things I learned were from the older boys. You'd go over one guy's house and he would have all kinds of Bob Crosby records, all the Chicago guys, another house would have nothing but Basies and small-group Billies, finally you got to Mayo Duca's house who owned every alternative of every single 78 that Louis ever made. That was Louis's buddy, when he came to Boston he'd stay in Mayo's house and do all his typing from there. So when I'd go there to hear records, Mayo always knew where he started with me and where he left off. Everybody came to the house. For me it was a little worse because I had to get the hell out of his house at ten o'clock and get home so I can go to school. Only I wasn't going to go to school, I was going to listen to the damned radio again. I had to hear all Mayo's stories about what Louis said before he made this record or that, and I'd say, 'I don't care. Play the record' but no, we had to hear them all. He'd play all these wonderful things and that was like a college for me."

Early Learning (ii)
"You heard all the comments, what the professional musicians had to say about everything, you learned a lot, and then you said something, and they said, 'No, you don't know what you're talking about. Shut up.' There was a lot of listening and also I'm playing with the radio all day long as well, with my horn. And by the time I'm 12, 13, 14, I'm playing gigs. I was playing parties when I was 11 and 12 years old. I knew all the tunes of the day because I played them with the radio. By ear. And then when I got to be a little older, about 14 and 15, when the older boys took off on Friday and Saturday from their gigs that they were playing to get more money, I would substitute for them. If the gig paid a dollar-and-a-half a night for me, you can't even imagine what I could do with a dollar-and-a-half. I could have the world's greatest time."

Earnings
"My father could be working all week, six days, like a horse, doing hard work; he was a cabinet-maker, and probably getting nine, ten, 15 dollars at most. I'm coming home with tips of three and four dollars a night with the promise of a taxi cab. They had to pay for my cab in front of the Silver Dollar Club all the way, a good 12 or 15 miles to where I lived, in these long, super-looking Packards and Cadillacs. Meanwhile the guy that went out to do the better gig wasn't making what I made on his gig. Why? Everybody liked this kid who knew every goddam tune. Short pants? Of course not, but I had to stay at the bar between two sailors or soldiers and not move for the entire intermission, which was not very pleasant."

Boston

"There was music in all kinds of joints, but also New York stars would come up to play sessions on Sundays. For example, there was a place called the Vanity Fair that all week would have some of my favourite people like Frankie Newton, Vic Dickenson, Pete Brown and a wonderful rhythm section with Kenny Kersey on piano. I'd wander in there on Sunday, and sit and listen to them and love that. Then there was the Savoy, which I later worked with some of the same people playing in there. Red Allen would be in there, all kinds of wonderful players would come up from New York: Coleman Hawkins would be there. The Ken Club had sessions on the Sunday afternoon and then there was the Hi Hat that had all kinds of people playing. There was a lot of things going on.

"So I got to know who all these people were. They were told around town there's a kid who plays pretty good stuff like that, and they used to ask me to play. I rarely ever wanted to play with them. I just wanted to hear them – I didn't want to go in for all that. I would never play with Coleman Hawkins. Jesus Christ! I had a record of his 'Body and Soul' that I got for eight cents, at my house that I destroyed (wore out). Think I want to sit-in with this guy, you gotta be crazy! I know a lot of people that would; I know people who would jump up on stage and play with Louis Armstrong. They have no brains.'"

Boston (ii)

"See, Boston's a strange town. They never liked you when you didn't make it and they never liked you when you did make it. They hated everybody and if you lived in Boston long enough you'd hate everybody. It was a town of sick provincialism. It was wonderful if you wanted to be a doctor or a lawyer or go to Harvard, but to be a musician was a very hard life in Boston. To make a living you had to do club dates for the most vicious people that ran those club date offices. On a Saturday night the scale was $11.50 and you were lucky to collect it in five weeks and to this day the practice still goes on in New York. They keep all that money in the bank for interest and if you don't like it that's your tough luck. For me it didn't make any difference because they never hired me unless somebody died. So when I got there they had a lot of trouble with me because I didn't read music. I knew all the goddamn tunes, rumbas and waltzes and everything that had to be played, and I'd play them and when they wanted me to play their way, I'd say, 'Bullshit'."

Club Dates

"Most of those big offices, they existed on debutant dates. Most of those people came out of being unsuccessful musicians, they played rotten and they thought you should play as rotten as they played, and they always got bands to think in their terms. Did you ever hear such silly music? This particular guy Harry Marchard had an account for Howard Johnson (he was a self-made man with 28 flavours of ice cream, became a zillionaire). Every other Saturday night he would hire Harry's orchestra for dancing in his home. He had a ballroom in his home! They couldn't get a trumpet player and they go for me, and there I was on the gig and Harry was not there yet, and they were going to go into their bullshit playing. I said, 'No, let's play the tune I was swinging on' and Mr. Johnson came up to me and said, 'Why doesn't the music sound this good all the time?' So I said, 'This is the way I always play.' He said, 'Why aren't you always here?' I said, 'They never call me. I'm here now because somebody must have died.' He says, 'You better be here from now on' and he went out and got a tray of drinks for the band. Then Harry Marchard came in and said, 'How dare you ruin my music?' called me every name under the sun. Up comes Howard Johnson and says, 'Never come here without this guy.' Harry says, 'He'll always be here' and then he says to me, 'You'll never be there.' I got so mad I took his library and all the music I wasn't reading anyway, and kicked it like a deck of cards across the dance floor. I never saw the place again."

Frankie Newton

"Frankie was a very advanced, marvellous phraser. He was very influential on me. If he played with just piano and drums – and I still think this way – the song was an entity in itself. It didn't matter to him whether he played a lot or didn't play a lot. At the end of the song he may just come and play the last four notes. That's how artistic he was. It was like a picture. I love that. I grew up hearing three-minute records, everything was on those things, whole concertos, a guy like Lester Young was known all over the world for a nice introduction he took on something.

"I played with all kinds of guys in that town. There was a guy, Ray Perry, who played violin and alto, he went with Hampton, and died very young for some reason. Slam Stewart told me during that time that I was going on Sunday sessions to watch Ray Perry and the rhythm section, Slam was at the Boston Conservatory studying bass and music. He said, 'I went over to Ray – Ray Perry would play the violin and sing – and asked if he would mind if I would take his style and use it for my bass. That's where I got my thing from.'"

Roxbury

"I lived in Roxbury (Boston's black quarter) but that wasn't the part of Roxbury they played. You had to sorta go downtown where they had the Hi Hat, Wally's Paradise, the Savoy, that was our quiet little 52nd St. Charlie Parker, later on in the 1940s, he was playing an engagement at the Hi Hat with a rhythm section and he thought he had an hour-and-a-half or two hours off and as high as he was he thought he'd go to New York and get himself whatever it was he needed to come back to play the next set. New York is a 250-mile ride if you're lucky. He got with one of his buddies and he said, 'If this car goes 100 miles an hour we can be in New York in two hours from now,' but he never came back. The club owner went out of his mind and brought him to the union, but he didn't know what union, because there were two (separate) unions, the coloured and the white union. Utterly stupid. Charlie Parker came back about a week later, forgot he was working at the Hi Hat and went to Wally's Paradise sitting-in for nothing, and in five minutes everybody in Boston knew Charlie Parker was there. The owner of the Hi Hat, who by this time had Serge Chaloff playing, ran over to Wally's and grabbed Parker: 'You took an intermission and five days later you come back and you're playing here, you come with me!' and took Charlie back to his place. Charlie had done this again after this and they still forgave him and let him play because he brought a lot of people, and he was wonderful. Jesus, that was funny."

Family Pressures
"I was still running around to people's houses hearing records and playing in joints. I was just carrying on doing everything. A compulsion? It had to be because it sure caused nothing but fights in my house, I can tell you that. Everyone fought about whose fault I was given an instrument in the first place. Everybody in the house was angry that I was involved in music because it was a disease they figured wouldn't go away. 'When will we start getting marks at school? When will we be able to get a job somewhere?'

"The only way that they realised that maybe I had something going was when they would begin to see little things; for example, in the newspaper they'd see somebody say something nice or when they saw me on television once in a while or when I'd make a record and they'd hear it and they'd say, 'Gee, he's not so bad, it's just that he can't make a living.' You couldn't really make a great living. They were more bugged about the fact that it was not a solid life. It wasn't so much that they hated music. When they told me when I was very young, 'Do you want to be in a life that has wild women, gambling, smoking, drinking and music?' I said, 'Oh boy, you just said the magic words.' When I opened the door to the Silver Dollar and smelled that beer smoke, cigarettes and whisky, it was the greatest perfume I ever smelled. Hearing music and guys playing was so exciting."

Glamour
"When you went to the movies and you saw Benny [Goodman] or any of the bands dressed up so beautifully and playing in one of those resorts or something, whether it was Miller or Artie [Shaw], you said, 'Oh man, what a life.' In Boston we had the RKO Theatre in which they had live orchestras and live things. The first live, big-time orchestra I saw was Jimmie Lunceford and even now I get a kick (thinking about it), the thing would rise and the lights and the curtains, and there they were with their beautiful

uniforms and their shiny horns. I stood for every show, you saw the two movies, an act from New York, dancers or a comedian, and then Lunceford's band would do their thing. I was probably looking at Jimmy Crawford and Trummy [Young], all the guys I would be playing with later. Oh jeepers. The next band I saw after that, a week later, on the same stage and I enjoyed it just as much, as rotten as they were, because they were live and good, was Clyde McCoy. See, I didn't care what it was, it was wonderful. I saw Benny there too, and Spike Jones for ever."

Spike Jones
"The alto player, his name was Zep Meissner, I'll not forget it. I was working in a club opposite the stage door entrance to the RKO Theatre, small street, so that anyone who came out of the stage door usually came through to the bar where we were playing. This guy Zep Meissner came in, he walked over to me and said, 'You got any cigarettes? You wouldn't have a Camel would you? I gotta have a Camel.' I thought he was crazy. 'Could I keep another one?' So I says, 'Keep the package'. He says,'Oh, here's a ticket to the show.'

"He got very excited. See because of the war cigarettes were hard to get. You could get, maybe, a package. So I said, 'I'll get you five cartons.' He gave me enough money and I got him about five cartons of Camels. Then he gave me this strip of these tickets for Spike Jones so whenever I had nothing to do I'd walk in and watch the show again and it was really quite funny. Very precise. Spike the leader, I didn't know this, was a magnificent drummer. The acts that preceded his show were these two black dancers from New York who danced to 'Sweet Georgia Brown' at this tempo (taps very fast) and Spike, to keep his hand in, would sit down and play the show for them. Nobody knew that was Spike. That's why he had such great timing. I ended watching them all the time and I brought millions of people in."

Bobby Hackett
"Bobby played around Boston lots of times. When I first heard him I wasn't that hip about how good he was and I went over to this trumpet player's house and he said, 'I'm going to play you a record of a guy, he comes from Providence, he plays around town here a lot of times. Now listen to this.' I think he played 'Ain't Misbehavin'' and he sounded so pretty to me, so lovely, and that's how I began to know who he was. Later on, in high school I used to go with the older guys on Friday nights to New York. It cost about four dollars and 12 cents for a train ride to New York, it was wonderful and three of us would get one hotel room, it'd be something like five dollars apiece for the whole weekend. It was a thrill, you know. He, Bobby, would invariably, on Friday, get on the train, and I got to know who he was and I said to him, 'You gonna be playing in Nick's tonight, huh?' Even then he was looking for someone to substitute for him so

he could drink, all of them, they were all the same, they didn't care, so he says 'You got your horn?' but I says, 'I'll be coming to Nick's to hear you' and he says, 'Bring the horn, it's a hard night for me there.' And you know the truth of the matter was in those days they went to work from about quarter to nine to four o'clock in the morning. Even Eddie Condon's when you went to work there it was nine to three. And no money! It was crappy money. But the guys liked to play and people spurred them on. There was a place next to Nick's called Julius's and that's where everybody went to drink, except Condon who did his drinking in the joint and met everybody so when he opened his (own) joint he knew everybody in the world. Very smart.

"We'd always start from the Village and work our way up and one night I went down there and Hackett said, 'You could do me a big favour, you know, sit-in and save my life for half an hour' and I went up and played. I think there was Pee Wee, a very unfriendly Brad Gowans, looked very angry at everybody, not just me, he didn't like anybody, and Joe Sullivan who kept saying 'What are we playing?' We weren't playing anything yet and he thought we were playing already, he was already stoned and a nice drummer by name of (Joe) Grauso, a very nice person, and we began playing. We played a couple of tunes and (owner) Nick Rongetti came running up to me and said, 'Who the hell are you? Why are you playing here?' "Cos Bobby asked me to,' I says. 'That bum, he's next door in Julius's when he should be here. Go and get him.' So I did that and told Bobby, 'Mr Rongetti is very, very mad at you and me.' 'Tell him to go to hell.' Bobby had a thing if he had one drink, he thought he had a lot of drinks, and he came in there and he was mad but he played. I just wanted to hear him play anyway and all the other guys for that matter."

Buck Clayton (t); **Pee Wee Russell** (cl); **Buzzy Drootin** (d); **Ruby Braff** (t), Newport Festival All Stars, publicity photo, 6th Newport Jazz Festival, Newport RI, July 1959.

New York
"Then we'd start wandering to a couple of other places. Willie the Lion was playing and I sat in with him and I'd have fun, he really liked me. And then we'd start going midtown and then to the (52nd) Street. Oh, that street. Frankie Newton was on that street,

Ben Webster would be over here, Coleman Hawkins, Lady Day was over there, Art Tatum. How could I go back to school on Monday after seeing this? Would you want to go to school on Monday? I had to do it. With the money I would get playing in those little places I'd save up a few bucks and I was pretty hip you know, going down to these places on weekends. The other guys were much older, they took care of me and they knew who they wanted to hear. Then when we had exhausted 52nd Street, standing outside the doors, there was a place called the Aquarium, a big, big place and I looked in the window and saw this black guy in a white suit and a big orchestra playing. It was Louis Armstrong (the Aquarium engagement was in spring 1946). I'd never seen him. I didn't know what the hell he looked like. With these revolving doors I'd have to hear the music every time the doors would revolve. I was losing my mind and I wasn't hip enough to those *maître d's* and bouncers when I stepped in and I'd run back outside. If I had any brains I'd have said, 'I'm just going to the bar, don't worry about it'. My friends were equally stupid. I told Pops (later) I had to catch a note or two every time the door revolved. He said, 'Why didn't you just come in and sit down?' I said, 'Because I didn't know what to do' and he laughed, he thought that was so funny. Even the notes that came out of that revolving door sounded good.

"Then we'd go up to Harlem to Minton's and to Small's. There were people jamming, it could be four in the morning, Roy Eldridge was playing with Coleman Hawkins and somebody else, maybe Charlie Shavers would drop in, it never ceased. When that ended and there was nothing else to do we went downtown to the big Nola's rehearsal studio and there was always big bands rehearsing and auditioning guys all night, and we'd sit there until about nine in the morning, listening to them and finally around twelve o'clock go to sleep. And then begin all over again on Saturday night. What a scene this was! On Sunday night I cried to have to get on that train and go home.

"I always hoped the day would come that I could live there. I graduated high school in 1945 and I'd begin going to New York and staying for a week or two and trying to work out a (union) card."

A Proper Job
"There was just nothing else I could think of to do. I wasn't trained to do anything. I took day jobs. I actually worked three times. You'll find this mighty interesting. Someone said, 'Why don't you go to an employment agency and ask them for a job that would suit you? Tell them that you didn't want to make a lot of money but enough to keep you eating. Don't tell them you want to be a musician because they won't hire you.' So I said, 'Oh, OK' and I looked up in the telephone book and found this guy. His name was Reingold. I told him 'I want a job just from twelve noon 'til six at night, answering the telephone and giving messages to somebody. You got a job like that?' He says, 'Sit down. Give me 45 dollars and I'll begin to work on this.' I says, 'What do you mean you'll begin to work on it? $45 is a

lot of money.' He says, 'You gotta pay me in advance. I'll get you a good gig. What do you do anyway?' Like a fool I told him I'm a musician. He says, 'OK where are you staying?' and I told him where I was. He says, 'You'll hear from me.' Next day he calls me, 'What do you know – I'm sending you to work and your first day of work you're going to be on Wall Street. Could anything be nicer than that?' I says, 'Gee, that's exciting. I can tell my folks I'm working on Wall Street. They'll be proud of me.' I didn't know what I was going to be doing on Wall Street. He says, 'Just go to this address, Stanley Transformer Company on Wall Street.' I went down there and walked in the place. 'Put on the smock. Go over to that table.' With five other idiots with their smocks on. And it's a transformer thing and they give you pieces of sharp lead, slates, that are to be wrapped around this transformer and you could cut yourself to slithers with this crap and you just keep doing this. I say to the person next me, 'It's not very much fun is it?' Nobody talks to you. All of a sudden, at 10.20, the bell rings and everybody throws off their smock and runs out to the fire escape and smokes. It's like a Charlie Chaplin movie. I ran out and I smoked. Then the bell rings and you run back in. So I says, 'This is not the kind of a gig that I want' and I threw the smock off and I went to the boss, 'Give me my bread. I'm getting out of here.' He says, 'Really? You haven't even worked until twelve o'clock.' So I says, 'Look at me, my hands are all cut up. Nobody talks to me'. He says, 'You didn't come here to talk, you came to work.' I says, 'I don't like it, give me my money.' He says, 'What the hell do you think you earned?' And he gave me almost four dollars."

A Proper Job (ii)

"I jumped in a cab downstairs. Took me back to St. James Hotel. I called Reingold. I says, 'Reingold, you've done it, what kind of a gig was that?' He says, 'All right. OK, that was the wrong job. Give me another chance. Take down this address.' I fell for it each time. I walked to the door and it was trillions of little Christmas trees, this big, and those things have to stand in a little piece of wood. The guy said, 'This is a drill, you gotta drill holes in this thing,' and he gave me a box of pieces of wood to drill holes though. I did this for three or four hours and I says, 'I can't drill any more holes.' He says, 'OK, would you like to wrap things?' I says, 'If I knew how, I wouldn't mind.' 'All right, go up to the third floor, tell them Harry sent you.' This should have been filmed. You go up to this third floor and there's literally a table the size of this room and a guy says to you, 'Fine, you come for wrapping? Have you had lots of experience wrapping things?' and I said, 'I've never wrapped anything.' He says, 'Nothing at all?' and he reached up with a hook and he pulled this thing and down came a car, this is really fun, a full-size replica of a real car for a kid to drive that has an engine in it and everything, on to the table. He says, 'I want to teach you how to wrap this car and you press a button and this thing will go away.' And he did this wonderful thing with huge pieces of paper and he just wrapped this thing. Marvellous. Then he says, 'Now you do it' and I says, 'Oh well, not yet, you have to do it a lot of times' and he says, 'I don't have time to stand here all day and wrap cars for you. I'll do it one more time and then you do it yourself.' He did it again. He says, 'I'll be back in a while.' I pulled this car down and I started to grab these gigantic pieces of paper and I became enwrapped in this thing. Not the car! And I couldn't get out and I'm yelling but there's nobody there to unwrap me and he finally came up and he said, 'Well, the car's not wrapped up but you are' and he had to unwrap me. And he says, 'This is not a good gig for you.'"

A Proper Job (iii)
"Once more I went back to Reingold. I said, 'I want my money back.' He says, 'We don't do that but I got something for you that you'll love. This is made for you. Look you're on 45th Street here, right? Right around the corner on 46th Street there's a marvellous outfit.' They take films that are made and bake these things to protect them for years. A very expensive process. I get up there and there's a girl who says, 'You have to know how to mark these, what to do with them and eventually when they're marked and attended to you take a wheelbarrow and you go up to another floor and then they begin their baking process.' I didn't know that the two people that are running this place hate each other like poison, as I'm trying to mark some film the wife comes in and she says, 'Why are you smoking in a place that has film, you idiot?' and I says, 'I'm sorry but the man that owns this place, the boss, just told me he wants me to smoke in here.' 'That's my husband, don't you ever listen to him again. He's a bum. Put the cigarette out.' He comes back and says, 'Didn't I tell you to smoke? Smoke! Smoke!' So here I am involved in this thing, she says no, he says yes. And they're fighting with each other and after about two days of this I told Reingold what's going on and I says, 'I can't take this. They're trying to kill each other and they're killing me and she also says I've destroyed about $30,000 worth of films by putting my hands on it.' He told me, 'Don't wear gloves. Destroy the film! I'm the boss, you do what I tell you', and she says she's going to take me to court for destroying Gypsy Rose Lee's films, so I'm getting out of here.' That was my last attempt to ever try to do anything (but music). It did me no good. I never worked again. It wasn't my scene, no."

Charlie Shavers
"I would get a night or two some place playing somewhere and later on I'd have to go back to Boston a lot of times and give up and play again in (local) places and then go back to New York again. By this time, this back and forth to New York and through people coming to Boston, I came to know a lot of fellows from New York. I came to meet Charlie Shavers and Buck Clayton and sometimes they would have calls for gigs they couldn't handle so I would do some of them. Charlie Shavers was a wonderful man that befriended me. Charlie was a very classy man. Matter of fact, when I was living in the St. James Hotel there was

envelopes of money being left for me every week. Sometimes 15 or 20 dollars. Charlie Shavers was leaving that money for me. I didn't know this and he would never admit to this. I caught him actually. Now a gig at the Metropole, for example, if you subbed for somebody, was something like 17 or 18 dollars for the night. It was really abominable. When Charlie asked me to play there because he had a gig with Tommy Dorsey, he said, 'I left a special package for you. You go to the bartender and get it.' And there'd be a 50-dollar bill in there for me. That's Charlie Shavers, baby. That's Mr. Class, you know. None of those other guys had that. He was wonderful.

"He saw me in a bar one night at one of the water holes for musicians and some guy said to me, 'How are things Ruby?' and I said, 'Pretty lousy, things are not very good' and he walked over and he said to me, 'Don't say things are bad. Take it from me. I know how people are' and I never forgot that. That was a place called Terrassi's on 47th Street where Buck Clayton had a little band with Kenny Kersey and a drummer. We were listening to him and that's when Charlie told me that. He knew the score, he knew how guys were like that, 'People don't care,' he says. 'If you tell them everything's great they'll hang around you.' What a musician! Had he lived he wanted to show me how to write and read and do everything. He knew that I knew Louis and I'd gone to Louis's house, so because he adored Louis I think he like me for that reason."

Newport Festival All-Stars, Tilburg, Holland, 15 April 1961. *L-r*: Pee Wee Russell (cl); Jimmy Wood (b); Ruby Braff (cnt); Buzzy Drootin (d, *obscured*); Vic Dickenson (tb); George Wein (*obscured* p, ldr) at left. Photo by Wouter van Gool. Courtesy Manfred Selchow.

Avoiding Bebop

"Well, I had already invested time playing the way I wanted to play. I looked at all those (bebop) guys like stylists. For example, Charlie Parker felt just as perfectly comfortable playing with me and Pee Wee Russell and Vic Dickenson as he did with anybody else. All he wanted to know was, 'What tune are we going to play?' Dizzy Gillespie was the same way. Even though they were innovative, I just thought, 'That's a wonderful way of playing the alto, I love the way he's playing the trumpet, like Pee Wee Russell's got his way of playing and that's lovely, and I love Vic Dickenson's way as well.' I wasn't interested in doing what anybody else was doing, so that was the reason I didn't pay it that kind of attention. Besides which I was still quite immature anyway."

Miles Davis

"If you think about it, Miles Davis had been playing with Bird all the time. If you'll notice, he wasn't playing like Dizzy or Bird either. He played the way he was playing. To the end of his life he never played like any of those fellows. I knew him when he was dressed in wonderful Brooks Brothers clothing – later he wanted to look as though he belonged to the ghetto, like he was apologising to the world!

"He used to come around to Boston and to play up there sometimes. His act was (rasps), 'Anybody got five cents?' Sounds crazy ... once again, he seemed always to be wanting to head into this ghetto feeling of things. And we talked a little bit later on when we were on tours together. I knew one thing about him, he was way above all the other cats in the sense that he'd say to me, 'Is that Bud Freeman over there? Did he play with Bix? I gotta ask him some things about Bix.' And he would. He loved Bobby Hackett's playing, and of course, Louis. All these people who pay lip service to him. Miles! Miles! Miles! ... how many times have they heard him say, 'Anything done by me or anybody was done better first by Louis?' Has it ever occurred to these people that if you like him so damn much, why don't you go listen to the things he has to tell you about? The trouble was, there were some vicious racial revisionists who didn't want these people to hear things like that."

Racial Revisionism

"That's a wonderful book by Sudhalter, incidentally (*Lost Chords: White Musicians and Their Contribution to Jazz 1915–1945* by Richard M. Sudhalter, OUP). You will love it

Ruby Braff Combo, Nice Jazz Festival, Nice, France, July 1987. *L-r:* Mark Shane (p, *obscured*); Jack Lesberg (b); Ruby Braff (cnt); Howard Alden (g); Chuck Riggs (d). Courtesy mr.jazz Photo Files (Theo Zwicky).

— I must say it! It shows you all the black and white guys that dug each other and how much they cared about each other's playing. I'm so glad this kid went and did this ten years of research on this book. It puts everybody in their place and gives them the respect they all deserve. If I had my way I would make it compulsory reading for every person that goes to school to study music. Now, the young black, and white, players, because of these people who'll not let them have information about all these kind of things, are not the beneficiaries of all the musical food that we dined on.

"They pay lip service to Duke Ellington – they don't even know the essence of Ellington is delicious melody embroidered over those great orchestrations. All Ellington's swinging phrases are elongated Louis Armstrong choruses! They don't know about all the different people that everybody listened to, so they are like dry nothing. They don't even know who Bird is, for God's sakes. They don't know who Lester Young is. They don't know who anybody is. I heard ten thousand wonderful different trumpet players playing when I turned the radio on. Now all the trumpet players sound the same, trying to play like Miles, or trying to play like Dizzy. The reason there's no individualism is that they have not dined on enough food. Will it be put right? That depends on people who have influence, like so-called critics. Let's put it this way, if they have political agendas, they're not serving music. Racism stinks from any side it comes from. This must be faced and realised. Either way! Even if I hated you like poison, let's say, and you played good, I've learned long ago that I have to separate that. If I were only to hear artists who I liked personally, I would probably hear about three people in my life!

"It doesn't go that way. You must separate one thing from another thing. If someone plays great music, you must give credit. The toughest black and white musicians I ever knew in my life that were great artists, when they heard someone play good, they went, 'Yeah, OK.' They didn't say, 'Well, man, he's white, or he's black.' That had nothing on earth to do with anything. They must return to that kind of a feeling – there are plenty of wonderful people who feel that way, don't think that there's not – but there's too much of an abundance of this 'whitey' thing, 'blacky' thing. This must be erased from art! It must leave."

Education

"If you were a young fellow playing an instrument, there is no magazine you can pick up, whether it's the *Jazz Journal*, or *Down Beat* or *Jazz Times* or a book in which all these names are not mentioned twenty thousand times. Wouldn't you say who the hell is Jack Teagarden? I want to hear Jack Teagarden. Fletcher Henderson knew him, he liked him, his trombone player liked him, the whole world liked him, Louis Armstrong liked him, why can't I hear Jack Teagarden records? Who's Pee Wee Russell? Who's Bobby

Ruby Braff – George Barnes Quartet, c.1973. Ruby Braff (cnt); George Barnes (g). Courtesy mr.jazz Photo Files (Theo Zwicky).

Hackett? Who's Bud Freeman that Ben Webster talks about all the time? Why is there no curiosity? We were curious about everybody.

"When I see *Jazz Journal*, it thrills me because it reminds me that I grew up with the old *Down Beat* which was like a newspaper – who's leaving the band this week, who's coming in, with pictures of everybody. I could hardly wait to get my next issue. Well, that's how I feel about *Jazz Journal*. They have feature stories which I love and I read, guys I've never heard of, and I say, 'Oh well, look what this guy did.' Beautiful magazine. Well, if people read these things, don't they want to know who these guys are who are in here? You see the name Benny Carter 55,000 times, don't you want to know anything about who he was? Why did *we* have more curiosity than them? It shouldn't be this way with any fellow who's earnest about wanting to play music."

Wynton Marsalis

"He tries to do what he can. Unfortunately, Wynton comes out, to me, of a more classical thing than a jazz thing, and as much as he's tried to know, he's still doesn't really know, in my mind. He talks a lot and says a lot of things, and the things he's saying are very good, but I never heard him talking about the people I just mentioned either. And that is disturbing to me. Giving lip service to Louis Armstrong's name is not enough. You must pay attention to *song*. Song is what inspired people to sing, and to embellish them and do something to them. Louis sang before he played."

The Jazz Century

"Jazz is *only* a hundred years old. A young man hits the stage in classical music, a pianist, or a violinist, he may be 24, 25 years old. You are looking at a full-fledged guy that's played the music of hundreds of years, quartets, baroque, he's conducted, he's done everything. You're looking at a poised man who knows what he's doing. Now, you've got guys going on the stage playing jazz, what the hell do they know about the stage, they don't know what they're playing, they don't even know what they're there for. They think they're there to just run up and down their horns all night. That wasn't what music was meant for. You're either composing or de-composing, in one way or another (laughs).

"Those concert guys play and listen to music hundreds of years old, and extend up to Bartók, and Schoenberg. We're only a hundred years old and you're trying to tell me that 1950 was 'before my time'. What do you mean it was before your time, you idiot? You got Jelly Roll Morton on records, you got everything, right up to now. In classical music you can't get a record of Chopin playing, you just have to imagine what he played like. You can't get Liszt playing the piano. You can't get Beethoven doing an interview, saying 'What?' which would be fun to hear (laughs). There is no excuse for anybody saying today, 'I don't know, that's a long time ago.' Get outta here, it's a long time ago!"

Contemporary Players
"I listen to all the so-called, in quotes, 'avant-garde' things, late at night because sometimes I'll catch someone and I'll say, 'Jeez, not only does that guy have a lot of chops, he's got some helluva good ideas.' You know, there's a young fellow, he's a very modern kind of a guy and I really like him, Tom Harrell. Unusual ideas, unusual thoughts. Matter of fact, I've got to call him and find him and talk with him a little bit. Now, I don't want to play what he's playing but that's nothing to do with anything. I like to listen to what's he's trying to say. There are people like this that I want to hear. There's a marvellous piano player in New York, Bill Charlap. He'll take you around a bend, I'm gonna tell you. He knows billions of songs. He grew up in a house where his mom was a very famous singer, Sandy Stewart, and he knows every tune, wants to know everything and will listen to anything you say. He worked with Phil Woods for the past few years, to learn what Phil is doing. Phil's a great alto player. Marvellous player. I've listened to Phil's things and I don't know what the hell he's doing with his music so I like his playing better when I hear him accompanying somebody like Lena Horne, with (Robert) Farnon. It sounds beautiful to me when he's playing tunes. Nice things."

Tunes
"I feel that Harold Arlen, and Duke, all those kind of guys are much better writers than me so of course, I want to play their tunes. I write originals, too, but I'd rather play their tunes. I don't (often) play originals because the people that are working with me in different places may not know them. I'm not going to make anyone uncomfortable. If they did know them, I still would only play two or three to a set and play standard things the rest of the time. People say, 'Well, Duke Ellington plays originals' and I point out to them, 'Duke Ellington's originals are part of the standard repertoire of this world.' Even he, were he alive going out playing dances, carries all the pop tunes of the day. Just hear some of those old dance records. He'd be playing 'Stardust' and everything. So if Duke Ellington does these things, are you out of your mind, you're a young player, no one's ever heard you, you make a record and you play me fifteen originals? Get

lost! There's something wrong with that. And it's not even respectable. That's ridiculous."

Howard Alden (g), **Jack Lesberg** (b), **Ruby Braff, Warren Vache** (cnt); **Scott Hamilton** (ts). Nice Jazz Festival, July 1988. Photo by Alan Smith.

Freshness
"It's always a brand-new song to me. A lot of the young players when they play a tune say, 'What are the changes?' They're just looking to play the changes. Are they 'Rhythm' changes? It's no good when you're just improvising on changes, there's nothing happening. When you have the format of this original beautiful melody first, you got something to build on. But first you have to like that, and understand it, and love it, before you can fix it. So for me, when I'm playing a tune, starting thinking of that song, how lovely it really is, I play it in a hundred different tempos. I'll slow it down, 'What does it feel like when you do this way or that?' so it's never boring to me because it's going in different directions all the time. It starts off as just a place I'm living in for a moment then I'm leaving. The worst thing, to me, is the constancy of one sound in a place. I don't like to hear one sound. I've heard string quartets or trios, and in the context of three guys playing, my God, all kinds of things were happening. Why do you have to go to a joint where there's a bass, drums, and a saxophone player, and the same thing goes on, he plays fours and then he takes a hundred choruses here, and the tune ends the same way?"

Audience Expectations

"See, the thing that saves me a little, I have in-look out-look. Before I play the tune I already know what it's going to be like for them. And if something is happening musically in the group where I know it's not going to sound the way I want it to happen, I'm ready to change it very, very fast. I'm going to be going out of this thing in a minute and going into something else. I know that Duke always had that – when he wrote something, he already knew what it was going to be like out there, but of course, he could depend on his band. I can miscalculate and say, 'Oh, I made a mistake' but I don't have to suffer through this. I can change it. My job is to see to it that they (the audience) have fun, they're not bored with this tune, and at the end of the tune, that I've brought them to a little better place than they were six seconds ago. Hopefully it's the same picture for the night. I don't want someone leaving saying, 'Oh God, if he did this again, I think I would have had to leave,' which I've had to do in my lifetime, leave a place because somebody was boring me to death. You've got to know these things."

Benny Goodman and His Orchestra, Capitol recording session for *B.G. in Hi-Fi*, New York, 9 November 1954. *Rear*: Carl Poole, Chris Griffin, Bernie Privin (t); Bobby Donaldson (d). *Middle*: Will Bradley, Cutty Cutshall, Vernon Brown (tb); George Duvivier (b) Mel Powell (p); *Front*: Paul Ricci, Boomie Richman (ts); Hymie Schertzer (as); Al Klink (ts); Sol Schlinger (bs); Steve Jordan (g); Benny Goodman (cl, ldr); Ruby Braff (t, soloist). From March of Jazz programme 2001.

Recording for Benny Goodman
"I was never in Benny Goodman's big band! I was called there as a soloist when they were remaking these things (for Capitol's *Benny Goodman in Hi-Fi.*). I never played in the band. I'd have had a nervous breakdown just sitting in a brass section. I wouldn't know what to do with that. I couldn't read anything or do anything. Benny was very beautiful to me. I was frightened to death standing there looking at this band. Here's Mel Powell and George Duvivier, all my favourite people. I was just there to play the choruses and I says, 'Why do you want me to do it?' He says, 'Oh, keep quiet, I'm the leader. I do anything I want. You just play when I tell you to play.' He must have liked something I did.

"I loved seeing him. I was so thrilled to just look at him. There he is, Benny Goodman. My God. He would say sometimes, 'What are you staring at me for?' 'Because I can't believe you're Benny Goodman.' There was never anything like him. Here's another thing for the revisionists: Charlie Parker adored Benny Goodman's playing and used to beg Red Norvo to get him in early at the 400 Club before all the people came so he could listen to Benny rehearsing and fooling around and playing. He called him the most unflagging instrumentalist he ever heard. Now, why haven't other people heard what Charlie Parker said? He said it many times, in *Down Beat* and different places. Why are these things removed from people? You see what I mean about this business? This bothers me."

Involvement in Education
"Nobody's ever asked me. Never in my life. I live an hour-and-a-half from Boston with all its schools and nobody's ever asked me to do anything. It amazes me. I have often looked on TV and watched them doing a show or discussion on Louis Armstrong and I saw people participating that don't even know who he was. It strikes me as strange that nobody's ever thought to ask me and I was a friend of Louis. I was one of the many trillions of singers, dancers and musicians who went to Armstrong University, from which you never graduate. There's no diploma because you're never through, you never pass!"

Academic Study
"Gone to (music) school? Yes, I would have given my life for it. I study all the time now when I'm home. I study writing, I study everything. I'm a novice but I love it. I love being at the piano all day messing with things. Had I done all of those things when I was younger I would have been writing for movies by now. I don't believe that anyone with any talent would have been any lesser for knowing more. Mr. Coleman Hawkins certainly didn't die from having been a cellist and having gone to school, and Stan Getz was not hurt by being able to read anything and do anything. I don't see where Duke

Ellington was hurt very much by becoming a great orchestrator. All I think knowledge would have done is enhance me and I would know more. Knowing how to do something, you just put more of it to what you do."

A Voice of Your Own

"Sure you know my sound, but you also know that when you hear Clyde McCoy so that alone is not enough (laughs). See, I don't come out of instrumentalists alone. My life has as much to do with Judy Garland, Frank Sinatra and Charlie Chaplin and two zillion other things as it has to do with Louis Armstrong. I'm just as enthralled with a Fred Astaire performance as I am with anything Lester Young can dream of doing. If you're not going to learn from the greatest performers in the world ... You hear all these people say, 'That's show business.' What the hell do they think Duke Ellington is, the greatest showman I've ever seen? What are we to do, forget about these guys? All those people mean something to me. When I'm out there on the stage playing, everything that I've ever heard and seen in my life is running through my heart and soul. I'm always learning from what they said. I remember Judy saying to me, about playing in Carnegie Hall, 'You play in a place like that, don't lose the intimacy of a club, think of that.' These are things you learn from great performers, you don't learn them from silly little guys playing a horn.

"What did Fred Astaire say about this? He said this. What did Frank say about this?. What did Bing say about this? I want to know what these people have to say and think. This is part of my life. I'm not interested in some mad alto player that is angry tonight because somebody is having fun with the audience. That's his problem. I like audiences. If they're not attentive, it's my fault, not theirs. There are no bad audiences, just bad performances. We have to learn how to play better, and do better, to make them happy. It's the truth."

2nd Timex All Star Jazz Festival, TV show, New York, 30 April 1958. L-r: Ruby Braff (t); Marty Napoleon (p); Chubby Jackson (b); Jack Teagarden (tb); unknown (d); Louis Armstrong (t). Photo by Jack Bradley. From March of Jazz programme 2001.

Looking Forward

"What I look forward to is just a chance to keep learning more. I would like some day to spend my life interviewing people. I'm a born reporter and I'm a good interviewer. All my life I've interviewed people like Louis and everybody – they never knew I was interviewing them but that's how I learn things."

Louis

"Oh God, how do I remember him? I remember him, from a personal point of view as being a wonderful, generous, lovely host. Great guy, great hospitality. Of course, I always will remember him for teaching the whole world, whether you sing, dance, play or write. He taught the whole world how to phrase, how to think about music. It's just uncanny. He plucked it out of the sky. Like his love for opera and all these things – everything that he heard he sucked into that wonderful brain, and out it came.

"None of these people are dead as far as I'm concerned, they're very much alive. Their music will always be with me and with all of us. I just turn on a Benny record, and bang, he's alive. That's what knocks me out."

Ruby Braff (cnt), New York, 1990s. Personal promo. Photo by Jay Anderson. Courtesy Dave Bennett.

Ruby Braff Trio* and guests, Bristol 1991. L-r: Frank Tate* (b); Ruby Braff (cnt); Scott Hamilton (ts); Jake Hanna (d); Dave McKenna (p); Howard Alden*. Courtesy Dave Bennett.

Braff on Record

"I probably made about 250 albums and a good many of them I wish were never made because I wasn't good enough to make them, but I will say this, and I don't mean it bragging, in the past recent years, I've really begun to know how to play so that when I hear me play, I'm no longer disgruntled about it. I can actually listen to it and say, 'Jeez, you know, that ain't bad. I like it.' I'm learning and I want to keep doing it. If I can ..."

First published in three parts as
'Rappin' with Ruby – Extracts from a Life' in
Jazz Journal, August 2002, January 2003 and May 2003

George 'Buster' Cooper

Buster Cooper, Duke Ellington Orchestra, Granada TV, London, 1963. Photo by Val Wilmer. Courtesy Val Wilmer.

Buster Cooper's 'blistering trombone solos' with Duke Ellington's orchestra made him a star. Clubs and festivals wanted him once he'd left Ellington – they liked his exuberance and crowd-pleasing quality – so he began to travel, visiting Europe regularly in the late 1980s, including an appearance at the 'Ellington '88' conference held in Oldham, England. I talked to him for publication in June 1988 before the conference and this was the piece that resulted. I also accompanied him to a November gig in a pub in Kings Langley, Hertfordshire, the following year, chatting to him while he prepared his instrument and sneaked 'a little taste' to set himself up for the performance. As always, he played with commendable verve and charmed everyone. Later, I was fortunate enough to hear him with the Statesmen of Jazz performing at a high school in Palmdale, north of Los Angeles in 1995.

Despite being 'the busiest black trombone on the West Coast' in the 1980s, a period which included a visit to Japan with Benny Carter and the formation of a well-received quintet with fellow trombonist Thurman Green, Buster and Sarah, his wife, became disenchanted with life in California. They returned to St. Petersburg for good in the mid-1990s and he has continued to play, fronting a trio at the Garden Restaurant for the past 15 years. Still in demand for the occasional Ellingtonian reunion, Buster remains a force for good in jazz. When I recently mentioned the possibility of retirement, his answer was, "Retire to what?" Asked why he still sounds so good, he says, "I'm not the one playing the instrument. It's God playing it through me. He's the best trombone player I know."

Beware the pigeon-hole that becomes a blind alley. Someone looking for a capsule definition to place and describe Buster Cooper's talents might suggest 'inspired by J.J. Johnson but plays in a more extrovert manner'. That's OK so far as it goes but the Floridian's style is far less deadpan and rather more vitally expansive in context than might be imagined from that reference. He's extrovert all right but there's a rewarding light and shade to his performances that's born out of a deep commitment to the horn – 'six or seven hours' practice a day' – and a professional's desire to respond to a variety of musical challenges. Stanley Dance called Cooper a 'lively spirit' and that seems a fair description to me. More important, Buster is his own man and in no sense a Johnson sound-alike. His crowded CV puts it this way – 'a world-renowned trombonist, from the hard-driving swing school'. There's plenty of recorded evidence to support this particular assertion and dotted around the discographies of major leaders such as

Buster Cooper (tb), unknown orchestra and location, Los Angeles CA, c.1980s. Courtesy Ernie Garside.

Buster Cooper (tb), Statesmen of Jazz, Mesa Intermediate School, Palmdale CA. 31 August 1995.
Photo by Peter Vacher.

Buster Cooper (tb), Buster Cooper Quartet, Bayboro Campus, University of South Florida, 1st music-and-arts festival, St. Petersburg FL, May 1971. Bass and drums unidentified. Photo by Tony Lopez for the St. Petersburg Times-Ind.

Lionel Hampton, Earl Hines, and principally Duke Ellington, there are a host of individual sides which attest to Cooper's jazz creativity.

Cooper and his friend, the cornetist Bill Berry, were in Britain to appear at the highly successful Ellington '88 event in Oldham and the positive impression gained then led to Buster Cooper's first-ever solo tour of Britain. He's a lean, athletic-looking man, unmarked by time and as excitable in his speech patterns as his powerful solo work might suggest. When we talked he told me that he was born in St. Petersburg, Florida (on 4 April 1929) and recalled that his father, a one-time blues guitarist, 'just loved music' but that his namesake cousin, George Cooper, a drummer, had been his true inspiration. 'He was at Alabama State, with Erskine Hawkins and Haywood Henry, and I idolised him. He inspired me to start on drums at first, in High School. I played for a while but every time I'd take my drums out, to pack them up, all the girls had gone.' Lester Young made the same observation and turned to the tenor instead. Daunted by this the young Cooper abandoned drums and graduated to the trombone by chance, spotting an instrument in a nearby pawnshop window.

St. Petersburg is a resort town but was rigidly segregated in those days. Despite this Buster was taught by a local white instructor, Vernon Yonkers: "He and I are very good friends to this day. He gave me the horn I play on right now." Eventually Buster joined his cousin's 16-piece band and he says that it included a number of good players among them, "one of the best pianists that ever lived, named Oscar Dennard. He was the one that set Cannonball (Adderley) on the right track. In fact, Cannonball and Sam Jones, the bass player, worked with my cousin's band later on down the years." Strictly a territory unit, the George Cooper Orchestra occasionally ventured into faraway Texas and Buster remembers getting stranded there in the summer of '46. "The job was cancelled and we stayed in this little town for two weeks. Really hungry but it was a learning experience. Made me feel like a professional musician."

Out of High School Buster began to work in his father's landscaping business, still intent on making music his career but uncertain how to promote that ambition. His elder brother Steve, a trumpeter who later became a fine bassist, was already in New York and Buster had thoughts of emulating him. As he said, "New York was it then." It took a call from another Florida musician, the saxophonist Noble Watts, then with the Nat Towles band in Omaha, Nebraska, to make up the young trombonist's mind for him. "He sent for me and I stayed with Nat Towles for about six months. It was a territorial band, so we played places like Fargo, North Dakota, and Bismarck, ND, and there'd be snow up to your neck. I hadn't seen snow before! Did I tell you Oliver Nelson was playing lead alto in Nat's band? And he was writing for the band then. I was the only trombone. Nothing but dances and it wasn't no romping band either. Still, Nat was an immaculate man."

A month after his return home Buster moved to New York. He enrolled at the Hartnett School of Music in 1950, supporting himself with daytime work in the garment district, met his future wife Sarah and was thrilled two years on when he heard that Lionel Hampton wanted him. Like most Floridians, he also looked out for opportunities to help home-state friends and was instrumental in recommending Nat Adderley to Hamp and incidentally assisted Cannonball's career aspirations. When the elder Adderley came up from Florida to see Nat he joined Buster, Sam Jones, Nat and the brothers Cooper for dinner at Buster's house."That night, when we got through eating, Cannonball asked if there was a place to play so I took him down to the Club Bohemia. Oscar Pettiford had the band and he let Cannonball play on the last set. He played 'The Nearness of You' and he ate it up! He played so good the next night he was working at the Club Bohemia. So I was the one that got him down there."

Lionel Hampton and His Orchestra, European tour, Basle Station, Switzerland, 23 or 24 September 1953. Standing L-r; possibly Clifford Scott (ts) or Oscar Estell (bs); Quincy Jones (t); Curley Hamner (dancer, d); Gigi Gryce (as); Monk Montgomery (b); Buster Cooper (tb); Art Farmer (t); Alan Dawson (d); George Wallington (p); Jimmy Cleveland (tb); Clifford Brown (t). Front: Billy Mackel (g); Al Hayes (tb); Anthony Ortega (ts); Clifford Solomon (ts). Photo by Ernest Zwonicek. Courtesy Art Farmer.

Buster's tenure with Hamp included the celebrated European tour of 1953 when the band's line-up of young stars, among them trumpeters Art Farmer and Clifford Brown, trombonist Jimmy Cleveland and saxophonist Gigi Gryce recorded in Stockholm and

Paris against Hamp's express wishes. The resulting fuss seems distant now but not so the memories of Brown. "Clifford was a sweet man and it came out of his horn that way. I remember one time when he got through his solo he was coming back to his chair and he had a frown on his face. I said, 'What's the matter, Clifford?' and he said, 'Man, I missed that C7th change.' But do you know what he did? He went home, got his mute and he practised that change all night long. Oh yeah, he was very dedicated. Clifford was a good pianist too."

Buster dropped out of the Hampton band for a while but was invited back, staying a year second time around in a trombone section that boasted Carl Fontana and veteran Al Hayes – "Fred Beckett was his idol." From there he started to freelance in New York, working the five–six shows-a-day grind with Reuben Phillips's house band at the Apollo Theatre in Harlem. Although this group bristled with jazz talent (trumpeter Money Johnson, tenorists Seldon Powell and Eric Dixon included) its musical possibilities were limited since so many of the top acts of the day were rock-orientated. However, the trombonist kept his jazz chops honed with short-term engagements with Max Roach, Johnny Griffin and Pepper Adams, finding the time to record for Prestige, including the star-packed Prestige Blues Swingers 'Outskirts of Town' (1958). He also played with the Lucky Millinder orchestra up at the Savoy Ballroom at this time and kept company with his brother. "We had a group called the Cooper Brothers during this same period with Eric Dixon, Lloyd Mayers and Jimmy Johnson, the drummer who used to play with Duke's band. We'd go in a club, like Count Basie's and stay there maybe six or seven months. We had a good following. We'd play anything with a good solid beat. Knock the people out." The fraternal duo also had the chance to perform with Coleman Hawkins. "He was beautiful to work with and he paid good too!"

Another good payer was Benny Goodman whose group Buster joined briefly before the Cooper Brothers took their combo to the Olympia Theatre in Paris, supporting singer Caterina Valente and later working with the marvellous entertainer Josephine Baker, and staying for over a year. It was arch-Ellington enthusiast Eric Dixon who persuaded Buster to respond positively to Duke Ellington's repeated calls in 1962. The trombonist then accepted a weekend date with Duke in New Jersey which stretched into a seven-year association, involving extended overseas tours and many recordings – in all an extraordinary life-enhancing experience. Looking back Buster said: "Once you go with Duke you don't have to make any more auditions. It was a learning institution for me – opened a lot of doors.

"Actually when I first went into the band I said to myself, 'Damn, the whole band is out of tune,' but it was me, my ears, 'cause I wasn't used to Duke's voicing." Buster remembered Duke's personal touch: "He tried me out the first night. Once he'd hear you he'd write for you. He'd write for his personalities, but never tell you *how* to play. Every

Duke Ellington Orchestra, London, February 1964. Ellington trombone section: Chuck Connors, Buster Cooper, Lawrence Brown. Photo by Brian Foskett. Courtesy Brian Foskett.

Duke Ellington and His Orchestra, Second Sacred Concert, St. John the Divine, New York, 19 January 1968. *Rear*: Alice Babs (v); Jeff Castleman (b); Tony Watkins or Jimmy McPhail (v); Cootie Williams standing, Herbie Jones (t); Steve Little, Sam Woodyard (d); Mercer Ellington, Cat Anderson (t). *Front*: Bennie Green, Lawrence Brown, Buster Cooper (tb); Paul Gonsalves, Jimmy Hamilton (ts); Johnny Hodges, Russell Procope (as); Harry Carney (bs). *Front*: Chuck Connors (b-tb); Duke Ellington (p, cond). UPI Photo.

musician there is, black or white, wanted to be in that band. I was very proud and honoured to be there." Buster left the band "because my dad had passed" and went back to Florida to "take care of his business. I bought me a home but I wasn't playing my horn."

Frustrated by this, Buster and his wife Sarah took off for California and relocated there, taking a chance on the freelance scene in and around Los Angeles. Thankfully Buster's career credentials and all-round musicianship earned him first-call status with Bill Berry's big band, the Nat Pierce-Frankie Capp Juggernaut and the Gerald Wilson Orchestra. In addition he was in demand for record dates, small-group gigs and occasional studio jobs, accepting the fluctuations of income that are inevitable in these circumstances. Through cornetist Jake Porter he was also involved with movie/TV walk-ons and could be spotted in series like *Moonlighting*.

Capp-Pierce Juggernaut, Playboy Jazz Festival, Hollywood Bowl, Los Angeles CA, early 1980s. *Rear L-r*: Nat Pierce (p); Jim Hughart (b); Frank Capp (d); Conte Candoli, Johnny Audino, Snooky Young, Bobby Bryant (t). *Middle*: Garnett Brown, Alan Kaplan, Buster Cooper (tb). *Front*: Ray Pohlman (g); Red Holloway, Herman Riley (ts); Marshal Royal, Jeff Clayton (as); Jack Nimitz (bs). Courtesy William Berry Jr.

Even so jazz has continued to be his priority and as we've seen he says, "I thank God for that." Doubtless British audiences passed on their appreciation in less mysterious ways when this swinging visitor let rip on that long-past solo visit.

Buster Cooper (tb), soloist with Harmony in Harlem, Ellington Conference, Royal National Hotel, London 2008. Photo by Chris Lee. Courtesy Chris Lee.

First published as 'El Busto' in
Jazz Journal, June 1989

Bill Berry

Bill Berry (1930–2002), London, 1997. Courtesy Bill Berry.

Bill Berry was short and dapper, and it seemed appropriate that he should prefer the cornet to the trumpet. As he said, "It's more my size." I first heard him fronting a student band at a concert in Ealing and immediately took to his crisp, swing-to-bop solo style. After participating in the 1988 Duke Ellington conference in Oldham, alongside his Los Angeles friend, the trombonist Buster Cooper, Bill began to tour the UK regularly as a single for promoter Susan May. It was in June 1989 that we taped this interview in London covering some of his career experiences and reflections on his life in Los Angeles, later published as a two-parter in Jazz Journal.

Two years on, we caught Bill again with a quartet at The Edge, a short-lived club near Marble Arch in London and shared a pre-gig meal with him. After that we kept in touch and I was delighted to observe him in action in California in 1995, leading the Statesmen of Jazz, including Cooper, of course, as they performed for an enthusiastic audience of young school children. Gifted with a persuasive manner and a cheerful personality, Bill continued to organise his LA Big Band and to conduct the High School All-Stars at the Monterey Jazz Festival (he was the MJF's musical director from 1987 to 1993) until his death in November 2002.

Widely lauded for his work with the Woody Herman, Maynard Ferguson and Duke Ellington orchestras and for his many other big-band associations, Bill Berry always seemed to embrace something of both swing and bebop in his playing. Talking in his hotel, I asked him first about his initial awareness of bebop, whose acute accents could sometimes be detected in his solos.

"Well I was only 14 or 15 years old. I'd just started playing. I had been raised on swing records. My parents were musicians. One of my favourite trumpet players was, and is, Bunny Berigan. My next-door neighbour was a kid my own age, his name was Dee Felice, he's a drummer in the States now. In those days in the United States you could go to a music store and they had booths where you could play the records. So, of course, we used to do that without buying them. Dee said, "You gotta come downtown with me" – this was in Cincinnati – "to hear this trumpet player play I Can't Get Started". Brand-new trumpet player, never heard of him and so we did. It was Dizzy (Gillespie) and I thought it was the worst thing I'd ever heard. About a week later I thought it was the greatest thing I've ever heard. I was so used to Bunny's record and this sounded totally different. I've been in love with Dizzy's playing ever since. He was a major, major influence on me.

"In those days also, Woody Herman's band broadcast every Friday night from wherever they were and of course he had beboppers in his band, in that particular band, in 1946. Then I heard Charlie Parker of course, and Sonny Stitt, and Miles. I was well into bebop; I was just a kid when it came out. I had all of Dizzy's big-band records and whatever you could buy in those days on those little independent labels. Zoot Sims and Stan Getz also impressed me when they started making records of their own as did my favourite trombone player of all time, Bill Harris. He really knocked me out and then I finally got to play with him."

Bill Harris (trombone), Woody Herman Orchestra, Capitol recording session, Hollywood, December 1948. Capitol Record's photo by Gene Howard.

Speaking of Harris, Berry recalled, "Bill used to do terrible things. When I was with Woody's band he always carried a mannequin with him and the mannequin sat in the trombone section with him. We drove cars in those days and Bill could only take two band members because the mannequin was sitting up in front. I remember one night in an after-hours barbecue place we were eating, it must have been three or four o'clock in the morning, and Bill, who looked like a college professor really, banged on the table and yelled for the waitress. He had gotten a bun that they put the meat in and he put his false teeth in the thing, so the poor waitress came over and he says, 'What is this?' and there's a set of teeth in the bread. Another night we were playing a country club, a very sedate, conservative club, and there was only one exit from the ballroom to the bar or whatever, so we took an intermission and there was this terrible

Duke Ellington Orchestra, 'pep' section, probably Boston Arena, 22 May 1962. *L-r*: Lawrence Brown (tb); Ray Nance, Bill Berry (t). *Rear*: Mercer Ellington (*obscured*, conducting, sub. for Duke Ellington recovering from surgery); Johnny Hodges (as). Courtesy William Berry Jr.

crush of people waiting to get out. What in the world was going on? When we finally got to the doorway, there was Bill, who was about 6´2˝ or 3´, big tall feller, lying flat on his back with his arms spread out right in the doorway and 300 people had to step over him to get out. Then, he liked dropping his pants. Standing in a bar and having a drink with his bright red corduroy band coat and with velvet lapels and no pants because they'd be down around his ankles. Standing there, very serious-looking. Oh, he was nuts but a great player. Totally original, too. I loved him."

Berry joined the Duke Ellington Orchestra in 1961. Given his enthusiasm for bebop, I wondered how this had impacted his playing. "I think that time with Duke made me go back further in musical styles," he said. "When I joined the band Shorty Baker and Ray Nance were in there and they both played absolutely gorgeously and very melodic. Not bebop! That had a big influence, I discovered during that period that about the hardest thing to play is the straight melody. That's almost impossible and you never hear anybody do it, but Johnny Hodges could do it, and Shorty Baker could do it, and make you cry. I mean exactly the straight melody, that's almost an impossible thing to do. Every player has certain habits, licks and so forth that they play, but in fact in Ellington's band they played the same solos, note for note, every night. I don't know how many times I heard those guys play the same tunes. I could, and can, sing everybody's solo but every night they were so touching, even to me. They were so perfect. I think those solos became part of the compositions. Even Paul Gonsalves playing 25 choruses of blues was almost the same. Duke didn't demand that or if he did it wasn't overtly. One time I made a movie with him and we recorded the soundtrack one day and then filmed it the next day and everybody knew exactly what they were doing on their solo but me.

"One time we did an album called *All-American*. This was the music from a Broadway show that closed the day after it opened or something (*All-American* opened on Broadway in March 1962 and ran for 80 performances). In the meantime we made an album and the Broadway composers were there and when Strayhorn and Duke got through with their music it sounded like they wrote it. Pure Ellington but they (the composers) were astounded, of course. About six months or a year later somebody who had gotten the album requested one of these tunes, a beautiful ballad, so they dug it up. Paul Gonsalves stood up and played the same solo he played six months ago. We'd sight-read it for the record and never played it since.

"Johnny Hodges just took me under his wing. (Trumpeter) Cat Anderson, also. All the guys were lovely but those two were extremely so. When I was there it was the height of all the Civil Rights business and we used to play black theatres in Chicago and New York, and the mood was not too friendly toward white people. At the Regal Theatre in Chicago even the black guys in the band were afraid to go there it was so rough. The first day we were there as always, you had a nine or ten o'clock rehearsal in the morning for the acts

Duke Ellington's 70th birthday party, White House, Washington DC, 29 April 1969. Willis Conover and the All-Star Band with guests Earl Hines, Dave Brubeck and Billy Taylor, hosted by President Richard Nixon. *L-r*: Dave Brubeck, Hank Jones (p); Jim Hall (g); Tom Whaley (Ellington associate); Paul Desmond (as); Earl Hines (p); Gerry Mulligan (bs); Billy Taylor (p); Mary Mayo (voc); Milt Hinton (b); Willis Conover (mc); President Nixon; Clark Terry (t); Duke Ellington (p); Joe Williams (voc); Urbie Green, J.J. Johnson (tb); Bill Berry (t). Courtesy William Berry Jr.

that were on the bill. We did the big rehearsal and then Johnny took me, before the first show, about noon, around to about three or four restaurant-bars in the immediate vicinity of the theatre and introduced me to the bartender or the owner. I didn't really realise it at the time but that was so I could go in these places all that week we were there. I don't think anybody else white would have gone, and if anybody gave me a hard time, the bartender would say 'Wait a minute, he's all right.' And that was all Johnny. He was beautiful to me; in fact to everybody, really. I made three or four records with Johnny, a couple of them playing vibes, as a matter of fact. I don't know how he found out I used to bang on vibes a little bit. That was after I left the band, but the very first record date that I did with him was about two days after I joined the (Ellington) band. Johnny used to call everybody 'young man' and he came up to me one night when we were in New York and he said, 'Young man, what are you doing Tuesday afternoon?' 'Nothing!' I wanted to say 'sir' you know, and I think he said, 'Well, would you like to make a record with us?' I said, 'Yes of course' and that was the very first Ellington record I made, with Johnny and Strayhorn. Duke wasn't there.

"Cat Anderson was very nice to me. He helped me a great deal because we didn't have music with the (Ellington) band. I mean we literally didn't have music and you just had to learn your part, make it up, and he was very helpful in that. I've told this story a million times but one night I said, 'Cat, what do I play on the end of this tune?' He says, 'Grab a note that sounds wrong and hold on!' And when Cootie came back in the band we were playing some tune and we got to the last note and I played the note I'd been playing for a year, and Cootie looked at me and he says, 'That's my note!' Jeez, he was there before I was born, he was right, it was his note so I found another one. Duke used to do that. Somebody would say at rehearsal, 'I think I got a wrong note in my part' and Duke would say, 'You're a musician, fix it. Find the right note.'"

Anecdotal evidence suggests that Cat was a pretty bristly sort of man. "He was, but not to me. A lot of people had differences with Cat. Everybody gets in moods and when he would get to feeling evil, as we would say, I would just do what they call drop the curtain. Just let him do his ranting and raving and not have anything to do with it. But he was lovely to me. The guys were human. They all had faults. It's a tough life and they'd been there, some of them, since before I was born. Harry Carney was one of the nicest people I ever met in my life. Anybody, anytime, anywhere. He never changed. You never leave that band. It's sort of a family thing. Buster Cooper and I are still very close friends and that's where we met. I haven't worked with Mercer (Ellington's son) in several years but I have worked with him since Duke passed, on many occasions. In fact I did about a year of *Sophisticated Ladies* in Los Angeles. Mercer was not there, but he was certainly involved.

"Woody was another great man who taught me many things. I remember the first album I made with him, I had a bunch of solos. You never like what you play, I guess, so I thought I had really messed up the end of some tune. I used to ride with him, just the two of us, and after we made the record, we were on the road driving along and I said, 'Jeez, Woody, I'm sorry I really screwed up the end of that tune.' He said, 'By the time the record comes out in six months you won't even know it. You'll love it.' And it was the truth. He knew that but I didn't know it. Oh yes, Woody was another beautiful guy.

"Maynard was an astounding musician. I don't know if you know this, but he plays every instrument that was ever invented. He can play anything. His was probably the most popular band I ever worked with. We would go to a town and Maynard was always a very sharp dresser so six months later we would go back to the same town and all the kids in the audience would be wearing what Maynard had worn six months before. I think we had three tunes in our entire library that he wasn't featured on. If Maynard was late for the job we were in big trouble because we didn't have anything we could play without him. I was with that band for about a year and that was a hard job because we played a lot of things with a lot of brass and there were only six of us counting Maynard. It was three trumpets and two trombones. I won't say we were

Maynard Ferguson Orchestra, unknown ballroom, Boston MA, late 1961. *L-r*: Bill Berry, Don Rader (t); possibly John Neves (b); Maynard Ferguson (t, ldr). Courtesy William Berry Jr.

playing Stan Kenton-type music but sort of like that and with half the number of brass players that Stan had. It was hard work. We used to play about half the year in Birdland which was a very difficult room to play in physically. It was covered with carpets, the walls, the ceilings and the drapes. It was dead acoustically. When you're pumping as hard as we had to with Maynard's band, that's really difficult. I went from Maynard's band directly to Ellington's band which was totally different. They played so softly sometimes that it was almost a whisper. The whole band. It was great. Way down. They never worked like Maynard's band. Just the opposite.

"I was in Thad (Jones) and Mel (Lewis's) band right from the beginning (1966) for the first three or four years. We were never really on the road. That was a one-night-a-week band and it was all the busiest guys in New York. I was very glad to be in on it. It was very interesting music, very difficult music but Thad was also a real beautiful, gentle swinger. After Ellington nothing ever came up to that level again. Duke's was the last road band I was with and the next big band I worked with was Thad Jones which was totally different, of course. A different approach completely, but to me nothing ever was as good as that Ellington band. Even Thad's band, that was a wonderful band, with the best guys in town and great players. Guys like Snooky Young and Pepper Adams. Snooky was a great jazz player, not too many people know that but he played great solos. He was one of the champs with that plunger mute."

Bill Berry (cnt), Los Angeles CA, 1970s. Personal promo. Photo by Patricia Willard. Courtesy Ernie Garside.

Berry was born in Benton Harbor, Michigan in September 1930, where his father, a travelling musician and bandleader, was playing a gig. "Born in the bass horn case!" he laughed. "I used to sleep in the bass horn case so they tell me. As far as being a bandleader, my mother told me that when I was two or three years old I had a white tuxedo and used to lead the band. It sounds silly now. Yes, my dad was a musician just about until the war started. Musicians were working during the Depression and nobody else was. On the road, but working. They would have done anything in those days. We're very close now but I don't think that I really knew him that well then because he was always working. At one point in the thirties after we got off the road, he worked at a day job running a lathe or something for eight or nine hours a day, five or six days a week, then he worked from six to eight-thirty in a dinner place, then from nine to one in a dance hall. Every night. He had three full-time jobs and in the meantime was taking a correspondence course in drafting. I didn't see him a lot but he was certainly working for the family. I always admired him.

"I never had any thoughts of being anything but a musician once I found out I wasn't going to be Batman. Or Sherlock Holmes! My dad and I used to listen to John Kirby's band broadcast Saturday or Sunday mornings and it was all music, all the way. I never had the kind of problems with parents that most musicians do. Everything was all right. I believe that in order to be any kind of musician, it's got to be 24 hours a day. No such thing as doing it part-time.

"'I was a studio musician for 15 years steadily but always made sure that I played jazz at nights because studio music isn't really music. It's sound effects for a movie or a television show. They don't want individuality. They want you to fit in like a cog in a machine. That's OK but it's not musical at all. So that's very frustrating. You play it because it pays wonderfully. That's a good reason. I'm not knocking it. The timing was just right for me. I did it from just about the time our son was born till he was 14 or 15 years old so I also had the advantage that a lot of musicians don't have, of being home with my family during those years. I didn't do any travelling in those days. I was too busy. We used to start making records or TV or radio commercials, at eight or nine o'clock in the morning. We'd do two or three of those and then I'd go to the (Merv Griffin) television show. I was so busy I used to send a substitute in to make the rehearsal for the television show while I was out making a record or something. But then after the television show was over I'd try to work (play jazz) at night. We used to be up 19, 20 hours a day. Every day.

"For the last ten years or so I haven't done anything but play jazz. I don't make nearly as much money as I used to but I don't care. I'm doing what I want now. My best friend (tenor saxophonist) Richie Kamuca died very unexpectedly. We always talked about what we'd do when the television show ended. We did play a lot together at the Half Note in New York and in LA but I thought, 'My God that could have been me,'

Bill Berry's Ellington All-Stars, Donte's Club, North Hollywood CA, 29 April 1976. *L-r:* Britt Woodman (tb); Nick Ceroli (d); Marshal Royal (as); Ray Brown (b); Bill Berry (t); Jimmy Jones (p). Courtesy William Berry Jr.

because it happened just like that. He got sick one day and died. So I said, 'I better do it now.' This is it. In California the people who do the studio work are generally hired by the writer, the composer, and as the young composers came in, and are coming in now, they hire their friends. Of course I'd do the same thing. That's perfectly natural. I wouldn't fit in to what they're playing anyway so why would they hire me? So everything worked out perfectly. I just think it's a natural progression. I was certainly ready to quit that stuff. When I was more or less forced to, I did it and it worked out just fine. When I do get an occasional studio call, I usually do it if I'm in town but I can't wait to get out. Everyone else is hoping they'll get an hour of overtime and I'm hoping we won't."

So why take on a big band of your own, with all the attendant hassles and problems? "I seem to have a talent for that. I seem to be able to get the music out of the players. It's nothing overt. Now, I get calls for the band so of course, I'm going to take them, so I guess that makes me a bandleader. It wasn't anything I ever thought of doing. The reason I started the band in the first place was because I'd been doing some writing and my wife said to get some guys together to play my charts. Yes, I still write

Bill Berry Big Band, Donte's Club, North Hollywood CA, 22 February 1986. *Front, L-r*: Jack Nimitz (bs); Lanny Morgan (as); Marshal Royal (solo as); Herman Riley (ts); Jackie Kelso (ts); Bill Berry (standing at right). *Middle*: Garnett Brown, Slyde Hyde, Buster Cooper (tb); Frank Capp (d); Dave Frishberg (p). *Rear*: Al Aarons, Frank Szabo, Johnny Audino, Conte Candoli (t); Chuck Berghofer (b). Courtesy William Berry Jr.

occasionally but like Duke said, I can't do it unless I have a deadline. Then I can do it but I don't enjoy doing it. It's very hard work for me because I'm not that good at it. It takes me a long time and it's difficult.

"I have been very fortunate because the only times, with a couple of exceptions, that anyone has left the (Bill Berry) band is because they had to leave town or they died. I had a band in New York for about six months (in 1970) but then we had to leave town because the Merv Griffin show moved to Los Angeles. From the original West Coast band I still have Jack Nimitz. He may be the last one left now. The original trombone players, Britt Woodman, Benny Powell and so forth moved back to New York but then Buster (Cooper) showed up out there. Marshal Royal has been with me for 18 years now. That's almost as long as he was with Basie and Lanny Morgan has been there for 15 years that I can remember. The tenor chairs have changed around more than anything else and of course when Cat and Blue (Mitchell) died we had to get a couple more trumpet players but Jack Sheldon had been there right from the beginning almost. He's indescribable but I love him and he's a great player. He hates to travel, hates being away from home. More so than any musician I've ever met. He works constantly in LA.

I mean two or three jobs a day. The band's an occasional thing, especially as I'm out of town so much but we usually work two or three times a month, usually different things. No place steady. No rehearsals. I got an award last year, a humorous award for the Least Rehearsed Best Big Band. But the kind of music we play, once you learn the arrangement it's different every time anyway. People say to me, 'Do you have a rehearsal band?' and I say, 'No, absolutely not!' I would say we rehearse about once every two years.

"What I'd really like to do and it'll probably never come to pass because it's too expensive, is get my big band over here in England. Excuse my immodesty but it's a great band and I know it would knock everybody out if we could get the money organised. Airplanes cost so much these days and I have to pay the band well because they're the best. It's a problem taking the band out of town even for a day or two. Thankfully they work for me for very little but it still costs a lot. We're going to Lake Tahoe, Reno, from Los Angeles for one concert and the airplane fare is something like $8,000 and it's only an hour flight. That's before you start talking about hotel rooms and salaries. So we don't travel much. It's a big hassle too. Just getting them to the airport, along with the music and the bandstands. My wife helps, and my son, he's been raised in it so he knows what to do and what not to do. For instance, for jobs that come in while I'm gone, he will hire the right people and take care of it. Which is great for me. He loves jazz and he's a very good musician. He plays piano and recently he's been writing vocal arrangements for a group he sings in. He's just graduated from university in film and TV production. He's always been interested in film. He was animating things when he was seven or eight years old. He works for a film distributor now. They distribute mostly bad films to third world countries but they also make commercials for cable television. They've got him hiring singers, voice-over people and things like that. It's a tough business to be in. It's like this one, there's no such thing as a steady job. It's from day to day. This business of playing solo like I'm doing now is so simple. I don't have to worry about anybody but me. It's much easier."

Berry always seemed to find compatible musicians for his groups. "It's very simple. If you want to play the kind of music you like with the guys you prefer, then you've got to be the leader. When you work for somebody else they're going to do what they want. I try to use the guys out of the big bands pretty much. These are musicians you respect. I usually use our rhythm section which is now Ross Tompkins on piano – Dave Frishberg was with the band from New York days until about two years ago when he moved out of town up to Oregon – Monty Budwig on bass and Frankie Capp on drums, depending on what kind of job it is. I get a lot of jobs where they say, 'We want you to do Ellington stuff' so then I will hire Marshal Royal usually, or Buster Cooper, or both, and if it's a job that requires more bebop, then I'll hire Don Menza or Lanny Morgan or Nimitz. Or I'll hire Gerald Wiggins, a wonderful piano player, when I can afford it. And then I've been using a great pianist named George Gaffney, who was with Sarah Vaughan, when he's in town. I sometimes use him with Andy Simpkins, the bass player. I believe in audience involvement and I think if the band is having a good time, if they're enjoying themselves, that'll communicate with the audience. And if they're not, that'll communicate as well. My first thing is I want the band to be happy.

"There's just so many good musicians in Los Angeles but there are problems in getting together. That town must be miles across. The San Fernando Valley goes for miles. Where I live is called North Hollywood and it's just over the mountain from Hollywood. I can get to Hollywood in five minutes but to go to the beach towns like Hermosa Beach, Newport Beach, anywhere down south, that's a good hour's drive. And that's if there's no traffic. If you live in the western end of the San Fernando Valley it's a two-hour drive. Everybody in Los Angeles says it's twenty minutes from everywhere to everywhere else, well it isn't! It may be the biggest city, territorially, in the world. You can go swimming in the morning in the ocean and go skiing in the afternoon in the mountains. People do this. It's totally different from any other part of the United States. I like California very much and I'm glad I live there but truthfully the reason that I live there at the moment is because of the big band and the musicians in that town. They're the best in the country. With the kind of work I'm doing I could live almost anywhere where there was an airport but you never get weather like that anywhere else. I haven't owned a top coat in twenty years!"

Benny Carter Group, rehearsal prior to Japanese tour, Los Angeles CA, 1983. *L-r*: Buster Cooper (tb); Harold Land (ts); Bill Berry (cnt); Benny Carter (as, arr). At *rear*: unknown; Buddy Collette. Courtesy William Berry Jr.

Are there opportunities to get together informally to jam in this extraordinary city? "Yeah, about six blocks from my house. There were four jazz clubs within a mile, two of them are no longer extant but the other two are a block apart from each other. One is called Alphonse's, the big band works there once a month or so but they have music seven nights a week and there's one up the street called MoneyTree which has music five or six nights a week. They have the Page Cavanaugh Trio on three days and they have Jack Sheldon for two days so if I'm in town and I feel like playing, like it's a Tuesday or Wednesday, I just go down and play with Jack. And he works at Alphonse's every Sunday and usually, unless it's an organised group, I could go into Alphonse's almost any night of the week."

Bill made it clear that the fraternity of jazz musicians in Los Angeles was something of a special elite within a larger musical community so I asked him if there were individual players who deserved wider exposure.

"Lots and lots of them, of course. Take Clora Bryant, the trumpet player. She used to work in my band. Did you hear the story about her just recently? She wrote a letter to Gorbachev and she just went over to the Soviet Union. They loved her. It was a strange thing they agreed to get her a band and to pay her but she had to get there herself. They couldn't pay her air transportation so we had a big party where everybody played and raised the money for her. There's that kind of community. We'll get together if somebody gets sick or has an accident, usually it's a tragedy but this wasn't. They had it at the Musicians' Union, it was an all-day thing, ten different groups played. And then there's Herman Riley, he plays tenor in my band. He's a great player. I've got several jobs next month when I get home and Herman is doing them. He's another one I sometimes use in the quintet. He can do it all. We went to Japan together last year (1988) with Benny Carter."

Benny Carter Group, prior to Japanese tour, Los Angeles CA, August 1987. L-r: Bucky Pizzarelli (g); Oscar Brashear (t); Bill Berry (cnt); Bill Bell (p); Benny Carter (as); Britt Woodman (tb); Sherman Ferguson (d); Herman Riley (ts); Cecil Payne (bs); Frank Tusa (b). Photo by Ed Berger. Courtesy Britt Woodman.

"Any regrets? No. Nothing is all good but I wouldn't trade any of it for anything else. I wish I had practised more and I wish I could work some more. I meet somebody, not musicians, when I'm some place like this and they say, 'Oh, you're on holiday' and I say, 'Well, no, I'm working.' I don't know that I've ever taken a holiday because I'm doing what I want now. I don't want to get away from it. You run into friends all over the world. I think jazz is more popular today than it's ever been. I remember one time about 12 years ago Richie Kamuca, Jake Hanna, Nat Pierce and I got a job at some little club in LA for one night and the entire audience consisted of my wife and my mother and father who happened to be visiting. In fact Nat was in bad shape in those days and we each chipped in two and a half dollars to give Nat ten dollars. We didn't make a cent. A year later we were making records with the exact same band. We couldn't give it away a year earlier. For many reasons, jazz has always been looked down on by the establishment but now they're giving people like Dizzy awards on national television and he gets invited to the White House.

"Certain people think you've got to be black to play jazz but that's like saying you have to be German to play Beethoven. That's ridiculous. I don't think that the real serious musicians believe that at all. Rex Stewart was crazy about Bix Beiderbecke. He loved him. After my time with Ellington, later on in New York, there was a strong view about white players among a minority but certainly not in Duke's band. Thad Jones didn't feel that way. This music was strictly American and now it's international. I play a lot in Japan with Japanese musicians. Great musicians. Here too. They're greatly influenced by Americans, naturally, as Americans invented it. I have a friend over there who plays in the Lester Young school and there's another one that they call the Johnny Hodges of Japan. Wonderful alto player. He doesn't sound like Johnny but he's in that groove. For example, I'm playing at the Pizza Express (in Soho) tonight and the sign says 'Bill Berry Quintet'. I have no idea who the other four people are but I'm not concerned about it because I know they'll be good. In the United States it used to be, not so long ago, that if you got pretty good on your instrument, you had to leave town no matter wherever you were. You had to either go to New York or

Bill Berry Quintet with special guest Tommy Whittle, Pizza Express Jazz Club, Dean Street, London, 1 June 1988. *L-r*: Bobby Orr (d); Bill Berry (cnt); Tommy Whittle (ts); Tony Lee (p). Photo by Peter Vacher.

Los Angeles because they're the headquarters. Still are. But now all over the country and not just in the States either, there are excellent musicians everywhere, who no longer have to leave their home town to be good. And that's fairly recent. Certainly well within my playing time.

"What was really extraordinary about Ellington's music was that it seemed to have a lot to do with love. I have seen that band play for an old folks' home or a kindergarten class, doesn't make any difference, they all got the message. That's very unusual. But Ellington could do it. I played for Ellington's 70th birthday at the White House and the waiters who work all the functions there said it was totally different from any other party they'd ever had in the White House. The Supreme Court was there, and the President, and the Cabinet, all the biggest people plus Dizzy and Benny Goodman, and all kinds of musical luminaries. Ellington was the kind of guy, when he walked in a room the light went on. Armstrong was like that too. Even if somebody didn't know who they were, they could feel the magnetism."

At this point I asked Bill to talk about the moments in his own playing when everything came out as he wanted it. "That's rare but when that moment does occur it's worth it all but the funny thing is, quite often, most of the time maybe, when you do play something that you really like nobody says a word; then when you play something that you think is terrible everybody goes, 'Yeah, great!' We've all talked about that sort of thing and nobody can explain it and you never know when it's going to happen. You can't plan for it. It'll happen under odd circumstances. I played with a rhythm section a month or so ago that were good but I wasn't expecting anything outstanding. Then right from the first note everything worked well.

"I've managed not only to know and meet, but to record with, a lot of my childhood idols. I've made a lot of records. For my own playing probably the best record I ever made was the *Shortcake* album on Concord. The first big-band album (*Hot and Happy* on Beez, 1974) I like very well too. That's long out of print. It was on my own label and that's why it's out of print! I sold it to Carl Jefferson (of Concord) but he never brought it out. He owned it and I don't, I'm sorry to say. (Trumpeter) Blue Mitchell plays a solo on 'Smoke Gets In Your Eyes' (that we sight-read that night on the concert) and well, it's phenomenal. I'd known Blue for years and he was not only a great player but a great person. Very gentle. I have known quite a few like Blue. I feel very fortunate about that like I feel very fortunate about everything. I have been in the right places at the right times. I've gotten to work with the best people in the world. That's always what I wanted to do.

"I feel I'm just getting warmed up. Like when I get back I'm working several jobs with Juggernaut (big band). I've been a member of that from the beginning, and then I'm working at Alphonse's with three different groups, one with a friend of mine who's a singer, one with a quartet and then with the big band. After that I'm going up to San

Francisco for a while then to Japan. I'm the musical director of the Monterey Jazz Festival and I also have the youth band at the festival, the California High School Band. I've been doing that for about ten years now and we always tour Japan with the youth band in the summertime so that's the next big thing that's coming up. After that we get back and it's the Monterey Festival for a week. I'll conduct the kids and Dizzy is going to work with my kids. He's also working that night with Billy Eckstine and then Illinois Jacquet's band. The Monterey Festival is a three-day affair but I'm there for a week. I'll play with an all-star group on the final night but I don't really know where I'll be playing otherwise. Then I'll be going to Japan for a one-night affair and then I'm doing some school things and another little festival where I'm also the MD, in Portland, Oregon, and then back to Japan until just about Christmas time. My son told me on the phone the other day that Benny Carter had called me to go to Japan which would make four trips there this year but I don't think I'm going to be able to make that one because I have this other thing in the middle that I must do.

"As to working with kids, well I seem to be able to make them make music. I don't know why but I'm good with kids, if I do say so. I seem to have a good rapport with kids. Quite often they'll want me to do an Ellington programme, for one thing, I have the music physically and nobody else does. The notes aren't all that hard, not like trying to play Thad Jones's or Don Menza's music but it's actually more difficult, especially with young people because it's so simple that it's difficult to play. I take some Basie things too and 'Moten Swing' is almost impossible for young bands to play. It's too easy and they don't know what to make of it. They can play a million miles an hour but this defeats them.

"Nobody's ever been able to define jazz. I often ask kids at a clinic or a class to tell me the difference between jazz and any other kind of music and the kids will say it's improvised. I'll tell them all music is improvised at some point – there was music long before there was paper and a composer has got to think of it before he writes it down so that's not it. Well, they'll say, 'It's got a steady beat' and I say, 'so has a march and so has a waltz.' You get all kinds of answers and then finally somebody will say that jazz swings. That to me is the answer. If a tape comes on in the elevator everybody in the world knows immediately it's jazz, even if they don't know (exactly) what it is, they know it's jazz because it has a different feeling from any other kind of music. Now then if that is the criterion then is that other stuff – the avant-garde – jazz, because it isn't swinging? It can be very good music but is it jazz?"

Adapted from a longer version
first published in two parts as
'Bill Berry in conversation with Peter Vacher' in
Jazz Journal, July and October 1990

Benny Powell

Benny Powell (1930–2010), Randy Weston's African Rhythms, Birmingham, UK, 1993. Photo by Brian Foskett. Courtesy Brian Foskett.

Benny Powell visited the UK many times with Count Basie but somehow our paths never crossed; I was always too busy chasing other Basie-ites for interview. We did meet backstage at Brecon Jazz in August 2004 where he performed with Randy Weston's African Rhythms Quintet but it was hearing Benny at St. Peter's in April 2006 that inspired me to fix the interview whose outcome is presented here. It's true that he was a little reluctant at first but we soon established a friendly rapport which continued via e-mail for a while. It's also correct that he was so pleased with this Jazz Journal feature (and my cover photo) that he ordered 50 copies of the magazine for distribution to friends and family. It's equally clear that a single interview like this could hardly do justice to a career that was suffused with variety and achievement. I was pleased, however, that we were able to home in on his early days in New Orleans, a facet of his life that most interviews skated over.

Benny died of a heart attack in hospital on 26 June 2010 following a routine spinal operation. Just days before, he had played at the annual open-house concert at the Louis Armstrong House in Corona, NY with an all-star band. It's especially appropriate that Fred Sater's fine photograph should depict this 'gentle, determined' man playing in his beloved St. Peter's alongside fellow trombonist Tom Artin.

The lofty atrium that encloses New York's St. Peter's Lutheran Church may seem an unusual setting for a jazz performance. More so, perhaps, because this modern worship space is shoehorned into the vast, glittering Citicorp building that stands at the corner of West 54th Street and Seventh Avenue in downtown Manhattan. An unlikely fusion of God and Mammon, you could say. Still, this is no ordinary church and Benny Powell was no ordinary jazz musician.

St. Peter's ministers to the Big Apple's jazz community, originally through Pastor John Gensel and then via Pastor Dale Lind, a genial, bearded man whose sibilant delivery was eerily reminiscent of broadcaster Garrison Keillor. The occasion that drew our attention was the Easter Day Jazz Vespers with Benny Powell and Friends in April 2006. Powell's music was a crucial part of the service as were his spiritual reflections, happily complementing the solemnity of the Eucharist and laying bare the trombonist's continuing gratitude for a life that might otherwise have been cut short by serious illness.

Mr Powell was a dignified man, with a reserved air, whose smile was sometimes slow to arrive. You sensed that he was waiting to assess your seriousness, to know whether your enquiries had some depth to them, before he opened up. Aged 76 at the time of our meeting, he lived alone in mid-town Manhattan in an apartment that was showing signs of age, with the detritus of life spread around. There was a piano to one side, small piles of CD albums and centre stage, a trombone on its stand. Mr. Powell had been practising.

The bare bones of trombonist Benjamin Gordon Powell Jr.'s career story are these: born New Orleans, 1 March 1930. Early experience with territory bands, joined Lionel Hampton in 1948, stayed three years, joined Count Basie in 1951, stayed 12 years. Played for Merv Griffin TV show in New York and Los Angeles. Extensive freelance work and recordings. Tours with Randy Weston, taught at the New School in New York and led own group. Vast discography.

It would take a whole series of interviews to cover such a career adequately but our time was short. Mr. Powell had an engagement to fulfil. Our first topic was a more personal one. I had been concerned to hear him refer to illness when he spoke at St. Peter's and asked him to elaborate. "It's been ten years since I had a kidney transplant – ten borrowed years," he explained. "It's a funny kind of disease. It certainly didn't debilitate me. I was still travelling and I never missed a gig. When I'd come to Europe with (pianist) Randy Weston, he always provided the greatest care; a lot of times he had the bus fixed up with a seat in the back where I could stretch out and get some rest. He's a very thoughtful man and I was grateful to be working for such a person.

"When I was born, they (the kidneys) both didn't develop at birth but the funny thing about that is you can last all these years on one kidney. It kept me out of the Army, which was great, as I'm a peaceful man. I didn't want to fight anybody so it worked to my advantage. Then I had dialysis for 15 years. Three times a week. After I got it straight in my mind, I never had a problem going. I adapted. When I didn't feel well, I could send in a substitute. Before I was faced with dialysis, I'd been with Lionel Hampton, Count Basie, Merv Griffin, and I said, wow, I have all of this done on one kidney. So I have nothing to be angry about. It certainly didn't deprive me of anything."

During the course of his participation in the St. Peter's service, Benny sang a couple of numbers, with lyrics that he had written himself. Was this a new venture, I wondered? "One of the songs I did yesterday was my own – in fact it's the title of my last CD called *The Gift of Love*. I thought I could write new lyrics to it, which would be appropriate for Easter Sunday. I had to do research from books I have and put my mind to it for a couple of days. I really enjoyed the experience of doing the research and thinking about just the right words. I told my pianist Sayuri Goto that I'm going to write religious lyrics to all my songs. She said, 'Wow, that could start a whole new career for you, at 76!'"

Obviously a man for whom spiritual considerations were important, Benny had an active connection with St. Peter's. "The church has a jazz ministry and I love playing there. I met the original pastor (Reverend Gensel) a while ago. They called him the

Night Shepherd. Lovely man. There was a pianist named Eddie Bonnemere who was very close to religious things and for a while we played a service every Sunday. Through that I became affiliated with the church and found that most musicians have a spiritual side that they seldom allude to so it has provided an outlet for this. We've had memorial services for Duke Ellington and all the greats."

Benny's New Orleans upbringing, like that of so many African-American performers, was coloured by intense religious observance. "I come from a loving family, a pretty religious family; well, my three sisters go to church more often than I do. We were taught spirituality, that there is a God and He enhances your life." I then asked Benny to talk about his early days in the Crescent City in particular as other interviews have tended to concentrate on his years with Basie. Indeed, as he observed, many people had no idea that he was from Louisiana as he'd left home for good when only 16. "My house was just on the edge of Louis Armstrong Park," he told me. "I lived on Marais and St. Philip Street. Things were pretty segregated during those days though not totally. Right around the corner from me was a white family. When we were very little kids, we played together but at a certain age there was a cut-off.

"My father died of a heart attack when I was six years old so I didn't know him very well but my mother was just the most wonderful woman you could imagine. She even put a down payment on a house; I don't know where she got the money from but she did it. She had a college degree but in those times it didn't do black women any good. So when my father died she started working as a domestic worker, ironing people's shirts. She worked in the French Quarter and while she was upstairs ironing shirts, I was down in the Quarter having fun. Being the seaport town it was, all races and cultures came into New Orleans. There were so many influences."

Benny's first musical leanings were towards the drums but at the age of 12 there came a Damascean moment at an uncle's house. "As kids get bored around grown-ups, I fidgeted around on the sofa; instead of sitting, I was kneeling and I happened to spy this trombone case behind the sofa. I asked about it, and he took it out and let me see it. Well, in New Orleans at that time, if you showed interest in anything, your parents immediately found you a teacher so that you could have some other outlet for your life's work. My mother found Eddie Pierson[1] as my teacher. He was a marvellous player, because he was pretty broad (stylistically). I don't know if he'd been with any of the travelling bands. He made sure I could read and he taught me just major scales, how to produce a tone, but when we talked about style, he liked Trummy Young and that kind of player. I was fascinated by that too, because Trummy Young was a smooth trombone player as opposed to somebody else who was a little more raucous. I met guys like Eddie Durham and Dicky Wells later but I didn't really meet any of the New Orleans trombonists who later were part of the Preservation Hall Jazz Band. I was like a bebop baby; I came up in the early 1940s. No, there was no music in the family but we all took music lessons because it was just part of your social upbringing."

Benny then mentioned an incident, which cemented his desire to play trombone. "I was sitting in the back of a car and it had the top down, and right behind us there was one of these social club parades and the trombonists were at the front. I saw this guy; he looked like he was having such a grand time, just marching. I was fascinated by his joy at playing and his pride, the way he walked, and the way when the musicians would stop somewhere and have some refreshments, the ladies were flocking around him. I found out, wow, he actually got paid for that. That's not a bad way to make a living. My mother called him over to have me meet him because I was so fascinated by the trombone."

Evidently quick off the mark, Benny remembers playing with Sidney Desvignes and Kid somebody – "there's a bunch of Kids in New Orleans" – before becoming part of the Dooky Chase Orchestra in 1945. "This was a juvenile band. Because this was during the war years, the forties, we had a pretty good success. In New Orleans there are many celebrations. So there's a social club dance almost every week. Dooky Chase Jr.[2]

Dooky Chase Orchestra, Laborer's Hall, Iberville St., New Orleans, 1945. *Rear, L-r:* Tony Moret, Theodore 'Teddy' Riley, Arnold DePass Jr. (t); Vernel Fournier (d); Leroy 'Batman' Rankins (b). *Middle*: Awood Johnson, Benjamin 'Benny' Powell (tb); Dooky Chase Jr. (t, ldr); John 'Picket' Brunious (p, arr); Doris Chase, Andrew Brown (voc). *Front:* Warren Bell Sr. (ts); Larry Smith, Charlie Gaspard (as); Sterling White (bs); Hilton Carter (ts); Curtis Trevigne (g). Photo by A.P. Bedou. Courtesy Tulane Jazz Archive.

played trumpet. His father was a restaurateur and he became a restaurateur too. Dooky Chase's is one of the most famous restaurants in New Orleans. Dooky was a very good-looking guy, looked like Desi Arnaz, and used to try and emulate Louis Armstrong by having a handkerchief as part of his persona. He organised us pretty well. We didn't record.

"We played stock arrangements from Basie and Lunceford, but there were some original arrangers in New Orleans, like the guy who played piano with Dooky Chase, his name was 'Picket' Brunious. He was a very fine arranger but we were so busy playing stocks and covers, we played his originals but they were mixed in with everything else.

"Vernel Fournier was our drummer; he and I went to grammar school together, along with Wilbert Hogan, another drummer. Vernel was one of my best friends. When we were kids, I had a record player so Vernel used to come over to my house and bring the records so we could listen to them. I remember a very cute incident with my mother. She heard that music so much until one time I walked into the kitchen and she's singing 'Oo-Bop-She-Bam'. I thought that was a lovely experience.

"Warren Bell Sr.[3], our alto player, was the one we thought was going farther than anybody. There's guys in New Orleans who develop that stay-at-home attitude. They have comfortable lives. He might have gone into some kind of business thing. I understand his son is now a prominent newscaster. Warren was part of the after-hours experimental scene and I was part of it too.

"Bebop, that was all we wanted to hear. Trumpeter Emery Humphrey (actually Emery Humphrey Thompson aka Umar Sharif)[4] had been to New York and he brought back some of the early bebop records. I remember 'Shaw 'Nuff' was one of them, and 'Groovin' High', the early things by Dizzy Gillespie and Charlie Parker. We were just totally blown away."

Once the draft began to impact the Chase band and "some of the guys got restless and decided to join the Army", Benny, armed with good grades from school, and still only sixteen, elected to go to Alabama State Teachers College. "As I said, my mother was a domestic worker but on her salary she sent me and all my three sisters to college. I chose Alabama because the famous Erskine Hawkins band had graduated from there and because I knew then I wanted to be a musician."

Accompanied by Fournier, who had also enrolled at Alabama State, Benny drove from Louisiana to Alabama, passing through Mississippi, then inhospitable country for blacks. "So many bad things had happened there. I remember one time we ran out of gas and we had to break the lock on a pump and steal gas. We were two frightened young men but fortunately nothing happened to us. We got there and we got back."

Benny's stay at Alabama State was short-lived. "The next year, when I came home during the summer break, Arnold DePass Jr., the trumpet player from Dooky Chase's band, was going with King Kolax's band. He had already been there for a short time and he was going to rejoin. They needed a trombone player so I talked it over with my mother and she gave me her blessing because she saw the opportunities were pretty limited in New Orleans. I joined King Kolax in Port Arthur, Texas. He was a good man, like an uncle to me. I was barely 17 and he took me under his wing. He was a high-note player and he had been with Billy Eckstine's big band for a while.

"King Kolax's band was like an offshoot from the Eckstine band. We were playing covers of bebop things – it was total bebop but bebop for dancing because we still had a beat. Kolax looked like Thad Jones, he was a very muscular sort of man. I was always fortunate enough to work with bandleaders who I admired and who liked me because I was a nice, polite kid," he said.

"We played in Port Arthur for a while and then started travelling throughout that area. There were things called territory bands at that time and that's what we were. It was really a small big band – maybe 12 pieces. We used to get stranded a lot. They'd get you a job and the job would cancel, and we didn't have the money to go on so we'd stay in that town until the Ferguson Brothers (agency) office in Indianapolis sent us money to move on. I remember New Bern, North Carolina, we got stranded there during the summer, and I used to go into the supermarket with this jacket, like an army jacket, with many pockets, and load up my pockets with stolen food, and pay for just a little bit of it and go out. We didn't have money enough to get a hotel room so we slept in the bus, up in the luggage rack or whatever. I was just a kid, what did I care?

"Anyway we got stranded again with King Kolax, this time in Oklahoma City, and somehow I heard of an opening with the Ernie Fields band out of Tulsa, Oklahoma. When we first got stranded in Oklahoma City, we were staying two people in a room. By the time I left, we had one room for *12* people. Six were sleeping in the room; the other six were sleeping in the park or walking the streets. I walked out of the front door as if I was going to the grocery shopping. Fortunately, our room was on the rear of the hotel and Vernel, who was with me in Kolax's band, lowered my bag down on a rope and I grabbed it and ran to the bus station and joined Ernie Fields's band in Tulsa."

It's clear that Fournier, two years older than Powell, and a prominent part of pianist Ahmad Jamal's later success, was important to the trombonist as both friend and mentor. "I liked his philosophy, he was a deep-thinking man, and he became a Muslim (as Amir Rushdan) in later years. We both travelled with bands and when he left New Orleans, he moved to Chicago (in 1948) so we didn't see each other for a long time. I came to New York and then I'd see him sometimes when Basie's band would go to Chicago. When I was first getting married, he said, 'Be faithful to your wife, do everything to have a good marriage so if anything does happen, you won't have any regrets. People do change after marriage; they just get other goals, other ideas for themselves.' That really influenced me."

Ernie Fields (ldr, tb), Ernie Fields and His Orchestra, possibly Tulsa OK, late 1940s. Ferguson Brothers Agency promo.

Ironically, both men went on to marry and divorce three times. "You would have loved Vernel. Lovely man. I guess we were like little old men, even in those days. We never fooled around or played pranks as kids did. We were so involved in the music, and we just wanted to play all the time." When I suggested to Benny that his move to the Fields band was a step up, an improvement, he was quick to correct me. "I didn't look at it that way. King Kolax wasn't working that much, Ernie Fields was," he said, flatly. "I was with Ernie Fields a year. He played third trombone. Well, he played enough to hold a trombone, and lead the band. Being the businessman he was, we worked pretty much. Predominantly black dances, but some colleges too. His son, Ernie Fields Jr. is a very important contractor in Los Angeles now – I worked for him couple of times with Aretha Franklin. He contracts TV shows.

"As fate would have it, Lionel Hampton's band came though Tulsa. He had just had Chips Outcalt, one of his trombonists, leave him in Oklahoma City. Betty Carter was Lionel Hampton's adviser into bebop and she knew who could play – he called her Betty Bebop, if you remember – and I found out later she gave me the thumbs up."

I asked Benny to comment on Hampton and his time with the band, so he paused, and said soberly, "Hamp was a very interesting man. I never did get very close to him. He was a pretty self-centred guy. Kinda selfish. When something wasn't right or he wanted to admonish somebody in the band, he would have a meeting just before the show. He'd get us all on stage and tell us how unworthy we were. He'd say, 'People come to see me. I can get out on stage and urinate on stage and people will applaud that.' He would go on and on like this, and when he was finished, he'd say, 'All right, gentlemen, let's have a good show.' I'd say to myself, 'Good show! I feel like crying.'

"On the other hand, he was an amazing musician himself and never did get credit for his musicianship because he was so visual. He was busy entertaining the people. He'd do anything for entertainment. He was a very modern guy and we had great arrangements but they were so covered up by show business. In the band, we felt Hamp was self-centred because he'd play all the time and never wanted to get off the stage. And he wouldn't pay overtime!"

I asked Benny about his relationship with the legendary Gladys Hampton, Hamp's wife, who acted as his business manager. "I got along well with her," he said. "I respected her, she respected me. I didn't have that much contact with her. She had been wardrobe person for Joan Crawford in Hollywood and she had a great business sense. A lot of time she got blamed for Hamp's selfishness. He didn't seem to care too much about business. He would make sure he got what he wanted. Other things we did, like radio shows, sometimes he didn't pay us." Benny's solo possibilities were limited due to the substantial presence of fellow trombonist Al Grey. "Hamp had his favourite players. In those days, and even in later days (with Basie), I lived in the shadow of Al Grey. When he got finished, maybe I got eight bars, maybe Jimmy Cleveland got eight bars. Jimmy was a wonderful player (died August 2008). He went into real estate – he owned a couple of buildings in Los Angeles.

"I don't remember too many of the guys but (pianist) Milt Buckner was there. He was a sweetheart. He played trombone also. It was the same thing as with Hamp – Milt's showmanship superseded his value in music. First of all, he was a short guy and kinda round, so he did comedy and clowned around. He was a great writer as well. Was I bored by playing the same things all the time? No, I was having so much fun, and so many wonderful experiences. I was a teenager still. I was only 17 when I joined Hamp; 21 when I joined Basie." Recalling his New Orleans origins, Benny laughed as he remembered an incident with Hamp. "We did a sort of anthology or history of jazz and there was a period in it that had (early) New Orleans music and being from there, I was supposed to play that, but every time I played, it came out like Jay Jay Johnson. In the end, the trombone part was played by a Japanese guy (Paul Higaki) from San Francisco!"

Knowing that Benny had always cited Johnson as his principal inspiration, I asked him if he'd known him personally. "To me, if it didn't sound like Jay Jay, I wasn't too much interested. I was with the new guys. I think I first met him down South. He was with Benny Carter's band. We became great friends; in fact, I have his bass trombone now. When he started writing, I was, like, his first-call trombonist to play jingles and things he had written for TV. He was a wonderful man. I guess Slide Hampton is the closest thing to him as a player and as a person too. We've known each other since we were teenagers. In recent times, I've played often in Slide's 14-trombones group, and he's been a wonderful friend and supporter, even now. I can find myself playing at the Blue Note with his ten or 12 trombonists and he'll always give me a prominent spot."

Benny left the other Hampton in 1951 and moved to Hull in Quebec. Why? I wondered. "Between racial prejudice and Hamp's pettiness, I got sick and tired of a whole bunch of things. I was the young kid and I wasn't one of his favourites. We played Canada with Hamp and then I quit and moved back there. I stayed for a while and when I came back to New York, I was working at the Apollo Theatre playing for the acts with Joe Thomas, the saxophone player who'd been with Lunceford. Charlie Fowlkes, the baritone saxophonist, was part of the band. He told me Basie's band was reorganising and if I was interested to come to a rehearsal. I did and I wasn't hired on the spot but began doing weekends with them. This was October 1951. We would go

Benny Powell (tb), Count Basie Orchestra, unknown location, 1950s. From the Otto Flückiger Collection. Courtesy Armin Büttner.

out for Friday, Saturday and Sunday, come back and Basie would give us dates for the next weekend," Benny remembered, adding that, "When Basie reorganised, Billy Eckstine gave Basie music stands and some music. Of course, Basie had his music but this was for a smaller band or left over from the so-called 'Old Testament' band.

"I was still freelancing around. In fact, I had solicited the job with Charlie Ventura as Bennie Green had left, and also with Illinois Jacquet, but meanwhile, I'm going out with Basie on the weekends. I kept asking Basie in different ways whether I was hired or not. He would never give me an answer. So I'd say, 'Well, Mr. Basie, how did the trombones sound tonight?' He'd say, 'They sound OK, kid.' That would be it. I think he was on to it that I was trying to get a 'yes' out of him but he liked dangling the carrot in front of the rabbit. That was part of his character. Then after me asking him so many times, and the band seeming to be working a bit more, the final answer I got out of him was, 'You're here, aren't you, kid?' This was as close as it got." From that laconic reply, there developed a formative, 12-year sojourn. "He was a wonderful man and he was sort of like an uncle to me. He realised I was a greenhorn kid from New Orleans. I learned from just watching him, how he conducted the band. He was a minimal guy."

Reflecting on his Basie experience, Benny emphasised the value of his exposure to older players. "I was only in my early 20s so I was taught everything I know by the older guys in the big bands. They taught me all about life. They passed things on to me and I try to pass them on but there's not the same situation now. There's not one big

Count Basie Orchestra, unknown location, c.1955. *Rear, L-r:* Eddie Jones (b); Sonny Payne (d); Freddie Green (g); Reunald Jones Sr. Thad Jones, Wendell Culley, Joe Newman (t). *Front:* Frank Wess (ts, f); Bill Graham (as); Count Basie (dir, p); Marshal Royal (as); Frank Foster (ts); Charlie Fowlkes (bs, b-cl); Bill Hughes, Henry Coker, Benny Powell (tb).

band to leave, and another to go to, like there used to be. I sat next to guys like Quentin Jackson; I got a chance to know Sweets Edison, and these guys were my mentors. They taught me without even realising it: how to carry myself, how to conduct myself, my manners. I never overstepped my bounds. They could see I was trying to live in the tradition. I watched how they dressed and I watched Count Basie, too. One of the things I most remember about him was what a gentleman he was. You could approach him with any lady to meet and he always stood up, whether it was your granddaughter or grandmother. They taught me lifestyle and values, because you could see what their values were."

Marshal Royal (as); **Benny Powell** (tb); **Frank Foster** (ts), Count Basie Orchestra, unknown location, possibly New York, 1950s. Photo by Popsie. Courtesy Chris Lee.

Speaking of values, I was intrigued to know how Benny had avoided some of the temptations that derailed the careers of his contemporaries. "We were so young and the company we kept, they were all pretty clean guys. I always avoided the drug scenes because I saw how debilitating it was to people. I never did believe that you should suffer just because you're a jazz musician! A lot of times guys were trying to escape the fact they didn't have any work. Life had done them a dirty trick so maybe they had lost respect for themselves and they were hiding it. Sometimes drug guys would infiltrate the band, one would get in and get another in, and Basie had to deal with that for a little bit. This was early on and instead of firing guys, he would just disband the band and formulate it again without those guys. Clever man."

Benny went on to describe how he used Basie's example to help him handle recalcitrant students. "Now that I'm teaching school, I ask myself how would he handle it? I had a class at the New School that wouldn't respond to anything that I told them to do. I don't have to depend on teaching but I like to teach, although I don't like to

Benny Powell (tb), on tour, possibly France 1980s. Courtesy Benny Powell.

grade papers and do all the rest of the stuff that teachers have to do. At any rate, I considered quitting. Well, I solved my own problem. I think I was talking too much. I have a composition that is quite complicated so I put it in front of them and they got so involved with trying to figure it out until they responded to the music. They were so busy they forgot to be the rebels that they thought they were.

"Fortunately I've never had any low points in my career or any periods when I didn't play – I've always been a musician. Never had to take a day job. I realised early on you had to be diversified plus I'm interested in a lot of things. Right now, my biggest asset is that I'm asked to talk about my early days and experiences. Even when I do lectures, I can't duplicate the Birdland days, the 1950s, the 1960s; conditions are just very much different. To me, a lot of jazz and its history is sociological. It's fed by many things, World War Two, the Civil Rights days, all of these provided a more lively background than now, and there was a greater sense of community with the big bands. When I have to do workshops, I try and explain swing, telling them first to understand the purpose for the music. The purpose then was to get people to dance. Bands played for dancers. These students have no idea about social dancing. I tell them that John Coltrane and even Elvin Jones had all been through this swing thing. They decided the way they wanted to play (eventually) but it wasn't like they started off there."

Production still: **'Jamboree'** [aka Disc Jockey Jamboree], director Roy Lockwood for Warner Bros., Hollywood, 1957. Still shows Count Basie and His Orchestra: Jerry Lee Lewis and Fats Domino also appeared. *L-r, rear*: Eddie Jones (b); Sonny Payne (d); Bill Hughes, Henry Coker, Benny Powell (tb). *Front*: Count Basie (p); Frank Wess (ts, f); Bill Graham, Marshal Royal (as); Frank Foster (ts); Charlie Fowlkes (bs, b-cl).

Benny said his Basie period "went by like a day or so". He recalls his section-mate Henry Coker who was "a marvellous player – played piano as well, but he suffered the same thing as I did because Al Grey was so fantastic, so aggressive, he overshadowed us both as far as the solo thing was concerned. Al was really a natural trombonist. I don't know how much he had studied but Al would say about people like him that nobody ever told him he couldn't do that kind of stuff so he did it."

Benny left Basie in 1963 – "I wanted to develop" – and said that his time with the band opened many doors for him. "When I got my first Broadway show or my first TV

Count Basie and His Orchestra, unknown location, c.1960. *Rear, L-r*: Sonny Payne (d); Thad Jones (cnt); Sonny Cohn, Joe Newman (t). *Middle*: Eddie Jones (b); Freddie Green (g); Henry Coker, Al Grey, Benny Powell (tb). *Front*: Count Basie (p); Billy Mitchell (ts); Frank Wess (as, ts, fl); Snooky Young (solo t); Marshal Royal (as); Frank Foster (ts); Charlie Fowlkes (bs).

show it was directly because I had been with Count Basie for all those years." Still, for all the myriad experiences of the past 40 years, he remains forever part of the extended Basie family. Honoured to be asked to direct the latter-day Basie band in Zurich, Benny told me how he had imagined he might stand in front of the band like Stan Kenton, "arms spread like an eagle". After listening to tapes sent by present Basie trumpeter Scotty Barnhart and watching a video, "It dawned on me the whole 12 years I was there, nobody stood in front of the band waving their arms. Basie would stick a finger up and the band would explode. We had some guest conductors; Jerry Lewis used to love to conduct the band, and they didn't know what they were doing, in fact it was distracting. I decided I wouldn't be one of those so I got a bar stool and sat in the crook of the piano. I made my initial announcements, 'This is Benny Powell. I'm proud to be conducting the Basie Band tonight.' Doug Miller, the tenor saxophonist would give me the tempo for each number so I would turn to the band and say, 'One, two' and they'd get started. I'd go and sit on my little stool and stay out of the way.

"Recently, the band played a concert at Carnegie Hall with Patti Austin and the sponsors had asked that some of the former Basie-ites be there. I agreed that I would be there. As it turned out I was the only one. During the concert, (leader) Bill Hughes announced that somebody from a former Basie band was in the audience, which turned out to be me and he asked me to take a bow. I stood up and did so. They turned the lights on. To be acknowledged in Carnegie Hall, it doesn't get much higher than that. Proud? Oh man, was I ever! One of the high points of my life. I thought at the time that Basie would be very proud of Bill for the way he was conducting. He was the last guy in the band you ever thought would be leader. He wasn't a self-promoter; he's always been very calm about things but he conducted the band and did everything in great style. Very dignified.

Dameronia with special guest Johnny Griffin, Uptown recording session, Englewood NJ, 11 July 1983. L-r: Cecil Payne (bs); Virgil Jones (t); Walter Davis, Jr. (p); Frank Wess (as); Don Sickler (t, ldr, arr); Benny Powell (tb); Philly Joe Jones (d); Larry Ridley (b); Johnny Griffin, Charles Davis (ts). Courtesy Charles Davis.

Count Basie Alumni Band, Stadttheter, Schaffhaursen, Switzerland, 7 May 1985. *L-r*: Nat Pierce (p); Freddie Green (g); Eddie Jones (b); Buddy Tate (ts); Benny Powell (tb); Gus Johnson (d); Harry 'Sweets' Edison (t). Photo by Rolf Baumann. Courtesy mr.jazz Photo Files (Theo Zwicky).

"I've been very fortunate to keep going year in and year out. I'm always reinventing myself. I teach on my own terms. One day a week. I play with a number of bands, mine included. I plan to do more writing and I'd like to do more music in churches. I've started singing my own material so I have three or four careers going at the same time," he said, breaking off to tell me that he had appeared, as an actor, in a TV commercial for Johnson & Johnson which seems to have brought him more fame than almost anything else he's done. He said he played and sang with the Duke Ellington Orchestra at Birdland on Tuesdays and then reminded me about the days, "When I would do a commercial from nine to 12, them maybe a rock and roll recording from two to five than I'd go and do a Broadway show and leave that to go to the Vanguard and play with Thad Jones's band."

Basie All-Stars, Nice Jazz Festival, Nice, France, July 1986. *L-r*: Eddie Jones (b); Buddy Tate (ts); Clark Terry (fgh); Gus Johnson (d); Benny Powell (tb). Photo by Alan Smith.

Poster for **Giants of Jazz VII concert**, South Orange Middle School, South Orange NJ, October 2004. Courtesy Benny Powell.

Powell said he had no regrets although he wished he'd learned to play piano properly. His only daughter lived near Atlanta and there were two grandchildren, one of whom, Faith, was born the year he received the kidney transplant. His sisters remained close to him – he had fronted a charity fund-raising concert with a 16-piece big band ("Cecil Bridgewater did the arrangements") and a 37-piece choir in Rock Hill, South Carolina, at the request of his sister. "We ended up raising $10,000," he recalled.

Benny Powell (tb), 350 W. 55th St., New York, 17 April 2006. Photo by Peter Vacher.

Naturally he was sad at the fate of his home town (we were speaking just a year after Hurricane Katrina had wrought its worst). "I feel it's been a mixed blessing. New Orleans has always been a kind of lie," he suggests. "They've always made it look like the happiest place yet thousands of people there are in dire need. At least, Katrina brought that to the fore. I don't know how much it will improve but I'm glad that side is uncovered."

The interview terminated, I suggested a photograph. With that, Benny disappeared, only to return with a different hat, a fresh shirt, and some added personal jewellery, while proudly holding "the trombone that Tommy Dorsey gave me personally". Just before I finally took my leave, Benny told me that his one unfulfilled ambition was always to play Ronnie Scott's in London. "I think my biggest audience was in France. I did the show *Ain't Misbehavin'* over there in '81, stayed a year but I've never even been in the door to Ronnie Scott's. Never seen it, don't know where it is. I wish I could have developed an audience in England. I've been asked to come to England but the fee was so small. Still, it may not be too late, it's not over 'til the fat lady sings."

New York trumpeter John Eckert summed up Benny as follows: "Benny Powell was a favourite person of mine. He was such a personable and sincerely friendly man. I can't think of anyone of his stature in the jazz world who came close. His playing was free of self-promotion and ego, as his demeanour would indicate, and contributed the same joy to any musical event as his personality contributed to any social event. He dealt with his health problems in a heroic manner and since I didn't know him as a close friend, although anyone who met him was given the impression he was one, I can just say that I admired him and am grateful to have met him."

First published as 'Benny Powell: If it isn't fun, I don't want to do it' in *Jazz Journal*, December 2006

---

[1] Edward 'Eddie' Pierson, born 1 August 1904, Algiers LA; died 1 December 1958, New Orleans. Trombonist with Sidney Desvignes on the riverboats in the early 1930s. Also with Sunny South band, Armand Piron and Young Tuxedo Orchestra of New Orleans. With Oscar 'Papa' Celestin from 1951.

[2] Edgar Lawrence 'Dooky' Chase Jr., born 23 March 1928, Fifth Ward, New Orleans. Played trumpet in Booker T. Washington High School band. Led his big band from 1945 to 1949. Later gave up playing and took over the restaurant that bears his name, from his father Dooky Chase Sr. Now retired. Restaurant still operates and is managed by his daughter Leah.

[3] Warren Bell Sr., born 2 April 1929, New Orleans. Taught by Theodore 'Wiggles' Purnell. Played saxophones at Booker T. Washington HS. Benny Powell was also in the band, as was drummer Wilbert Hogan. With original Dooky Chase orchestra on alto; also played tenor and baritone. Played in Army bands at Fort Dix, New Jersey. After returning to NO, was with Dave Bartholomew big band, recorded with Ray Charles and Fats Domino. Member of AFO (All For One) modern jazz collective, along with Ellis Marsalis and Alvin Batiste. Took day job with chain of food stores. Bell died on 22 November, 2006. Warren Bell Jr. is Associate VP for University and Media Relations at Xavier University, New Orleans.

[4] Emery Humphrey Thompson (aka Umar Uthman Sharif), born 1927, New Orleans; died 16 October 1998, Norcros GA. Taught music by grandfather Prof. James B. Humphrey. Percy and Willie Humphrey were his cousins. Turned professional while at Booker T. Washington HS. Played with Dooky Chase Orchestra then worked with Herb Leary and Valmar Victor big bands in New Orleans. Recorded with Luis Russell in New York; was with Louis Armstrong's orchestra in 1947 and Lionel Hampton in 1948, then with Louis Jordan, Big Joe Turner and Lonnie Johnson. Gave up playing on becoming a Muslim; resumed in 1975 in Chicago. Returned to NO in 1979, played in big band at Fairmont Hotel and worked with Barry Martyn. Played for Broadway show *Black and Blue*. Recorded with the Lincoln Center Jazz Orchestra in 1991. Retired to live with his sister near Atlanta. His son Jamil Sharif is a trumpeter in New Orleans.

Plas Johnson Jr.

Plas Johnson, tenor saxophone, Cambridge, UK, 1989. Photo by Brian Foskett. Courtesy Brian Foskett.

Talking with the distinguished tenor saxophonist Plas Johnson in his service apartment as he prepared for his evening gig at the Pizza Express in London's Dean Street way back in March 1993 proved to be something of an eye-opener. Here was a highly successful studio musician who had a fancy house in Studio City within easy reach of Los Angeles yet who seemed to yearn for a different kind of recognition. He wanted, he said, to take his chances as a jazz soloist. In the intervening years since this interview was published, Plas has continued to tour, often appearing at European jazz festivals but not in Britain, sometimes performing with the brilliant expatriate African-American organist Rhoda Scott. He still sounds good, still gets 'hot' in four bars and knows how to swing. How satisfied he feels now, I don't know, but hearing him again at Ascona in Switzerland more recently was a joy.

For virtually three decades Plas Johnson Jr. was among the busiest of studio musicians in Hollywood and Los Angeles. His blues-oriented 'signature sound' enlivened countless recordings by artists of every stripe and hue. It's a fair bet that almost all the 'hot' tenor-sax breaks or solos on rock and pop records emanating from LA since the mid-fifties have been by Plas.

His discography is endless and exotic; sessions with Googie Rene, the Piltdown Men, the Coasters, the Pets, Boots Brown and the Blockbusters jostling for space among those for Fats Domino, Ray Charles and Little Richard. Of course Johnson's contributions to some of these now-forgotten chart-chasers were uncredited – he was just another pro doing a job – but along the way he created a reputation for the musical 'bon mot' which later made him the first choice for mainstream album producers and film composers. Most famously, his was the prowling tenor saxophone on the soundtrack version of Henry Mancini's 'Pink Panther Theme'.

When we met up, Plas spoke first about his Louisiana origins. "I was born (in 1931) in Donaldsonville, about 60 miles up the river from New Orleans. That's where my mother's family was located. They were completely musical; my aunt was a singer, her name was Florida Richard, she married a guitarist whose name was Willie Francis, one of my uncles played piano and sang, and another played trumpet. My mother played the piano and my father played the sax and the banjo.

"I guess you know my brother Ray's a pianist, he was one of the really best blues and boogie-woogie pianists in LA around '54 when we got there, and he still plays and does singles in restaurants and nightclubs. That's how he works, 'cause he likes to sing." Do the brothers work together today I wondered? "Not at all," Plas said, laughing. "We talk but I guess we quit playing together back in the fifties. Work was very tough at

Publicity still: **'Feather on Jazz'**, 13-part series for Universal TV, produced by Leonard Feather, Hollywood 1967. Still shows scoring session with Plas Johnson (ts); Benny Carter (as); Joe Comfort (b); Unseen: Frank Rosolino (tb); Harry Edison (t); etc. Courtesy David Meeker.

that time, this was before either one of us was doing much recording. I got a job in Long Beach with a quartet where we played dance jazz music and sang four-part harmony, but Ray split. He went somewhere else and got another job. He liked playing what he liked to play. I'm only willing to do that today. He was willing to do that when he was 25 years old!"

Ann Young with the Charlie Blackwell Trio, Stardust Room, Long Beach CA, 1955. L-r: Ann Young (voc); Charlie Blackwell (d); Plas Johnson (ts); Ray Johnson (p). Courtesy Plas Johnson.

The Johnsons had relocated to Donaldsonville from New Orleans for economic reasons."We probably were starving in New Orleans, it was during the Depression. You got as close to family as you could then. They helped feed you, and they would give you a sofa or spread the kids around so you could survive. I just know we almost never had enough," he added. Plas is sure that these bruising experiences coloured his views about his chosen career."I was very much into the insecurities of our business even though I was considered a talented young player. My brother and I had worked and made money; I would say we sent ourselves through High School. From the age of 14 and 15 we bought our own clothes, our own car, stuff that kids today expect their parents to do. We made enough to take care of ourselves. Even beyond that I still had this feeling of insecurity so when I got out of the Army I went to Los Angeles and I tried to enlist in a trade school. It seemed like a natural thing to do but the counsellor there rejected me. I don't know why except he was a white man deciding the fate of inner-city black kids.

"I was 21 years old, I had graduated High School and I said I'd either like to take carpentry or auto mechanics. He said I needed pre-requisites for these courses. What the fuck is a pre-requisite for an auto-mechanic course? Anyway, I wasn't heart-broken; I enrolled in a school of music instead which was a decision made for me by someone else but as God would have it, it was the right decision. It helped my reading, my understanding of music harmony and notation, my ear training."

By the early 1940s the Johnsons had returned to the Crescent City."You had the parades, you had the blues clubs, and Mardi Gras which was a week of music and celebration. By the time we were 13 or 14 we were playing on the (carnival) floats. I had started on soprano saxophone when I was 12 and by 14, I was quite good at it, playing mainly by ear. It wasn't a choice. I guess it was the cheapest thing in the pawnshop: I became a saxophone player."

With brother Ray on piano the two youngsters were soon up and running musically: "He and I were a band, all we needed was a drummer. Then my cousin Renald Richard started playing with us on trumpet, so we had two horns but no drums. Eddie Blackwell became our first drummer, Tony Bazley was our second drummer, and they both started playing with us when they were about 13! We had the hardest time getting Eddie to play a backbeat. He could do it but he put it down. He was dead into Max Roach. He could play good and he enjoyed playing with us. Maybe we were the only ones that would hire him at the time.

Plas Johnson (ts), Johnson Brothers combo, New Orleans, 1947.
Courtesy Plas Johnson.

"We played what we liked, what the people liked, what they danced to. We definitely weren't a jazz band and we weren't jazz musicians, but we liked bebop. We got away with playing bebop; Dizzy Gillespie had some two-and-three horn arrangements out then. Nobody was writing in the band so it was a good thing for us and the people dancing, they didn't know it was bebop! All the young players around then were influenced by bebop. You would hear it on the jukeboxes. That music took root."

Territory big bands like those of Buddy Johnson and Lucky Millinder visited New Orleans, as did prominent black performers such as Dinah Washington, Louis Jordan and Earl Bostic. "In fact we played opening for many of these bands[1]. The Union had a situation where out-of-town bands would have to hire as many local musicians and we got some of that. We were about 17 then."

The city's racial divide was absolute in those pre-Civil Rights days. "I knew no white players. Segregation was just what the word says. It was complete. Our High School was all-black, all the guys we played with were black, and we played mostly in black places. When we did play in white places it was for only white people. It was only black musicians on the stage. In fact [trumpeter] Jack Sheldon was telling me about some place in the South where he tried to sit-in with a black band and he was taken off the stage by two detectives who were in doubts about his sanity. And that went on in New Orleans also. Unless you worked in the French Quarter you would never get to know or hear white musicians. People like [clarinettist Irving] Fazola you heard on the radio but the concept of a mixed band didn't occur.

"I felt strongly about it, of course. It's like being in jail, especially when you know there are other places in the country where people didn't live this way. We all had a false concept of the North which didn't have the segregation laws but which was just as bigoted as the South but that's not what you think about. You look around and you say, 'Hey, I've got to get away from this.' That was in my mind all along. You couldn't aspire even to be a policeman or a fireman, and that's not great aspirations, is it? We had a city of 40 per cent black people and we did not have one black policeman. Many times you had the most intelligent, the most highly educated, and even the most athletically inclined blacks leaving the South, going to colleges in the North. That has changed now of course."

The urge to leave town arose from the need for professional growth as well as the desire to loosen the straitjacket of segregation. "Not that we didn't have a lot of good people there who could play. There was a lot of jazz going on around the city. There was a young big band, came up around the forties, Dooky Chase, which was excellent. The musicians that stayed were respected, but we were looking for fame and fortune and they weren't rich, and they weren't famous. But they were good. I'm thinking of a saxophone player that got offered to go with Duke Ellington, a guy called Son Johnson. He stayed in New Orleans but it looked like everybody else who left became famous. Benny Powell came from there and he left. If you were going to shoot for national fame, or go to the top of your field, you had to get out of New Orleans. There wasn't a recording scene there at the time, you had fly-by-night recorders who would come in, take whatever they could get, leave town, and not pay any royalties, and sometimes not even pay scale. So I jumped on the first band leaving town."

The group that gave the fledgling saxophonist his first on-the-road break was that of bluesman Charles Brown. Brown, a singer-pianist, had achieved enormous success with 'Drifting Blues' and other hits. By now, Plas was a tenor saxophonist, having graduated from soprano to alto and then to tenor, "as soon as I could afford one. My first biggest hero was Illinois Jacquet – the hottest of the Texas tenors. That's all I wanted to sound like. I also liked the ballad playing of Gene Ammons and Don Byas. I didn't hear much of Lester Young. We didn't have a great record collection and that kind of jazz wasn't really played that much on the radio; you were more likely to hear Illinois Jacquet and Gene Ammons who were selling hit records at the time.

"Charles Brown was a great musician. I always respected him highly. Of the jazz bands on the road at that time it was one of the most musical to be in. He had all good blues players, and some good jazz players. Clifford Solomon was on tenor, the drummer was Cake Wichard, a terrific drummer, Wesley Prince, from the Nat King Cole Trio was on the bass, we had a good blues guitarist and Buster Bailey on the tenor. Three tenors in all. Clifford was a bebop player, the hip one in the band. He had already been with Lionel Hampton and with Roy Porter.

Plas Johnson (ts), US Army, Camp Roberts, near Paso Robles, central California 1952–53. Plas Johnson, second from left, others unknown. Courtesy Plas Johnson.

"We did 29 and 30 one-nighters in a row. Charles was hot to pop! He had one hit right after another. We did sometimes 400 miles a day in a Cadillac and an Oldsmobile, new, with a truck for the instruments. He paid me well, more than I was offered by Lionel Hampton and he was working six nights out of the week. We ran into Joe Liggins, Amos Milburn and Roy Milton out on the road. Sometimes we'd have two bands together. Roy had Camille (Howard) on piano, Jackie Kelso and two other saxophones, and they were swingin'.

"This was on the blues circuit, the chitlin' circuit; we only got past the Mason-Dixon line for probably two, three cities. Everything else was in the South or the centre. Charles was an idol then, he would be like James Brown later on. You put Charles Brown in a small town in Texas and he was a headliner. Charles handpicked his musicians and he let them play. It was the best of all worlds for me."

This idyll ended abruptly when Plas was inducted into the Army in 1951, aged 20, fetching up in the California desert. He managed to spend some off-duty time in San Francisco, running into a "slew of great saxophonists" including Teddy Edwards, Pony Poindexter, Leo Wright, John Handy, and Jerome Richardson at all-night jam sessions. "Hearing all these great saxophone players put a good fix on me. Left an impression to this day."

Plas managed to secure local gigs in places like Santa Cruz, Salinas, Monterey and Watsonville, staying on in California when his military service finished. Brother Roy came out to join him there, as did their sister. In fact he says, "Los Angeles was a terrible let-down. You always figure you're better than you are so we started going out to booking agents' offices and stuff. I mean, a ridiculous thing to do. We didn't have a job, we didn't have a decent place to live and we were working jobs in the downtown area of LA for five dollars a night. Less than we were making in New Orleans, so it was a shock. Still it was always fun to be playing music, even for bad money.

Plas Johnson (ts) with Jimmy O'Brien (p), Stardust Room, Long Beach CA, 1955/56. Courtesy mr.jazz Photo Files (Theo Zwicky).

Plas Johnson (ts), 'getting hot', unknown location, Los Angeles CA, mid-1950s. Courtesy Dave Clarke.

"Eventually I got some work with Johnny Otis, then I got a call for a couple of recording sessions. There were bandleaders around town who had access to various types of work, clubs, whatever was going on, they were into it. They always had a job. You'd made it when these guys picked you as their saxophonist, then you worked. Clora Bryant (the trumpeter) and I were talking the other day about a piano player named Poison Gardner. Everybody around town knew Poison and he was one of those personalities. I got some work with him then I met (drummer) George Jenkins, Dinah Washington's first husband, and got some work with George. It was nice for it seemed everybody who heard me liked me. I knew a lot of tunes and I knew how to play off the melody and play jazz, even if I didn't know the chord changes to the tunes."

Plas Johnson (ts), Benny Goodman Orchestra, Disneyland, Orange County CA, 30–31 May 1961. Pianist and bassist unknown. Courtesy Plas Johnson.

Johnson's fortunes improved after he made it out to the Capitol Studios in Hollywood with Otis. "I ran into Dave Cavanaugh, who was an A&R man there. He was an ex-tenor player and liked my playing so immediately started calling me for solo chores with Frank Sinatra, Peggy Lee, Nat Cole. He also included me on 'Session at Midnight'. They did a couple of albums on me also, which were neither fish nor fowl. I've had to live them down ever since! Rhythm and blues all of a sudden became very white but Leon René was still active with Class Records. He had Eugene Church and Bobby Day, and I did a lot of his work, and for Modern, Specialty and Eddie Messner's Aladdin label so I played on a lot of hit records. The tenor saxophone on those records was very prominent and my style was in vogue. But I still got hired by people like Les Baxter and the serious background music writers. It was like a crossover period for me. They wanted what I could do and I was the only one who could do it. I'm sure if they had a white tenor player who could play like I played I wouldn't have got the gig," he emphasised.

Plas Johnson (ts), personal promo, Los Angeles CA, mid-1950s. Courtesy Chris Lee.

Plas had qualities which other saxophonists found hard to match. He put it this way, "I could get HOT in four bars. If you had a really hot blues singer I could carry it a notch higher. They were playing music I was raised on and not necessarily doing it well so I was a vital element that gave it authenticity and more fire. Many times there was no music and I played the solo, I might have played the intro and then played riffs behind the singer on the way out. It wasn't always music that I necessarily liked to play but I still did it."

Billy May recording session, Time-Life 'Swing Era' series, Los Angeles, 1969–1970. Plas Johnson (ts); with Jack Nimitz (bs); Billy May (cond). Courtesy Plas Johnson.

Plas Johnson (ts), JazzAscora, Switzerland, July 2004. Photo by Jonathan Farber. Courtesy Jonathan Farber.

Studio calls meant that jazz took a back seat. Plas became an all-rounder, playing "everything that was expected of reed players, piccolo, flute, alto flute, bass flute, bass clarinet, alto, tenor, bari and soprano saxophones. Now I'm slowly selling them out although I still like to play baritone and alto." Then the studio situation changed. "I was getting less and less interested in recording. It had gone to 16-track. All the good fun and excitement had passed for horn players. You never heard the rhythm section any more, they were on before you got there, and you never saw the artist. That's two of the greatest perks for a hornman gone."

Plas enjoyed a quarter-of-a-century plus of studio activity embracing "masses of work for Motown" and 15 years on the Merv Griffin TV show, working there with many fine jazzmen. "Jazz players fit quite well into the studio scene. You're asked to do something that many of the better-trained classical musicians can't do well, and that is to take your experience and adapt it to a style of music they're trying to create in three hours, all without rehearsal."

That challenge has largely dissolved now. "It's not there to do any more. I guess I could hustle on the outer fringes of what there is to do if I wanted to, which I don't. Look at me, I don't want to die in the studio! I want to play music which makes people feel good."

First published as 'Travel the World and Play Jazz' in
Jazz the Magazine for March 1994

---

[1] The 'New Orleans After Dark' column in the *Pittsburgh Courier*, 1948, reporting on the star-studded Dawn Patrol show at the Golden Leaf Cocktail Lounge: 'Music was supplied by the Johnson Brothers combo, a young, capable aggregation composed of Edward Blackwell, drummer; Renald Richards (sic), trumpet; Plas Johnson, tenor-saxophonist, and Raymond Johnson, pianist.'

Carl 'Ace' Carter

Carl 'Ace' Carter (1931–1996), Cleveland OH, 1980s. Courtesy Ace Carter.

Pianist Ace Carter's period in the limelight was brief. Shortly after this interview took place, he left the Count Basie Orchestra for the second and last time and settled back into jazz obscurity in Cleveland, where he died of kidney failure on 20 September, 1996 aged 65. For such a fine player, his discography is tantalisingly brief too; a session with the singer Little Jimmy Scott, a pair of albums with the Basie orchestra, a Concord date with Basie trombonist Robert Trowers in 1992 and surprisingly, a 1981 recording with bluesmen Johnny Shines and Robert Jr. Lockwood. The great Cleveland-born saxophonist Joe Lovano rated Carter highly as a player and told me he was something of a 'ladies man' while local jazz historian Joe Mosbrook cited Carter as 'a leader on the Cleveland jazz scene who played with some of the best small groups in the city'. Carter was cordial and welcoming when we called on him in The Hague and clearly enjoyed the opportunity to talk about his career, a highlight being the week he had spent in London with the Basie band and Ella Fitzgerald just a few months prior to our meeting..

Back in July 1990 at the time of this interview, the little-known pianist Ace Carter was the man whose touch and flair was to be decisive in perpetuating the Count Basie Orchestra's distinctive sound. In the words of Frank Foster, its director at the time, 'this is no ghost band' but one whose purpose was not only to present the classic Basie repertoire but also to breathe fresh life into the concepts pioneered by the band's great originator. Carter's role in this, whether in introductory passages, in his solos or in those characteristic sign-off phrases, was crucial. He had to avoid anything overtly florid while maintaining his individuality. He needed to blend perfectly with the rhythm section and somehow to suggest Basie's minimal style without producing a parody. A difficult assignment but one that Carter on recorded and live evidence seemed to manage very satisfyingly indeed.

When we met during the band's sojourn at the North Sea Jazz Festival in July 1990, I asked Carter first to comment on the challenges involved. "Knowing that I had a role to fulfil I was very aware, naturally, but I'm very fortunate that they put no restrictions or pressure on me. It was up to me. I had an advantage due to the fact that I just enjoy playing so I didn't let that (expectation) become a barrier to me. I hope I bring a sense of enjoyment so that the rest of the band members could enjoy the whole scenario. Since you probably will hear me first I'm the one who has to set the mood. With that rhythm section (completed by guitarist Charlton Johnson, bassist Cleveland Eaton and drummer Duffy Jackson) we set the atmosphere. We have fun and I think the whole thing about the Basie band is having fun. Enjoying the whole situation. If it becomes a grind to me then I don't want to do it. I must have fun."

Carl 'Ace' Carter

The Count Basie Orchestra directed by Frank Foster, North Sea Jazz Festival, The Hague, Holland, July 1990. L-r: Ace Carter (p); Charlton Johnson (g); Cleveland Eaton (b); Frank Foster (dir, ts); Kenny Hing (ts); Duffy Jackson (d); David Glasser (as); Danny Turner (as); Clarence Banks (tb); Bob Ojeda (t); Mel Wanzo (tb); Doug Miller (ts); Mike Williams (t); Bob Trowers (tb); John Williams (bs). Photo by Ian Powell. Courtesy Ian Powell.

Carl Carter's nickname of 'Ace', now his professional name, was "bestowed upon me by a school chum when we were in Junior High School in Youngstown, Ohio". Although headquartered for most of his career in Cleveland, Ohio, the tall, dignified pianist was born in Youngstown (12 April 1931) when "it was a big steel town; of course all of that is dead now. It's almost like a ghost town. Very tragic." Carter's father moved back to Alabama when his son was still very young so his mother became "the breadwinner and the motivating force of our staying together. She remarried but she brought us through all this and she remained the motivating force in our lives." Every Sunday the young members of the Carter family spent the whole day in church where their mother was an active member and Carter remained thankful for that. He said it had a big effect on him in later years and the church involvement also helped his musical development. "When I was approximately four we had an old-type bellows organ that you pumped at the church and I used to sneak back there during services. The sound of certain chords fascinated me," he said.

There was no church choir but the aspiring musician sang in the junior choir at school. Heavily influenced by gospel music he also liked to sit at the old player-piano at his godparents' house. His family moved to another side of town around 1941 and as his sister was going to study to be a classical pianist, Carter's mother bought a piano.

"She (my sister) studied for five or six years then she just gave it up. The piano was sitting there so I started fooling around with it." Playing at first by ear he tried to emulate the lady pianist at Mount Calvary Church but soon looked for other influences. "I had learned to play the shuffle rhythm on the piano from listening to Louis Jordan and his Tympany Five. The first real professional job I had came because I could play that shuffle rhythm. That's all I could play; if they got away from shuffle rhythm I was lost! I was about 14 and these old gentlemen came by the house and asked my mother could I play a job for that night because their regular pianist who was a lady, she'd taken ill. They begged my mother and I guess she saw the look in my eye and knew that I would want to give this a shot.

"Elwood Moss was the bandleader but the fellow that caused all the problems was the drummer. His name was Ernie Stephenson, they used to call him Mix. He said, 'Why don't you turn to music? You can get more girls.' He's passed on now but I said if I ever see him in heaven I'm gonna kill him because to this day I haven't got a girl," Carter laughed. "They were very influential in my life because I was the baby in the band. They would take care of me and try to prevent me getting into any pitfalls. We were playing a place called the Ohio Tavern, Friday and Saturday. I was still in High School and we made seven dollars a night. That was good money, believe me.'"

Carl worked with Moss for three or four years at the Tavern, backing local performers and taking part in jam sessions. "We had Harvey Satterwhite on saxophone, Ray Fulham, trumpet; Elwood Moss was the bassist and Ernie Stephenson was the percussionist. We played like Louis Jordan. Same instrumentation, I was singing too, whatever was popular at the time. They really encouraged me."

Around the time that Carter left High School, fate in the form of the great alto-saxophone star Norris Turney, intervened and set a musical career in proper motion.

"Norris was appearing in Youngstown at a place called the Blue Bird and his pianist Joe Nesbitt was going to the Army. Norris had heard me at a jam session, we'd have them all the time, used to go on to the wee hours of the morning. Every weekend. Until daylight. I was fortunate to come up at that time because we had two major ballrooms and all the bands came there plus we had theatre shows. I was lucky enough to meet Basie, Lionel Hampton, Erskine Hawkins, Buddy Johnson, Andy Kirk, Lucky Millinder. All of these bands would come through the New Elm Ballroom; we had plenty of sessions with Woody Herman and Stan Kenton too. They said Youngstown used to be the hottest town between New York and Chicago. That was during the war years. There was an army camp called Camp Shenango[1], right on the state-line and on the weekend the soldiers would come in town, with plenty of money to spend. Norris had a quartet and his wife at the time, Aretha, was the singer with us. He had Junior Raglin, one of the great bassists of all time and Joe Collier out of Dayton, Ohio, was on drums. We opened in Fort Wayne, Indiana, and it was my first time really being away from home but I was caught up in it so much that part didn't matter." The group moved on to Louisville for the Kentucky Derby, playing straight-ahead jazz. Carl recalled Turney then as "a dynamite saxophonist" and their association lasted about a year until the band broke up.

Carl 'Ace' Carter (piano), Cleveland OH, 1970s-1980s Courtesy Joe Mosbrook.

Back in Ohio Carter started work at a new nightspot, the gangster-owned Cotton Club in Cleveland, staying in the house band until 1952. He remembered visitors like Cab Calloway and Ella Fitzgerald. Former Ellington bassist Joe Cooper[2] led the band and Mel Wanzo, the trombonist later with Basie, was a member along with Ray Fulham and Bobby Yeager on drums. Carter transferred to the Sportarie Bar, working with (guitarist) Tiny Grimes's Rocking Highlanders ("I refused to wear the kilts," he said) for a week and with Red Prysock and saxophonist Rusty Bryant. After a spell in Akron, Carl moved back to Cleveland. "There was another band called Pops Teasley, he was a bassist. On that band we had Curtis Peagler who was with the Basie band later and Rusty Bryant again, also Elvin Maddocks, the drummer."

The pianist then took on a lot of solo work, sometimes playing for go-go dancers. He became a great admirer of Art Tatum and recalled an after-hours spot in Youngstown which was called Harris's and "whenever Art would come to town, he'd be there. Art caused me to have the lambasting of my life from my mother because I stayed out all night to hear him. She thought it was a joint, a devil's place."

Cleveland provided plenty of opportunities for work although Carter did venture out on the road again with Jimmy Coe, a saxophonist, in a septet, again with Ray Fulham on trumpet, Ellington Nelson, baritone saxophone, and Mingo Jones on bass. "We toured the south in '56 on a big rock and roll package. We had Linda Hopkins, Little Willie John, Camille Howard, playing clubs in the black community. Jimmy Coe stayed active in Indianapolis after that, playing and leading a big band." Carl then rejoined the Joe Cooper band which was playing by now at the Ebony Lounge, a top location for black entertainers and for jam sessions involving the likes of Clifford Brown and Max Roach.

Later in the sixties Carter formed his own cocktail group with bassist Al MacDonald and a singer. Known as the Counterpoints they worked around North Dakota and

Minnesota before returning to Cleveland to more solo jobs and concerts – a pattern which continued more or less until the call came from the Basie office. How had that come about, I wondered?

"I was working very well as a single in Cleveland. Tee Carson had back problems and they needed a pianist. There was a guitarist on the band then, Paul Weedon, and we used to work together in Cleveland a lot, and Mel Wanzo the lead trombonist, we go back a long way and they recommended me. They called me and I said "OK, I'll give it a shot.' Now I'm glad I did but at first it was pretty slow in coming together. I'm not going to say I was intimidated by being in the Basie organisation but it was a new type of thing being with an organisation of that reputation. Trying to do well and not making too many mistakes.

Carl 'Ace' Carter (piano), Count Basie Orchestra, UK tour, backstage, London, October 1990.

"I left the band, not because of that but because I didn't care about the travelling any more. I was getting older and all the flying and the bus connections gave me a back problem. I never experienced pain like that in my life." Doctors told Carter to rest and to carry a pillow with him and he was better prepared when the second call to the Basie colours came not too long before we met. "Now I can handle it," he said. "I love the guys in this band. I love the camaraderie that we have and I enjoy visiting new cities and meeting the people but even so I will give it up and go back to being a single. To me the challenge of being a single is very exciting. I've been very fortunate and I'm thankful. When I look around I know things could be much worse. A lot of my friends got involved in other things like narcotics and they passed on. Oh I strayed yes, but I would always come back to some of the teachings of my youth. I'm very grateful to have been part of the entertainment scene and for as long as the good Lord lets me stay there I'll probably be part of it."

Adapted from the article
first published in *Jazz Journal*, January 1991

---

[1] Camp Shenango in Western Pennsylvania was a WW2 holding point for trained soldiers awaiting deployment. In 1943 it was the site of the 'deliberate fratricide' of black soldiers by white soldiers after a black soldier attempted to buy a beer from an army PX for whites only. The attack resulted in one fatality and another six men being injured, all of them black.

[2] It has been impossible to verify bassist Joe Cooper's claim to have played with Duke Ellington. As Dan Morgenstern says, 'We have all encountered musicians, who, having possibly subbed one or two nights with a name band or leader, claim alumni status. This is probably another such – if even that.'

Herman Riley

Herman Riley (1933–2007), tenor saxophone, Jimmy Smith Quartet, London, 1996. Photo by Peter Vacher.

The black music community in Los Angeles has always included a number of versatile saxophonists able to cope splendidly in big bands, play commercial sessions, excel in small jazz groups or provide gritty support for rhythm and blues artists. Plas Johnson is probably the best known of them, but others like Clifford Solomon, Jackie Kelso and Bill Green were not far behind, at least in the estimation of their fellow professionals if not the wider public at large. One who regularly earned the appreciation of his peers was Herman Riley, an outstanding tenor saxophonist whose substantial discography and wide-ranging employment reflected his status as a resourceful soloist and fine section man. At the time of this interview Herman was appearing with the Al McKibbon Trio, the Bill Berry big band and when the road called, the Jimmy Smith Quartet. It was his sojourn with Smith at the Rhythmic in London in February 1996 that brought this opportunity to build on an acquaintanceship which had begun in Los Angeles a year earlier. After Smith died in 2005, Herman continued to play in local clubs until he, in turn, succumbed to a heart attack in April 2007.

Herman was a solid, well-built man whose muscular physique seemed to mirror his playing style. "I've always stayed physically fit," he said. "Ever since I was a kid I've been involved in athletics. I used to get up early in the morning and run four, five or six miles, when I was nine or ten years old. Then I got into basketball, and into football and baseball. Did all those things until I decided to play the music. Suddenly all my friends were outgrowing me. They were taller, wider and stronger than me so I knew I had to change my thoughts about being an athlete. I always knew I wanted to do *something* of worth, and I always wanted to *belong* to something of worth. That made it easier for my family, because it helped them to help me. I was very teachable!

"So I got into the music. This friend of mine named Roy Henderson who became a fine jazz flute player in Oakland, we'd be playing at his house or mine from one o'clock Saturday until one or two in the morning Sunday. We'd be practising, studying the sounds of Gene Ammons or Lester Young or Coleman Hawkins or Illinois Jacquet, and listening to Ellington and Basie. And quite a bit of listening to Kenton too. Also I really would like to thank Norman Granz for bringing so many artists down to New Orleans especially during those years. I saw Charlie Parker just before he died; it was the concert of '54 with Stan Kenton's orchestra. Lee Konitz and June Christy, Candido and Dizzy Gillespie. Boy, Bird baffled them saxophone players in Kenton's orchestra. They were all back there trying to take notes on how he approached different chords and phrases."

Herman Riley

Herman Riley was born on 31 August 1933 in New Orleans. His home was in Algiers on the other side of the Mississippi. "In those years Algiers was quite a fine residential area, like a suburb of New Orleans. I lived in Orleans Parish and over there we had some great musicians, people like Mr. Harrison Barnes, the trombonist that played a lot in those brass bands, and Freddie Kohlman, one of the greatest drummers. Gordon Jenkins sent for him during the fifties. Later I met Bucky Pizzarelli and Bucky told me how much Zoot Sims loved Freddie 'cause Freddie had a very perfect feel for the drums.

"Of course there was an old man that was before him, we called him Happy Mathews[1]. You ever heard of Happy? I know that man was born in the 1800s 'cause his family were close to my family. He used to play in all of the brass bands in the City and in Algiers too. And that's the first one that I saw with that cymbal nailed to the top of the bass drum, holding his mallet in the left hand and playing that special beat. That same beat is very profound and pronounced in Ahmad Jamal's 'Poinciana'. The drummer on that is from New Orleans, Vernel Fournier. Vernel is comparable with June Gardner and Earl Palmer, and they got it from Happy Mathews and Paul Barbarin and those guys. Musicians come and go from New Orleans but that rhythm is always there."

Talk of Algiers brought Red Allen to mind. "Red Allen went to school with my uncle and my aunt and I was told many stories about him as he grew up. His father was also a trumpet player and I understand Henry was one of the modern young men then and he'd be in the back line of the band right next to the second line and his father would say to him, 'You don't play that kind of stuff in here.' Henry was a strutter, they used to call him the 'Big Shot'. He was quite a colourful man."

Herman lost his father early. "He was a longshoreman and he got killed when a winch broke loose and he was standing in the line of fire. Bled to death. He was a nice person who did the best he could with what he had." Herman's mother, Nell Brooks, was a local jazz singer and his grandmother played a little piano. Herman grew up with music as an everyday element of the household and remembered his mother rehearsing with Freddie Kohlman's band. "They used to party – there'd be many times I'd be sitting in on the party and they would drink mint gin and give me Cokes and things. I must have been about three or four years old. Mom was known all over the city – she was like a Bessie Smith. She had a golden voice, one of those beautiful voices, and what made it go even better was her awareness of rhythm and feeling. She didn't get the recognition – never made records. I didn't realise just how good she was until I came back when I was professional and heard her sing in church. Every church we went to they would be asking her to sing. Unaccompanied. She sung and *swung* so hard it gave me chills. She had changed over to gospel from jazz years before. In those days people were very misled and they didn't know the worth of the music. My grandmother would say, 'Nell, why don't you stop singing for the devil and come sing for God?' They associated jazz with the bordello houses and that ugliness still stands today."

Herman said he was fortunate to study at L.B. Landry High School in Algiers – "one of the best in that town" – which recruited children from the sixth grade onwards. Pianist William Houston Sr. was the music teacher. "He was president of the black musicians' union at that time. He noticed a lot of talent and he also did a lot of helping and developing. We had it all there in the school, like once or twice a week, we'd have an assembly and he'd play for us. And he'd play jazz, things like Avery Parrish's 'After Hours'. Once in a while he would bring in some of his friends including a saxophonist named Sam 'Hold-That-Note' Lee and that's where I said I want to hold a note like that.

"They would all come play for us at our dances, people like Dave Bartholomew, Roy Brown, Sidney Desvignes, Herb Leary and Paul Gayten. Incidentally, Paul's wife Odile taught me and my wife in High School. Houston had a big band too and it goes 'til yet. He's dead but his son, William Houston Jr. runs the music now."

Herman saw Illinois Jacquet in 1948 and knew straight away that he wanted to play the saxophone. "Got me one second-hand, a silver-looking horn and I played around for a while. Six months later I was in the High School band – we were playin' jazz on the football field – and in the next six months I was on the street playing professionally. I'm very disciplined, just like with my athletics. I'd practise, practise, practise." He remembered a routine of regular weekly classical concerts, often at Loyola or Tulane Universities and says that he'd had eight years of study of European music by the time he moved on to college (Southern University in Baton Rouge) as a music major, where he played bassoon and picked cello as his "major strain". Herman was also appreciative of the support from his local community which, surprisingly perhaps, was integrated. "The city council-man was our across-the-street neighbour. The Jewish people were right there on the corner. All of us were family: we looked out for each other. There wasn't no colour thing.

"Matter of fact, I organised a jazz band when I was in tenth grade. I got all the best players in our High School, I bought some Stan Kenton music – 'Intermission Riff' and 'Eager Beaver' and 'Midnight Sun' – and we went up to my grandmother's living room and we played it. Only Roy Henderson and another guy named Earl Daniel Farrell still play. Did you ever hear of the drummer Stanley Williams?[2] Well, his son was a drummer in High School. That kid was very talented – ultra-talented – but he chose to play football. We were playing in a little local club. Clubs were there then – around the corner from the house. That was a way of life and that's why the music was so much better. Now, it's a business – it's an insult. Anyway, some good Algiers musicians – a guy named John Love – came in and they gave me a job. From there, the word got around. They used to call me Little Brooks 'cos the Brooks family raised me and one day after class, William Houston said, 'Herman, get your horn. You know this song?' It was

'September Song' and I played it. Hearing my concept, my approach, he laughed and he said, 'Go ahead, Herman, you got a new style going on here.' It knocked him out to hear I had musical imagination. So, around the time of the Carnival season, he borrowed my music. He'd just put his big band together, which consisted of all the faculty people from City of New Orleans. Later I played with that band. He was a master; matter of fact, he was a musical innovator."

It's clear from Herman's reminiscences that the black High Schools in New Orleans were a fertile source of jazz talent. Hay's Chicken Shack, a city restaurant, would invite each school's jazz group to play and broadcast on Mondays. Herman remembered Ellis Marsalis from Gaudet (private) School first as the tenor soloist on 'Red Top' and talked about Ellis's piano and strengths already evident at that early age. He still marvelled at the competitive zest and facility shown by youthful trumpeters like Tony Moret, Emery Thompson and John Fernandez (later Wynton Marsalis's teacher) on Dizzy's bebop showpieces. For Herman, bebop was a step too far at the time: he saw himself as a rhythm and blues player, plain and simple. There were bebop players around and he mentions altoist Warren Bell "who studied with Bird" as a profound influence later on. Then there was "a guy named Renald Richard, a trumpet player who wrote songs for Ray Charles, he lives in New York now. I understand his son is a good trumpet player." Another who helped was drummer Earl Palmer (also based later in California) who "hooked me up with Don Robey's Peacock label. I used to make a lot of those early record sessions and it put a lot of money in my pocket. Used it to pay my folks' light bill. I was still in High School then – I was real well-rounded with all the music I was doing!"

Herman was drafted in 1953. "'They took me out of school (college). The Army did me a dirty trick; they were mean to me. They wouldn't let me get into my music at all. Two years of my life that I'll never get back. I had to scuffle like the Dickens – there was a lot of racism in the platoon." He served both in the US and in Germany in the artillery on a '105 Howitzer'.' After demob Herman tested the water in New York for a short spell, alongside musicians like tenorist Tina Brooks, trumpeter Bill Hardman and guitarist Les Spann, all youngsters trying to break into the modern jazz scene of the day.

Herman had married Thelma and started his family when very young and determined to finish his education he abandoned New York to move on to Los Angeles and then to San Diego, California. While playing in the Elks Club there with trumpeter Froebel Brigham he encountered Mustapha (Kirt Bradford) the one-time lead alto for Jimmy Lunceford's Orchestra, who offered him theory and harmony lessons. "And I haven't stopped studying since," he told me. "Brigham was the doyen of San Diego's black music scene and the man who gave people like Harold Land and Walter Benton their starts." Still alive at the time of this interview, Brigham was then over 80 but badly paralysed. Land, Benton and Teddy Edwards all came down to play guest spots with Brigham and Herman recalled other musicians on the scene including drummer Leon Petties, pianist Adam Cato, saxophonist Gene Porter and the ex-Hines trumpeter Walter Fuller. He also spent six years working in a hospital to support his family, juggling this with his classes at San Diego Music College and his music gigs.

Herman Riley (ts, bs, fl), Los Angeles CA, 1980s.
Personal promo. Courtesy Herman Riley.

In 1963 Herman felt confident enough to finally move back to Los Angeles. "I used to come up from time to time to hang out with (saxophonist-educator) Bill Green and (eventually) joined his quintet. The club we were playing in was called Marty's on 58th and Broadway and that was six nights a week. I played there for three years. First it was Bill Green, myself, Art Hillery on organ and drummer Donald Bailey. No bass. Then it was Bill, myself and (trumpeter) Bobby Bryant. Bill had transcribed 'Cottontail', Charlie Parker's 'Just Friends' and the guy from over here, Tubby Hayes, we had transcribed his thing on 'Soon' and Bill and I would play those things. Bill was just getting into the studios then and he said, 'Herman, when I'm not here you take care of the situation.' Finally he got so busy we had to get another man. At the time Dolo Coker, George Morrow and Philly Joe Jones and myself were playing in a group together so I said, hey, get Richard Boone. So Richard came in and played with us. I went out one night to a party which Count Basie had at Larry Hearn's Memory Lane and Boone got his trombone and came over and sat in. Basie heard him and he hired him. So Bobby says, 'Who can we get now?' so I said to get Hadley Caliman, the tenor player, who was a good musician. So we eased him in as the other tenor player. The guys liked him and he had a lot to offer but he was in and out of jail with that drug thing. Now he's an educator up in Seattle with Julian Priester, the trombone player. They teach at a college there. Finally Bobby took over and we got Henry Cain, organ player from Indianapolis, along with Donald Bailey on drums."

Jimmy Smith Quartet, unknown US location, 1990s. *L-r:* Terry Evans (g); Herman Riley (ts); Jimmy Smith (org). Photo by P. Baldwin.

Herman's original motivation in coming to Los Angeles came from his desire to play for TV shows, motion pictures and jingles. "New Orleans was an industry of nightclubs but in Los Angeles *music* was the industry," he said. Soon Bill, Plas Johnson, Buddy Collette and Jack Kelso were pointing him towards job opportunities as the studios were deliberately hiring more black players. He was anxious to pay proper tribute to Green (who died in 1996). "Bill Green was like a student of the instrument as well as the music. You had to walk up to him and literally take the horn out of his mouth. And if it wasn't the saxophone it was the flute or it was the clarinet, or it was the English horn, the oboe or the bassoon. He did all of them. Of course he had good training – he was in the Navy band. He was very energetic. We'd play difficult songs together and people like Sonny Stitt and Wes Montgomery would come in and sit in with us and Eddie 'Lockjaw' Davis or Roland Kirk too. It was quite a challenge."

Herman Riley (ts), **Curtis Kirk** (d), **Hugh Bell**, (t, voc), unknown (b) & (p). Unidentified Los Angeles club, 1980s. Courtesy Hugh Bell.

The group's popularity meant that they outgrew the original Marty's. While waiting for the new Marty's On The Hill to be finished they were out of work so singer Della Reese invited them to play and record with her. The resulting album, *One More Time*, on ABC Records helped to revive Reese's then moribund career. By this time Riley's own conception of the tenor was influenced by John Coltrane and Sonny Rollins – "there was a wealth of their music out there" – and he talked warmly about the advice given him by Rollins, Land and Teddy Edwards, who told him to "try to make the horn sound like the human voice."

Herman saw his career achievements as the culmination of a learning process started in New Orleans. Always the perpetual student and something of a historian of

Cab Calloway Orchestra, Disneyland, Orange County CA, c.1984. *L-r:* Jeannie Cheatham (p); Louis Spears (b); Jimmy Cheatham (b-tb); Paul Humphrey (d); Ray Brown (t); Donald Cooke (tb, contractor); Snooky Young (t); Buster Cooper (tb); Leslie Drayton (t); Herman Riley, Fred Jackson (reeds). Cab Calloway (voc, dir, *standing, right*). Courtesy Jeannie Cheatham.

the music, he acknowledged that even Jimmy Smith's apparently simple music required a lot of thought. "All of a sudden he start playin' in and out of the blues keys, adding different colours. You've got to be on your toes because anything might come at you. This man is a *mess* with his playing! He wants you to play with a lot of fire, a lot of energy, to be colourful and creative. He still speaks of creativity. Even in his old age, he's still *reachin'*. Although it's the blues you try not to lock yourself into one-four-one-five-one which are the blues changes but you try to be more musical. The blues *is* jazz. All of the sevenths are there and all of the things you can do from a seventh chord. You have to show your versatility in order to get that kind of respect. There's always somebody ready to challenge your thoughts but I feel pretty comfortable in saying that I can play in any kind of setting now. You can't make a living being one kind of artist, it's too narrow," he averred.

Asked to dip into his three-decade bran-tub and highlight some potent moments from his freelance career Herman picked an all-star tour to Japan in '73 and some LA gigs with Quincy Jones, live TV shows, stints at the New Grove in 1970 (contracted by J.J. Johnson) and trips to Hawaii with Sammy Davis Jr., playing the new Bill Cosby TV show (music by QJ), more trips to Japan (and recordings) with Benny Carter, sessions with Nelson Riddle, a CD with Roger Neumann's big band, recording with the Capp-Pierce Juggernaut, playing with Mercer Ellington's band in Scandinavia and Italy, recording with Jimmy and Jeannie Cheatham for Concord, touring South Africa in '74 with Monk Montgomery, playing Disneyland and San Francisco with Lionel Hampton, and LA with Woody Herman's small band, doing a couple of stopovers with Count Basie and sixty one-nighters on the Greyhound

Herman Riley (ts), Herman Riley Quartet, 3rd Annual Desert and Big Band Jazz Party, Palm Springs CA, 28 December 2003. Photo by Gordon Sapsed. Courtesy Gordon Sapsed.

bus with Louie Bellson and Pearl Bailey – "I never will forget that." All that plus a 12-year association with Jimmy Smith.

"Every music setting, I don't care how bad it is or how good it is, I get something out of it. If it's bad I'm in there working on something better and every time I put the horn in my mouth I'm working on something. I give great respect and homage to being a jazz musician because without that approach I would not ever have known anything about any other music. Jazz opened me up to learn about other music. I'll never throw away nothing that I learned. Right now I feel blessed. I'm a basic person and not greedy as far as material things and money go. My philosophy is that as long as I'm inhalin' and exhalin', I'm going to make a living."

From my close personal observation, Herman Riley was an accomplished instrumentalist, and an underrated soloist on both tenor and soprano, whose talents may never have been fully appreciated within the international jazz community. He cherished his roots in New Orleans music and especially the blues, retaining the strong spiritual values which were gained in childhood, yet remained open to new experiences. His peers thought highly of him and in his quiet yet confident way, he knew he had much to offer.

Herman Riley (flute), Herman Riley Quartet, 3rd Annual Desert and Big Band Jazz Party, Palm Springs CA, 28 December 2003. Photo by Gordon Sapsed. Courtesy Gordon Sapsed.

First published in shortened form in *Jazz Journal International* in February 1997

---

[1] Nathaniel 'Bebe' Mathews and Ramos Mathews were both born in Algiers and were known as parade drummers. I can find no reference which shows the nickname 'Happy' for either of them. Their brother, Bill Mathews, was a well-known trombonist who played and recorded with Oscar 'Papa' Celestin.

[2] Stanley Williams visited Britain with Kid Thomas Valentine in 1983. He had become a regular at Preservation Hall after his return to New Orleans from Chicago. In the forties he was with Fats Pichon on the SS *Capitol*, later touring with the Benny Carter big band (replacing Max Roach), before playing the Garrick Show bar in Chicago with Henry 'Red' Allen and in Adam Lambert's Brown Cats which featured a youngster named Miles Davis on trumpet. Williams died some years ago.

Lanny Morgan

Lanny Morgan, alto saxophone. Los Angeles, 2000. Photo by Steve Maruta. Courtesy Lanny Morgan.

As the opening to this piece indicates, I caught up with Lanny Morgan on a hot, sunny day in 2003 while he was staying at the Bull's Head in Barnes, in London. He was preparing for his evening appearance there as we talked. I thought he was frank and straightforward and I admired his playing enormously. With the help of his PR executive wife Marty, Lanny assembled and sent me a batch of great photographs to illustrate the interview and we kept up contact whenever he returned to the UK. This was often at the behest of the Essex-based promoter Susan May, the widow of saxophonist Spike Robinson, and Lanny became a very familiar figure on the UK club circuit. More recently, he has stayed closer to home and is releasing an impressive sextet recording, which may well be the 'dynamite' album he was hoping to make.

We're sitting in a high-ceilinged room in a handsome Georgian building looking out over the Thames. It's a blissful May day and an eight is exercising on the river below us. They're pulling away strongly while a lone sculler takes his time, pottering along, enjoying the air. It's easy to forget that we're just miles away from the centre of London.

The room is awash with clothing and papers, and the other possessions of its temporary occupant, mostly spread out on the bed. The distinguished alto saxophonist Lanny Morgan is in residence and we're talking in his room at the Bull's Head pub in Barnes. As many will know, the Bull has been presenting jazz on a daily basis for 40 years or more and Morgan appears there regularly when he's on tour in Britain. Over the years, he has become a close friend of the pub's proprietor Dan Fleming, who provides him with a base, hence the confusion of clothes, instrument cases and tour schedules that surrounds us.

Morgan lives in Van Nuys, California, and is generally thought of as a West Coast musician. While it's true that much of his professional reputation stems from his time on the coast, Morgan is originally from Des Moines in Iowa (born there in 1934) and cut his teeth in jazz with a number of road bands, most notably that of Maynard Ferguson. Although at the time of our conversation in 2004 he was making his living from a mixture of calls, from big-band sessions to studio jobs and solo tours, Morgan, it seems to me, was always at his happiest when blowing in a club with a compatible rhythm section. He's a stimulating soloist whose boppish inclinations have never deserted him and whose unquenchable desire to play is still manifest every time he performs.

Morgan began by lamenting the playing situation in the Los Angeles area for someone like himself. "There are, possibly, four jazz clubs out there that are suitable for small groups and of course, they go round the cycle, and everybody takes their

Buddy Collette (reeds) & **Lanny Morgan** (as), North Sea Jazz Festival, The Hague, Holland, July 1988. Collette was appearing as a soloist and Morgan was with Supersax. Photo by Peter Vacher.

turn," he explained. "There's really no place for big bands any more, except every once in a while, Ken Poston promotes an event, and some of the big bands do that. I remember when I was a kid, there used to be, like, seven to ten active, busy jazz clubs in Los Angeles. We had Jazz City, which is boarded up, Peacock Lane, it's a parking lot now, The Haig, which has been torn down, Tiffany's, that's no longer there, the Parisian Room (I played there with Supersax a lot), Zardi's, which is now a porno theatre, and the Lighthouse which is still there but it's mostly a kid place. Every once in a while they'll book a jazz group; this man named Ozzie Cadena, he's very active in that area so he'll maybe book somebody into the Lighthouse and then up the street there's a place called Sangria that he books people into. If you're at the Lighthouse, you play from, say, five to eight, and then they tear everything down and the kids come in.

"So what do I do? Actually, what I do is kind of a mish-mash. I do clinics and concerts with college bands. I come here (to England) a couple of times a year. I'm a member of (drummer) Frank Capp's band and I do whatever work he has when I can; we did a record with Keely Smith and we're due to tour in Japan. Frank is a contractor, a fixer, so we went down to Palm Springs recently and played behind Jack Jones.

"I do Bill Holman's band – I've been over here (to Europe) a couple of times with Bill's band. Once we did five countries in ten days, and then in 2002 I came over with a Tribute to West Coast Jazz. It was Bud Shank and myself, Teddy Edwards and Bill Perkins, Mike Brignola (from Woody's band), Joe LaBarbera played drums, Pete Jolly and Chuck Berghofer. We did two concerts; one in Verona and one in Lyon (for Lyon read Vienne). Actually they were two of the best-paying things I've ever done. I went

Terry Gibbs Big Band, Playboy Jazz Festival, Hollywood Bowl, Los Angeles, CA, 1990. *L-r:* Lou Levy (p); Jim Hughart (b); Terry Gibbs (vib); Frank Capp (d); Bob Cooper (ts); Conte Candoli (t); Alan Kaplan (tb); Pete Christlieb (ts); John Audino (t); Med Flory (as); Snooky Young (t); Charlie Loper (tb); Lanny Morgan (as); Bob Enevoldsen (tb); Steve Huffsteter (t); Jack Nimitz (bs). Courtesy Marty and Lanny Morgan.

back and told Bill Holman how much and he said, 'Jesus, how can they pay that kind of money?' With him I think we made $400 a concert for four or five concerts but for this thing we played in Verona, before we went on the stand, they gave us in cash $2,000 apiece and then we went to Lyon and they gave us another thousand so we were over here for five or six days – two concerts and we made three grand. Those things don't come along that often!"

Morgan's father was a bandleader. "He was Harold Morgan and I'm Harold Lansford Morgan – I'll never forgive them for either one of those names. A lot of people call me Lance or Harold or Hal, and I don't like those either," he grimaced. "My dad had the staff band at WHO in Des Moines, Iowa, when Ronald Reagan was the sports newscaster. He told me Reagan didn't know anything about sports either – he had to read everything. My mother wanted me to be either a concert violinist or a doctor. She didn't want me to do what my father did. She actually made him promise not to play his horns at home."

The family's move to California in 1944 came about almost surreptitiously, it seems.

"We moved out there at the end of August, ostensibly for a visit (to Morgan's maternal grandmother) and then when September came around, and they enrolled me in school, I realised it wasn't just a visit. I was really heart-broken. As it turned out, it was a good thing.

"I came home from first grade with a violin and played that for sixteen years and then my dad started me on clarinet in junior High School. I used to practise all the Artie Shaw things and the Benny Goodman things. I didn't start to play alto until I got out of High School. My dad was playing with this little band – he was kinda finished in the business by that time anyway – but he played on weekends, like three horns, tenor, alto and trumpet. Bebop was just coming in and the tenor player was a big bebop fan. My dad wrote out 'Ornithology' so I got a hold of that part and it was really interesting. By that time I had started listening to Gene Norman who had a thing called the East Side Show every night – the first alto player I heard was Art Pepper. Walking to my violin lesson on Saturday mornings I was whistling 'Groovin' High' and I couldn't relate that to the violin.

"During the last year of High School, I knew I wanted to be a musician, not a doctor. I discovered the alto just about a month or two before I graduated, so then it was signed and sealed. The saxophone really did it for me. My parents were separated for a while so my dad wasn't around but he later came back and was all for it. He was a very good Dixieland clarinet player but when I started to play saxophone, I never had any formal lessons not even from him. I used to go in my room and close the door and I would take Art Pepper's solos off records and try and take Stan Getz and Bird off; some of the more complex ones were a little difficult for me. At the same time I was taking harmony and arranging at Los Angeles City College so it all tied together. My dad would hear me practising and he'd say, 'You gotta play something with a melody' so I got that heat from him all the time. I tried to argue with him but finally I let it go. It's much like the avant-garders were to the beboppers and the beboppers were to the trad players. I just let it go and did what I did.

"The All-City Orchestra, which I was a member of on violin, used to rehearse at City College and that was probably the first school, even over North Texas State, that had a jazz band. One day we went up for rehearsal for the All-City Orchestra and Bob McDonald the band teacher had kept the saxophones over. I knew I wanted to do that. Right after I got out of the High School I went to City College and auditioned for that band and failed. Flunked the audition because I didn't know anything about saxophone. I didn't even know what some of the keys were. I went to work in a department store and practised night and day. Next semester I passed the audition.

"Bob Florence was in that band and there was a black trombone player, Lester Robertson, who passed away a few years ago. Later, (tenorist) Pete Christlieb was in the band. Bob had a quartet I was a member of – Ken Gregg was the bass player and

Don Myerson was the drummer. It was patterned, too much so, I thought, on the Dave Brubeck Quartet. There were structured things, counterpoint and fugues, all good experience for me as it did get me into playing tunes that were not blues or 'I Got Rhythm'. Bob picked a lot of tunes that were difficult and even though I didn't play them very well, I was exposed to them. See, in those days, there were a lot of dances for fraternities and sororities in City College, and they would always hire a little band. So you'd go off and make $20 or $25. People danced to standards then, ballads like 'Polka Dots and Moonbeams', so we would play a little bit on them. They didn't know the difference. It was a good training ground."

Looking back, Morgan laughed about another part of his musical apprenticeship when he played strip clubs while he was in college, remembering that 'Harlem Nocturne' and 'Night Train' were the favourite numbers with the 'artistes'. "I worked a few strip joints when I was in college. One was called the York Club in Los Angeles. I remember they (the strippers) all had exotic names, like Lisette or Zelda. This one, I don't remember her name, was quite elderly. Maybe 45 years old, a little flabby, and her act involved a parrot sitting on top of this gong on a stand. When she gave it the cue, the parrot would fly away for a minute and then hit the gong with its beak, and climb back up on the top of the gong. On the music it said, 'begin when parrot hits gong' – this was only a three-piece band, piano, drums and me, and I was playing tenor then. Well, of course, she gave it the cue and the first thing the parrot would do was to crap all over the gong. So we changed the music to say, 'begin when parrot craps on the gong'."

An inner-city boy himself, Morgan was chary about venturing down on to Central Avenue, LA's black main-stem. "I guess it was safe enough but like any place that's busy, with jazz people and drinking, and so forth, it wasn't the place for a kid to be. We used to go to the Hollywood Palladium. All the big bands would come through there and we'd stand around the bandstand, mostly for Stan Kenton and Woody Herman. Art Pepper, Milt Bernhart, Bob Cooper or Bud Shank, these guys were our idols. Later they became friends of mine, of course."

Morgan first tasted the rigours of the road straight from college with bandleader Charlie Barnet, a man who combined a whole-hearted commitment to the music with a hell-raiser's life-style. "It was only about a three- or four-week tour but I idolised him because he was a pretty wild guy, he had all that money and was able to be just completely independent. He had his tall leader's stand and he had a band boy named Wilson who always kept a couple of fifths of booze underneath that stand for him.

"One time we played a country club in Great Falls, Montana, and this was a long narrow room with big plate-glass windows looking out on the river. Charlie said, 'They want us to be kinda quiet 'cos the acoustics here are pretty live, so brass will play in buckets, saxophones, if you've got any rags, stuff 'em in your horns.' Charlie was playing his dance book, old stuff, so we played very soft, but they kept complaining, complaining. Finally this one guy came up and Charlie turned around, he says, 'Fuck 'em, take it out, we're going to blow the fucking place down.' So we took it out, and I swear to God, you could see the plate glass windows shaking. Of course, the people left. I don't know if he got paid for that gig or not but I admired his spirit.

"You know that band was kind of nondescript, but we got to play that book, all of those old Paul Villepique things, which were great, like 'Lonely Street', and then 'Pompton Turnpike' which actually was a nice chart, and we played some of the modern things too. Gary Frommer was the drummer, a baritone player named Ernie Small was in the band, he was on the Harry James band before, and Bob Edmondson and Richie Gilliam, trombones.

"The piano player in the band was named Ike Carpenter and he'd had a pretty good band in the rhythm and blues days. He took the band up to Lake Tahoe and we stayed there for the three months of the summer, working under his name, at one of the casinos. We got to play behind Nat Cole, Mel Tormé, a lot of people with very good music. It was mostly the same people from Charlie Barnet's band, except Gary Frommer had to go, he was Art Pepper's drummer at that time and Don Payne, the bass player, he had to go back too, so they got some people to come down from San Francisco to join the band. Barre Phillips came in on bass and Bill Smith came down and played lead alto. I was playing tenor and alto.

"Ike was OK, but he was very forgettable as a player. He was quite a drinker, and he was gay. We got to Lake Tahoe the day we were going to open that night, and we had to find places to stay, and it was kinda filled up already. It was the beginning of summer. Ike had this place they had given him right next to the casino, which was very convenient and he kept saying, 'You know, I got a big bed in my room, we can get three of us in it if you want to do that,' and of course, everyone dropped that like a hot potato, and said, 'No thanks, Ike, we're OK, we can sleep in the car for a night.'

"But I liked Ike, he was a nice guy, it was just that his lifestyle was a little strange. When he got drunk, it became even more blatant. He and Charlie Barnet were in a place, when we were on the road with Charlie, in Wyoming or Montana, in one of those shit-kicking cow towns. The only place that was open was a steak place, so he and Charlie were in there, both very drunk, but Ike was very loud, and some girl said something to him and he misunderstood her. I could tell he didn't even know where he was, and he said, 'Listen, baby, don't talk to me like that, I got something here that will split you right open' and of course, everybody in the place looked and said, 'Who's this asshole – maybe he'd like to get split wide open?' When I saw that, I passed on my after-the-gig drink and just walked over to the hotel. The next morning, after the hangover had subsided, he would be just a beautiful guy."

Morgan's experiences in touring big bands were often short-lived or casual, a consequence of the changes then underway in popular music. Even so, the work was formative and reasonably lucrative. "There was a bandleader called Luis Arcaraz, they used to call him the Mexican Glenn Miller. He'd come up from Mexico two or three times a year, and I would always do it with him, sometimes I played alto, once I played baritone with him. It was a real salsa kind of band, very good too. He brought a couple of people up from Mexico, in the rhythm section, and they would burn. We played a lot of Mexican dances even going as far east from California as Denver. It was wonderful. Those people can *dance* like you wouldn't believe – they've really got the moves. There was a lot of good Latin bands in Los Angeles then – we had a ballroom called the Zenda Ballroom, it's since been torn down to make way for a freeway, that was the big Latin place. So I did about three tours with him and then there was a guy named Tommy Alexander, we did one album with him for Liberty. Actually it was quite a good record; I had a feature on 'All the Things You Are' written by a guy named Ken Downing from Tulsa who was quite a good writer, since passed away, and another thing on 'We'll Be Together Again'. I wasn't really very happy with either one of them but it was my first actual recording experience. I just wrote it off to being green and hope that no one ever listened to it!

"I played second on that band. A guy named Bob Young played lead alto, Bill Trujillo was in that band – he went with Kenton after that. Then the band broke up and re-formed and I played lead alto. Got a lot of valuable experience doing that. The leader was a crook; he was a con man. He left us stranded in New York. No way to get home. No money. We all had to find gigs so I wound up doing a lot of work with Eddie Grady and the Commanders: they had four trombones, three trumpets, and two saxophones with Ernie Caceres as the other saxophone. Ernie played bass saxophone and baritone, and I played baritone and alto. Ernie was a good saxophone player. I worked with that band for probably two months and got enough money to get home. The lead trumpet player, who'd been on Tommy Alexander's band, drove us home, right across the country. He and his wife and his baby, with me sitting in the back seat. Later on Eddie Grady moved to the coast and I worked with him a little bit out there too.

"I'd become pretty good friends with Bill Perkins. He'd been on Bob Florence's band and he called from San Francisco in 1956 and said, 'Lanny, would you like to come on Stan Kenton's band? I think Lennie Niehaus wants to leave so sit tight and I'll give you a call.' Finally he called me back and he said that Lennie had decided to stay a while longer. I had to have some money so I went on the road with Frankie Carle. I stayed there for three months while Lennie was deciding whether he was going to leave or not. Frankie would do a little jazz here and there but it was just whatever you could make of it. He was tolerant and lenient about that. I played lead alto – there were four saxes, I can't think of anyone you might know except Ralph Muzzillo who used to play lead trumpet with Benny Goodman's band, and Ernie Small on baritone. It really was a very good band.

"It didn't do my jazz reputation any good but it was a gig, it paid good and as an example of how Frankie treated the band, we had to go to Denver and we had our own Pullman car. Everybody had their own compartment. It was a two-day, two-night journey and when we got there, they put our car on a siding so we could sleep as late as we wanted to. We got up at 11 or 12 o'clock, got off and checked into the hotel, and went to a rehearsal. It was nice all the way through.

"When I was on the road with Frankie Carle, I got a telegram from home which said, 'Call home regarding induction notice'. I had been drafted. I had to write them a letter and have Frankie Carle say that I was indispensable to him, and I asked for enough time to finish this tour because I needed the money and wanted to put my affairs in order. On 18 January 1957, I went in the Army for two years. I went to Fort Ord, up near Carmel, near Monterey, it was about a minute's walk from the beach, such a beautiful place, and I tried to stay there as cadre, as permanent personnel, as it was so close to home but they didn't have room for me so they sent me to the 4th Armored Division at Fort Hood, Texas. The armpit of the world! I was there for about four months.

"They don't induct you as a musician. I started one Basic Training programme and got pneumonia, I was in the hospital for about six weeks, then I did another one, and at the end they called me to take the band audition. I hadn't touched my horn for four months – I had it with me but I hadn't played for all that time. Fortunately the person who auditioned me was Allan Beutler, who played baritone with Stan's band in the early sixties. I played a little bit for him and he said, 'We'll get you in.' I got to play a lot of jazz at Fort Hood but then they sent us over to 7th Army in Stuttgart, where they had the big entertainment units. Five or six of us auditioned and I made it. They were just putting together a jazz show but it wouldn't be for a few months so I went out with a variety show called *Ain't Misbehavin'* and did that for three months.

"On the jazz show was Leo Wright, myself, Eddie Harris, Don Ellis and Cedar Walton. It was a big 17-piece jazz band called Jazz Three. We travelled all over Western Europe playing military bases. Don Ellis did a lot of writing for it, plus we got some things from Eddie Sauter. A great experience. Didn't have a uniform on for all that time hardly. Had a 24-hour pass every night. That jazz show lasted six months, then I went with the 7th Army symphony which was a 104-piece orchestra – very good – they'd draft these guys in from all the big orchestras in the USA. They were doing some Gershwin things so I was with them for four months then I went back to my own unit. I got out on New Year's Eve, 1958."

Three months short of his 25th birthday, Morgan was back in Los Angeles and contemplating his next step. "I always envisioned that I would like to spend some time

US 7th Army Jazz Show, Jazz Three, Germany 1958. *L-r:* Eddie Harris (ts); Lanny Morgan (as); Leo Wright (as); Merle Ellis (ts); Dick Van Cleave (bs). Courtesy Marty and Lanny Morgan.

on a band, six months or so and get off, form my own band and record and tour," he said. "You can't do that any more. You've got to have the support of the record companies but they don't want to take a chance."

In the event, Morgan earned his jazz spurs in the elevating company of star trumpeter Maynard Ferguson, but only after a short but stimulating association with trombonist Si Zentner and a valuable series of recordings with the little-known Rey DeMichel Orchestra. "Si had a band with four saxes and he was going to Liberty to record with a new arm of the label. There was going to be more jazz so he had to expand to five saxes. He asked me to come on the band – actually made a chair for me. I played second alto and all the jazz. Did two albums with him, then I played with Rey DeMichel who nobody's ever heard of, but we did three really good albums with him. Teddy Edwards was on one and Buddy Collette was on another. I played lead alto and got to play a lot of jazz. Terry Gibbs had just started the Dream Band and (alto saxophonist) Joe Maini used to go to Vegas and play with Ray Anthony so Charlie Kennedy would move over and play lead and I would come in and play second. Of course, that was really a thrill for me."

Maynard Ferguson Orchestra, Brooklyn Paramount, New York, 1960. *L-r*: Maynard Ferguson (t, ldr); Charlie Sanders (b); Lanny Morgan (as). Courtesy Marty and Lanny Morgan.

Morgan's jazz career took off after Willie Maiden called him to replace Jimmy Ford in the Ferguson band. "Jimmy had fallen asleep once too often on the bandstand. He used to have a pill to go to sleep and a pill to wake up. Anyway, Maynard finally fired him. I loved Jimmy, the Great White Bird they called him, and every time we hit Houston with a band, we'd go to hear him but he'd be too drunk to play. We did a concert together at Houston High School a couple of years before he died (Ford died in 1994) and we got along really good. Jimmy was another Chet Baker, he could have been one of the bigger names but he just didn't want it to happen for some reason."

Morgan knew the band (he'd subbed on baritone a few times) and Maynard knew him. "The air was just crackling with the excitement. The band was new, everybody loved it and Maynard was a big hero." Although he was starting to get some studio jobs – "Bud (Shank) would throw me some things once in a while" – Morgan opted for the jazz life and moved back to New York to join the band. "I decided I'd rather play a lot of bebop rather than make money," he says now, ruefully. Arriving just in time to make a rehearsal on 30 March 1960, his 26th birthday, Morgan stayed with Ferguson off and on for the next six years.

"Maynard's band was on the way up," he emphasised. "He was incredible, you know. After that first rehearsal he went to a dentist and had six front upper teeth filed down ready for caps. They made them overnight so he went and had this bridge fitted. We opened at Birdland that night and he played his ass off. Birdland used to go from 8.30 to 4am and the band had the last set and he was still playing notes off the end of the piano. It was just amazing. When he played lead with the band, like an octave or two octaves above the band, it just lifted you right out of your chair."

Maynard Ferguson Orchestra, Brooklyn Paramount, New York, 1960. *L-r:* Steve Martin (out of picture) (d); Willie Maiden (ts); Jerry Tyree (t); Lanny Morgan (as); Chet Ferretti (t); Joe Farrell (ts); Rick Kiefer (t); Frank Hittner (bs). Courtesy Marty and Lanny Morgan.

For all his agreeable personality, Morgan recalled that Ferguson could be hard to pin down when it came to a pay increase. "(Drummer) Rufus Jones came on the band and he had that single-stroke roll and it would get so fast, you couldn't see his hand. So he was a great asset – people would just go nuts over him. You had to time your asking for a raise, because if you got there after Rufus, you were out of luck. If you could catch him and Rufus hadn't got to him first, you might be able to get something."

Disgruntled by a typical Ferguson refusal, Morgan upped and left the band. "I was away from the band for about eight months and was really starving; had to borrow money, couldn't pay the rent. We had two kids by then and I remember having soup and cheese and soda crackers for three straight days. Nothing else. It wasn't all glamour!" Fortunately for Morgan, Ferguson pulled the plug on the big band at about this time and recruited him to join his new sextet.

Morgan looks back on his period with Ferguson with more than usual pleasure. "I thought the music was top drawer all the way, with writers like Slide Hampton, Willie Maiden, and Don Sebesky. Maynard had a contract with Roulette and he wanted out of it. So he conspired to do three or four albums quickly and said, 'Anybody in the band that wants to write something, you must do some.' I never did, but Don Menza and Don Rader wrote some really nice things. We did all the albums in a row and I always thought even the ones written hurriedly were great. Benny Golson had written a couple of charts for the band, Oliver Nelson had written a couple of things, and Al Cohn had, too.

Maynard Ferguson Orchestra, saxophone section, Connecticut, 1963–64. Ronnie Cuber (bs); Frank Vicari (ts); Lanny Morgan (as); Willie Maiden (ts). Courtesy Marty and Lanny Morgan.

"It varied, but maybe three or four times when I was on the band, it was the best band in the world. Nobody could touch it. It was actually a compact big band, just two trombones, three trumpets and four saxes. We had a dance book but that was jazz, too. During every college or High School dance, we would have a half-an-hour jazz concert in the middle and they would be 50 or 60 deep around the bandstand, listening and yelling. That's kinda disappeared now."

The fact that Ferguson's band was racially integrated seems noteworthy in retrospect. How relevant was it, I wondered? "It didn't make any difference to Maynard. Actually it didn't make any difference to any of us. Slide Hampton was on the band at various times, Jaki Byard, Rufus Jones, Harry Hall, trumpet player, and Charlie Greenlee, trombone player who's since passed away, he was there for a while. I can remember going down South to Richmond, Virginia, places like that, where the black players had to stay in separate hotels and they couldn't eat where we eat. If we were playing a gig and needed to hit and run, we'd have to stop at a diner and get their food to go. One night we stopped at a gas station, just outside of West Virginia and some white guys in a station wagon, and some others in a pick-up truck, got out with chains and they were headed for us. We just left the pump and got away. This was the middle sixties. It was terrible down there."

Morgan was also eloquent on the racial mistrust that began to manifest itself in New York during the Civil Rights years. "I hadn't paid attention to skin colour until I went back to New York and that whole thing started. There was a lot of protest music going on at places like the Five Spot. I thought it was all bullshit really. The arts have always been used to express discontent and that's fine, but come on, the other (white) people involved in it (jazz) didn't have an easy time either. We whites weren't

Maynard Ferguson Orchestra, Boston Ballroom, MA, c.1964. Maynard Ferguson (t, ldr); Linc Milliman (b); Willie Maiden (ts); Lanny Morgan (as). Courtesy Marty and Lanny Morgan.

oppressed as a race or as a people but at the same time, I can't help what my grandfather did. I'm not going to take the rap for it. It's been done, it's been said, let's move on," he said.

Morgan remembered an incident when the Ferguson band played the New Orleans Pavilion at the New York World's Fair in 1962. "After the gig, we had to walk a long way to where we had parked. Of course, they put the musicians in the next county! We were walking with Maynard and his wife Flo, and Charles Mingus. Everyone was talking nicely, Mingus was a little drunk, I guess, and all of a sudden, he picked up a garbage can and heaved it through the stained-glass window of the Pavilion. Well, security was on him just that like and they took him to jail. He was so unpredictable."

Ferguson's sextet lasted for a little over a year. "After Birdland closed, we played the Metropole in New York, the Living Room in Cleveland, all the jazz rooms. Willie Maiden played tenor, I played alto, Tony Inzalaco was the drummer, Ronnie McClure played bass, Mike Abene, piano, and Maynard was on trumpet, of course. A good band. We did one record called *Six by Six*.

"It's been reissued with four charts I hoped they would never put out. We did it at Capitol in New York, and by the time we came to those last tunes, most everybody was wasted. I'd been drinking gin, and I was playing with my shoes off and my shirt out. I think I was trying to get 'outside', playing changes that weren't there, hoping Mike would go with me but he never did! It just sounds wrong. Still, the original six or eight tunes on it were good."

Cast adrift when the sextet folded – Ferguson had gone to India and found his guru – Morgan looked around for work, and like many musicians before him, began to teach, also hooking up with a catering house to play weddings on the weekend. Later, he was lead alto at the Copacabana, one of New York's best locations, backing "all the big stars of the day – seven nights a week". Jimmy Cleveland and Richie Kamuca were in the band, too. Morgan formed a quartet with the sextet rhythm section and began to play guest shots for jazz clubs. Juggling these assignments brought him a passable living, and he still found time to respond to a call to join Howard McGhee's occasional big band. "We did quite a few jazz festivals and I had a good time with it. Clifford Jordan was on that band, and Frank Rehak was on trombone. Maggie was wonderful, always carried a quart of gin in his trumpet case. Sonny Red played second alto, and I guess he'd been a boxer. You couldn't even look sideways at him and he would be paranoid. He had all the solos, well, most of them, and one day we played something where I had the solo and he comes on and says, 'Why should he get all the solos?' Howard handled it. I just let them go. Otherwise, it was a joy on that band. He kept it together for a year or so.

"There was another band I played on, with Billy Mitchell, the tenor player. He put it together with essentially the same personnel. We'd do concerts in the summer in parks and play in the local ski bowls. Billy and I were pretty good friends, we lived fairly close to each other on Long Island. You'd call around Billy's house and he looked like a hobo who'd just gotten off a freight train yet when he went out he was impeccable. I've never seen anyone that sharp."

Morgan recalled that Mitchell planted 'grass' in a ravine near his home. "When it got ready, he'd pick it and process it." Then came the day when the city authorities came though the ravine with bulldozers and mowers, cutting down all the weed growth – including Mitchell's precious 'grass'. "He was just beside himself," Morgan laughed, adding that Mitchell, clearly a man of many parts, also used to build pool tables. "I think he did pretty well with that."

Although he'd made decent money in his final year in New York, Morgan jumped at the chance to return to Los Angeles in 1969 and go into studio work. He bought himself an arsenal of instruments: adding alto flute, bass flute, clarinet, bass clarinet, soprano saxophone and tenor saxophone to the alto, baritone, flute, and piccolo he already possessed. He also had to learn to play recorder. He remembered one gig where he had nine doubles (instrumental duplications) but says he never saw himself as a studio musician but as "a jazz musician who was fortunate enough to get a few studio jobs to survive". Even so, a typical day might include three record dates plus a TV show and the next, a movie soundtrack and a couple of TV things. At first, he would cover for other busy studio players who had more calls than they could handle, but then, "I got so busy I would have to call somebody else, too. It was a very nervous business. Still, I made about $22,000 in my first nine months in LA. That compares with $3,000 in my best year with Maynard!" Suddenly, he was financially secure: "It's like hanging the golden apple in front of a drowning man – it did get me for while."

Supersax, departure for European tour, Los Angeles CA, May 1978. L-r: Lou Levy (p); Jack Nimitz (bs); Lanny Morgan (as); Don Menza (ts); Conte Candoli (t); John Dentz (d); Med Flory (as); Jay Migliori (ts); Fred Atwood (b). Courtesy Marty and Lanny Morgan.

In 1975, Morgan joined Supersax, the ensemble that sought to replicate Charlie Parker's lines harmonised for five saxophones. Conte Candoli played trumpet with the group: "He was just a sweetheart. When he was right, there were very few trumpet players that could touch him. He was always bubbly, full of life, and funny. His big thing was the 'Tonight' TV show that lasted for over 20 years. They taped it in the afternoon and

Supersax, Carmelo's, Sherman Oaks CA, early 1980s. Jay Migliori (ts); Rex Reed (ts); Med Flory (as); Lanny Morgan (as); Jack Nimitz (bs). Courtesy Marty and Lanny Morgan.

were through by seven o'clock so he could work at night. Live TV was my thing, too. I did a lot of shows as a sub. A lot of times you'd record for (pop and rock) sessions where they had the rhythm tracks already laid down and you'd just go in, put the cans on and sweeten things. But then all that live TV stopped."

Capp-Pierce Juggernaut, Ottercrest Jazz Weekend, Ottercrest OR, 1982. L-r: Frank Capp (d); Bob Maize (b); Red Holloway (ts); George Bohanon (tb); Med Flory, Lanny Morgan (as); unk (tb); Gene Goe (t); Bill Green (bs). Courtesy Marty & Lanny Morgan.

When trumpeter Bill Berry relocated to Los Angeles to play the Merv Griffin TV show, he re-formed his big band, and called Morgan to sit alongside Marshal Royal, one of the last real stylists of lead alto. "I liked all the guys in the band and it was a real swinger when it needed to be," Morgan added. For all his involvement with Supersax and the Berry band, and his occasional subs with the Frankie Capp band, the collapse of a secure income encouraged Morgan to join singer Natalie Cole's substantial entourage in 1992. "I travelled all over the world with her, Europe, Bangkok, Hong Kong, just with lead trumpet, lead alto, rhythm section, background singers, and then there was this whole extra crew, wardrobe, lights, sound, covering 18 more people. The longest tour I ever did was when I first joined her and that was ten weeks. We'd have these sleeper buses, state of the art, like the rock and roll guys have. It was very good financially. They would give you $50 a day in the States – over ten weeks that's $3,500 and we used to live on that. Then you'd come home with a big chunk of cash. I have a lot of respect for Natalie. She's right on the pitch all the time; she's got great feeling and she can be a sweetheart." Morgan stayed with Cole for seven years in all, although "towards the end, she wasn't working that often. You were out for a week, and then you were back for ten weeks. In 1999, she went to a more contemporary format and she got rid of the band. That was me, the drummer Harold Jones and bass player Jim Hughart."

Morgan struck me as a tough-minded, experienced artist who knows his own worth and is simply looking for a fair crack of the whip. He has strong views on the

Lanny Morgan (as); **Dick Berk** (d); **Jack Nimitz** (bs); **Andy Simpkins** (b); **Lou Levy** (p). Gilberto's Rancho Cucamonga CA, c.1980s. Courtesy Marty and Lanny Morgan.

jazz establishment and its promotion of young Turks seemingly at the expense of mature players like himself. He said he'd like to make some money, but leant back and reflected: "I'm not a kid any more so solo work is what I really want to do. I still play in Bill Holman's band and Frank Capp's band but I really don't get an awful big kick out of big bands any more because there's not really a lot of chance to play. At my age, I can't project too much into the future but I would like to do as much as I can for myself. I'm not trying to set the world on fire – I just want to play."

Brabant Philharmonic Orchestra, Ellington Concert, arranged and conducted by Ron Pronk, Eindhoven, Holland, 1999. Soloists, *L-r*: Bobby Findley (t); Bill Perkins (bs); Andy Martin (tb); Lanny Morgan (as); Pete Christlieb (ts); Ron Stout (t). Photo by Adrian Korsner. Courtesy Marty and Lanny Morgan.

According to writer Scott Yanow, Morgan is 'one of the great bebop altoists', and I concur with that view. His performances are intense, often coruscating affairs, his fluidity and drive of a very high order. Morgan's discography is extensive, yet he said: "I've never made a record I'm completely happy with – if I had the time and the right personnel, I think I could make a record that would really be dynamite." For sure.

Published in two parts as 'Lanny Morgan: 'The Apprentice Years'/'Bebop and Beyond' in *Coda*, March–April 2005 and May–June 2005

Ellis Marsalis

Ellis Marsalis Jr., New Orleans LA, 1989. Photo by Matt Anderson.

When I asked if I might interview the pianist and educator Ellis Marsalis he suggested that we talk over breakfast at his hotel, the Bel Air in The Hague. He was appearing at the 1990 North Sea Jazz Festival with the Heritage Hall All Stars, a rather desultory band of New Orleans musicians whose stylistic approach seemed far too unsophisticated for a musician like Marsalis. As might be expected, he was erudite and clear in his opinions and assessments.

Ellis retired from the teaching post at the University of New Orleans, to which he refers in the interview, in 2001. Since then he has stayed close to home, playing local clubs like Snug Harbor on Frenchmen Street and appearing at the French Quarter festival with his brilliant quartet with his son Jason on drums. In the years since Hurricane Katrina, Ellis has been active in setting up a musical centre, the Ellis Marsalis Center for Music, sometimes performing with his sons to raise essential funds. It's evident that he's a determined (if occasionally didactic) individual, as befits the son of the first African-American (Ellis Marsalis I) to own and run a supermarket in the highly prejudiced city of New Orleans. What follows is the interview as it appeared in Jazz Journal in 1991, the emphasis on Ellis himself rather than his talented sons, Wynton, Branford, Delfeayo and Jason.

Preferring to stay off the road, Ellis has built a formidable reputation as a teacher of music in New Orleans. He is currently Director of Jazz Studies at the university there. He has also appeared regularly with his own groups and those of other leaders but, surprisingly, has recorded relatively rarely. In recent years Ellis has been seen more often in Europe, sometimes touring with New Orleans bands as a 'special guest' and he was tenorist Courtney Pine's partner in a series of well-received UK concerts in December 1990.

We met prior to that British visit and I first asked Ellis to comment on his current musical concerns and priorities. "My priorities are shifting. That is, during the year from, say, late August, September, through May, I'm teaching at the University of New Orleans. I'm the Director of the Jazz Studies programme there, which is in an embryonic stage and in the process of development. And also, I'm trying to play and keep my hand into that. The reason why I say that the priorities are shifting is because some things from time to time require priority over others. The business of putting a group together, the business of playing, of trying to write, core curriculum development, all these kinds of things."

The new course is clearly significant. "I think it is. There seems to be a move underway in the United States to develop jazz programmes at the college level, which

I'm hoping will turn out to be a plus." But the pianist's involvement with jazz education goes back some way. "Formally, when I say formally I mean in terms of actually having a job which by definition was to teach jazz, it started in 1974 at the New Orleans Center for Creative Arts. This was at High School level. It was a programme which started out with a government grant and the person that I think was responsible for the grant was Mrs. Shirley Corey. It was a three-year government-supported grant and at the end of the third year the New Orleans School Board liked the kind of thing that we were doing and said 'We'll pick up the programme,' which meant that they just paid the teachers' salaries.

Marsalis Family, USA, 1991. Ellis Marsalis (p); Branford Marsalis (ts, sop); Wynton Marsalis (t); Jason Marsalis (d, vib). Sony promo. Photo by Anton Corbijn.

"The school is still going on and I stayed there 11 years. It was an arts High School that ultimately had five disciplines; creative writing, music, visual arts, theatre and dance. So we were not hindered by football programmes and lunch programmes and all those things that take up a lot of time. Branford was there, Wynton was there also, Terence Blanchard was, Donald Harrison was, Reginald Veal came for a year and a saxophone player named Jesse Davis, he was also there for a year. There were some people who achieved local and national status like Stanley Stephens, the drummer, Chris Severin who is playing with Dianne Reeves, Kidd Jordan and his little brother (trumpeter) Marlon Jordan. Harry Connick Jr. also spent a couple of years there.

"I think the school helped those particular players who went there but I think there's also another stream of development (in New Orleans) that came by way of the brass bands, which doesn't have anything to do with school. The Dirty Dozen Brass Band was a front runner to the Rebirth Band, then there's another called the Pin-Stripe Marching Band and there may be some others I don't even know about 'cause these kids have a very high profile and other kids who are in school see them and look at doing the same thing.

"I wouldn't say this is necessarily the best way but I think it's a sign of a healthy culture when things like that happen. I don't know that there is a 'best way'. There are some situations for which formal education is indispensable to a certain level of development and there's also a way that it's a hindrance for a certain kind of development which needs to be nurtured culturally, especially when the education is foreign to the culture. Where music is started in America is foreign to some of the indigenous cultures. Most American music is taught with European concert music as the primary objective, so that means that the exercises, the literature, the modus of expression, the sound production – all the things that have to do with music and the sound of music as taught in institutions – are aimed at the development of people to perform or sing European concert music. So if there is another form of music that is derived from a different cultural or racial process, it can become a deterrent. It's not automatic. Most of the people that I've named are people who have studied this music to a point. The problem that we have is when the music begins to dictate philosophy, and to dictate values so that blues is not valued very highly because it's not taught in a school or something like that. Then we begin to get the primary/secondary approach to culture. I remember once in a panel a guy asking me, 'How can we get some scholarships for some of those guys in the brass bands to go to school and study music?' and I said, 'Hey man, if it ain't broke, don't fix it. I'm not even sure that they should go!'"

I then asked Marsalis about his own youth. Was there any equivalent support for him? "I'm looking at it in retrospect. When I was a youngster I didn't know what was out there. I stayed right in the same neighbourhood with (veteran banjoist) Papa Albert

French but I was very old before I really could appreciate who Papa Albert French was. I remember hearing Papa Celestin's band when I was in High School but the most impressive thing to me about that particular band was the drummer, whose name I don't even know. This guy sat up erect and had a sound on the drums and a press roll that was like tearing a piece of tissue paper. It was immaculate. I remember there was a tenor player, there was a banjo, drums, probably bass, piano, probably Jeanette Kimball. I had known Jeanette Kimball because her husband at the time, Narvin Kimball, was related to our landlady. We were living like, upstairs in her house and I would see him all the time. I didn't have any idea who Narvin Kimball was, except that he was 'Bubba'. So there was a lot of indigenous interaction that didn't necessarily lead to any kind of knowledge. That came from a lot of eclectic experiences; no one particular thing. I don't even know if I could put them all together so that they would make sense.

"I started playing piano when I was at the Xavier Junior School of Music. I was in a piano class. I was there primarily as a clarinet student, studying clarinet with a nun and eventually would go to college and major in music with clarinet as a main instrument. I was really not interested in jazz on clarinet and I wasn't that interested in being a classical clarinettist. There wasn't that many opportunities for black musicians in symphony orchestras anyway and if there was, I wasn't interested in it. So I went on fooling around with the piano and eventually, when there were no other piano players left to call, different people would call me, to come to a jam session or go to somebody's house and play. It got to be more and more and finally, by the time I graduated from college I decided, 'Maybe I better go learn how to play this instrument.' I was 20 which was young; usually students don't go to college until they're 18. I went a couple of years early – things were a little different then, you could go early. So I decided to learn how to play this instrument a lot better. I had (had) some lessons and I'd practised, all of that. I wasn't aware of that many pianists in New Orleans but by that time I knew about Art Tatum and Oscar Peterson. I knew about the bebop piano players but people like Fatha Hines I found out about later."

The impact of a musical form such as bebop on a city like New Orleans has always offered an intriguing prospect. "It was probably the same as it was any place else. Most people didn't even know that it existed. There was a core of musicians that was involved in trying to perform it. It did affect a lot of things in America's popular music across the board. But for the most part, New Orleans was going on about its business.

"New Orleans is a Caribbean town. Not only that, it was a proletarian town. It was a poor people's town. The cultural aspect of New Orleans emanates directly from the poor people. The activities of Mardi Gras, for example the pomposity of Rex and Comus, is constantly being underscored by the jazz band in the street. They get equal billing. All of the different ethnic groups in New Orleans have people that play music. The Italians have musicians. Jewish guys were players. Everybody had people who was playing some kind of music. The emigration of the Eastern Europeans brought some very excellent teachers to the shores of America but what they did was to perpetuate their cultural music that they left in Europe. It became then like the law of diminishing returns because as America began to develop, in search of itself, the music that ultimately established the primary ingredients of American music was that of black America, because no other music evolved."

At this stage of his own development, had the fledgling pianist decided on a performing career? "I never thought about career at all. Not until much, much later. It was always easy to perform in New Orleans. As a result of that, New Orleans offered me an opportunity of making extra money sometimes, if there's any such thing as extra. Let's say additional sources of income. There were times when (music) was the only job I had but this had more to do with consciously making decisions of things that I didn't want to do, more than making decisions about what I did want to do. I didn't want to be a schoolteacher, in the ordinary sense. I wasn't interested in having marching bands, although I did that when we had three kids and I took a job in a small town, Breaux Bridge, Louisiana, and spent two years there as band director and choral director. I left and came back to New Orleans after two years and worked at the Playboy Club for a while. Eventually, I worked with Al Hirt from 1957 until 1970."

New Orleans is famous for its musical families, of course. Were there musical antecedents in the Marsalis family? "No, not in my family. In my wife's family. My wife was related to Wellman Braud on her daddy's side and Alphonse Picou on her mother's side. But there was nothing in my family. My daddy's people came up from Mississippi and we didn't even have no blues singers in the family! No, there was none of that."

The younger Marsalis generation has earned widespread fame and attention. Has their renown refocused the way that people look at Ellis himself?

"To some extent, I don't know how much, but one of the things that I did not do, I did not lose my skills so consequently I was able to take advantage of some things as a player and also make some connections through their connections. But for the most part I've spent my energies in the last 15 or so years developing teaching skills for this music. That's something that I see as very important. I play because I can, not because I have a particular ambition in terms of a performing career. If you're going to have a performing career, you have to devote 100 per cent to it. Because of the fact that I was teaching music and experimenting with jazz curricula, it enabled me to stay in touch with it and also to continue to develop as a player to whatever degree I could. There's some people who are coming back into playing music after being 25–30 years as a civil servant, doing some other kind of job and they're good players. They're doing this as a way of shifting their life's base but see, I never was into that. I was always involved with music. It's just that it was never directly as a performing musician with a recording career and management. I didn't really do that. But I was always able to play."

Publicity Still for 'Mister Rogers' Neighborhood' programme – 'Fathers and Music', PBS TV, airing July–August 1990. *L-r:* Branford Marsalis (ts); Fred Rogers (show host); Ellis Marsalis (p, seated); Jason Marsalis (d); Delfeayo Marsalis (tb). Photo by Walt Seng.

Aside from Wynton, Branford and trombonist-producer Delfeayo, does the Marsalis clan boast any other upcoming talents worthy of note? "Well, we have six sons altogether. Our third son is in business with some of his college buddies. He's a computer consultant in Baltimore, Maryland. Delfeayo is number four. Our fifth son is autistic. He's 19 years old and he is at home with us. Our sixth, Jason, the last one, is 13. He is a drummer. Very talented in music. Will he come through? I don't know. We'll have to wait and see. He has a good chance and he has definitely the potential."

And what of the pianist's extended family, the many students who have emerged and attained success? Jazz educator Marsalis must take pride in their achievement?

"Well you have to realise, man, that was my job. This was not something I did as a hobby. If you train somebody to do something and they do it, all right, you feel good about it but then that's what you expected. That's what that's all about. I'm definitely glad for them, and a certain amount of it is (my) success but there's an even larger picture because there was a lot of (other) teachers involved. Even in the structured part of it, there were teachers from the symphony who taught these kids, there were private piano teachers who taught them, teachers who were teaching theory, teachers who were teaching them chorus. It was a whole process. Sometimes these questions are asked of me and they seem to be directed towards a belief that there was a kind of a Socratic circle and like, this great teacher was sitting around with these people. It didn't happen like that."

At this point it seemed appropriate to mention another Louisiana-born musician/educator, the clarinettist Alvin Batiste. "Alvin and I go all the way back to elementary school and we been playing together off and on for years. Even now. We did the Chicago Jazz Festival together a couple of years back. We've done a revision group of the American Jazz Quintet, which was an early group we had with Edward Blackwell on drums. Alvin just retired from Southern University but he went back on a part-time basis and is dealing with the Jazz Institute at another level now."

I was interested to have Ellis's view on the short-term future for jazz. After all, he's alongside the young musicians in whose hands its development must lie. His response was characteristically pragmatic. "I think the future looks bright. I don't really separate jazz from America and its development. It's like being on a ship − if somebody torpedoes the ship and the ship goes down, then everything on the ship goes with it. If America's future is bright, then I think the music's future is bright."

Some people maintain that jazz today is no longer of interest, or relevance, to the black community. "Well, it never really was, in the sense that they talk about jazz. See, jazz was a practical music in the beginning of the 20th century. It was America's music. It was the music that ultimately freed white Americans from the imperialism of European concert music which was really not a part of their acculturation. Not only that, I read some guy from England said that hearing jazz during the war freed them from the misery of having to listen to them Strauss waltzes! There was a point in time when the music no longer served, mainly, the interests of the black community. They also became influenced by other outside aspects. The compartmentalisation came, ultimately, with rhythm and blues. Those names really don't mean a whole lot because the elements of the music are the same. The names were changed for different reasons. The recording industry used to record all black popular music under 'race' and at some point, the National Association for the Advancement of Colored People entered a class action suit to dismiss that name, so the industry came up with rhythm and blues, which was the same identification, being black. Eventually, by the fifties, as young Americans began to become more enthralled with rhythm and blues, it became necessary on the part of the merchants to change the name because they wouldn't be able to sell it to the white community. So, eventually, rock and roll became the term and it sorta usurped r&b. Now, as that evolved, the compartmentalisation, the demographics of race, sex, age, income, dictated concentrated markets so then you got heavy metal, blue-eyed soul, which are white artists, you got a revision of r&b, now you got rap."

With the new course in mind, what hopes did Ellis have for it? "I don't know. It's too far to go, too much work to be done, there's courses to be developed and that's gonna be contingent on the kind of students we get plus what kind of finances we get to support the programme. I'm not saying that in a pejorative manner. The optimism is there but I can't make much of a projection because I'm not really sure how long it's going to take to do what. We have a good institution in the University of New Orleans. If that remains constant, then I think a lot of things will evolve. We go to all the (local) schools, we get some students that hear about the programme, there are European enquiries, some people come because they run into my children and they say 'you ought to go', so it's a lot of different things. In the final analysis, we're going to have to be responsible for recruitment and for what they call retention and development."

With that, this articulate and thoughtful musician and educator had to be on his way. Given his track record I'd suggest that jazz talent-spotters keep an eye (and ear) on the progress of his new course. After all, the extraordinary 'proletarian' city of New Orleans has already contributed mightily to the development of jazz, whether through

Ellis Marsalis (p), at home, Hickory Street, New Orleans LA, 20 February 1998. Photo by Derek Drescher. Courtesy Derek Drescher.

the products of its 'indigenous culture' or via musicians who have embraced the kind of structured programme that Marsalis oversees. The chances are that each route will continue to offer value for decades to come.

First published in
Jazz Journal for August 1991

Houston Person Jr.

Houston Person, Statesmen of Jazz, Brecon Jazz, Brecon, Wales, August 2006. Photo by Peter Vacher.

I first heard the tenor saxophonist Houston Person play at the North Sea Jazz Festival in The Hague in July 1984 when he was still touring with the singer Etta Jones. I enjoyed their quartet set but not enough to mention it in my festival review in Jazz Journal. Mea culpa. Still with headliners like Miles Davis, Cleo Laine and John Dankworth, Dave Brubeck and Dizzy Gillespie to contend with, I guess I could be forgiven for the omission. So my next encounter with Houston at Blackpool some 20 years later was a genuine eye-opener, the authority of his playing and his impressive demeanour marking him out as the star he so clearly is. He was back in Britain the following year with the Statesmen of Jazz and continues to be on the wish-list of every jazz party organiser and festival director.

Since this feature piece first appeared, I've observed Houston in action with his quartet on his home turf at Harlem's Lenox Lounge and as accompanist to the singer Ernestine Anderson at Dizzy's Coca-Cola Lounge in New York and more recently as a participant in the 2012 Norwich Jazz Party. He's a take-charge player, muscular in his bearing, who you sense knows exactly what he wants to do. He says little on the bandstand, letting the music speak for itself: the emotion is controlled, simmering rather than overt. Houston directs his career himself and stays busy as a touring soloist and accompanist to singers and with his regular group. He also continues to oversee many album sessions for HighNote Records.

Houston Person was lying on the bed, head resting on brawny arms, gazing intently at the television. Outside the sun was shining and couples were strolling along the promenade. Ancient tramcars were making their clangy way to and fro. It was a Sunday morning in May 2005 and Blackpool was looking good. Well, this end of town anyway. Further down, the so-called Golden Mile beckoned with its strip of tawdry amusement arcades and fast-food outlets but we were well away from all that. In fact we were up on the sixth floor of the Hilton Hotel, ready to talk with the burly tenor saxophonist about his life and times. He was here in England's northern seaside playground as part of Tom Baron's Jazz Weekend, appearing with the Statesmen of Jazz.

Initially it was the TV that engaged us, as Blair and Bush made their pitch for the continuation of hostilities in Iraq. We were at one, Person and I, it seemed, in feeling short-changed over the involvement of our two countries in what we'll call the Iraq situation. There followed a lively discussion on the topic that will stay unreported, except to say, as Person did, that these are just the sorts of things that any concerned citizen should seek to talk about.

Houston Person (ts), backstage, Blackpool Jazz Party, Blackpool, UK, 1 May 2005. Photo by Peter Vacher.

To me there are few greater pleasures in jazz today than hearing Person build a solo, standing tall and teasing a melody in his warm-toned way, terse at times, fulsome at others. It's easy to see him as an anachronism, a present-day throwback to the tenor stars who dominated mid-period jazz. I was anxious to know what Person made of all this so I asked him first how he defines his style. There was a pause. "Well now, I don't. I never thought about it. When I was coming along I worked mainly with my sound. I was not trying for a real virtuosic technique because I learned your sound was your identity. Illinois Jacquet was my main influence; a lot of people say Gene Ammons, a lot of people say Lester Young but I tend to lean somewhere between Lester Young and Jacquet," he explained in his slow-burning, languid way.

So, no room for the likes of Coltrane then? "There were so many guys with different approaches; you had John Coltrane, Johnny Griffin, Hank Mobley, a lot of guys. I think everybody brings something to the table. The main thing is that you don't want to be overly influenced by somebody," adding that an identity of one's own is crucial. "That's the way you're going to really make it in such an individual music as jazz." So what does Person bring to the table himself? Another pause, longer this time. "The legacy of jazz, which is the blues, a danceability to the music, swing, and a good emphasis on melodic improvisation. That's what I try to do. A *big* part of my thing is keeping in touch with the audience. I'll put it this way: I'm not one to turn my back on the traditions of *real* jazz. That's my philosophy."

When I ventured to question whether Person's kind of jazz still has validity in the African-American community he was quick to respond. "Of course. I play for African-Americans all the time because it (my music) has all those elements. Only because it has

Houston Person (ts) **and Byron Stripling** (t), Newport Beach Jazz Party, Newport Beach CA, 18 February 2008. Photo by Gordon Sapsed. Courtesy Gordon Sapsed.

those elements. When you go past those elements you've lost them," he said. Person likes/wants to play for dancers: "See that's the way it was when I was coming up. I play dances all the time. I request it. I tell people, 'Why don't you just play a dance?' I get joy out of seeing people dance. When you know your music is making people dance, then you do your improvisation toward that. You know how long to play, so you edit yourself."

Person's band is that modern rarity, a group with a settled personnel. "Stan Hope plays piano – he's been with me now for about 25 years. Stan's the only piano player I've ever had – when I went from organ to piano he was the man. He's a great guy, from Atlantic City, New Jersey, and he played with Hank Mobley, Clifford Brown, all those people during that time when things were happening around Philadelphia and Atlantic City. On drums I've got Chip White, he's been with me for about 20 years. He's from Peekskill, New York. He played with (singer) Tom Waits and he worked around New York with a lot of local bands. I have a new bass player, Per-Ola Gadd. He's from Sweden – he studied with Niels (-Henning Ørsted) Pedersen – and he's been with me now for about three years. We have a vast repertoire – that's another thing I stress, too – not too many originals but a lot of jazz standards, classics, and a lot of Duke Ellington. Duke Ellington's music was made for dancing. People get mad when I tell them that jazz is basically dance music. Why take the dance out of jazz? It's madness."

Houston Person (ts), HighNote Records promo, New York, 2000. Courtesy Brian Peerless.

We left that question hanging in the air and moved on to origins and other things. Houston Person Jr. was named for his father, and was born in Florence, South Carolina, the birthplace of trumpeter Taft Jordan, in 1934. "My father worked for the Agriculture Department and my mother was a teacher. I grew up there during the period of segregation – I know you want to ask about that – there's nothing to say about it except that it's an experience. We woke up every day and survived and still managed to get our education and fight for equality. All this without welfare or affirmative action! In my community, you wouldn't even think of graduating High School, you (only) thought of college. If you didn't have the funds, the community would help you to get to school. You had to make yourself as good as you could be."

Person grew up in a middle-class, aspirational black family, surrounded by music. "On the radio I was required, absolutely required, to listen to the Metropolitan Opera every Saturday at one o'clock for an hour before I could go out and play baseball or football. We had one local jazz band, that was Nat Green and his All-Stars, great bebop band, we had gospel groups and I was in the church choir. My parents encouraged me to get involved in everything. In school they wanted me to do all kinds of extra-curricular activities, sports, music, drama, all of it. My mother made sure of that.

"I started playing when I was about 16. My father gave me a saxophone for Christmas and I played it. I got in the band in my senior year at High School and my band directors (Hamilton Flowers and Charles Young) thought I had a knack for it so they took special time with me. Then I went on to South Carolina State College in

Orangeburg, majoring in English and music and that's where I worked with Aaron Harvey – he'd been with Tiny Bradshaw – he helped me a lot. Played college dances in the dance band, that sort of thing. When I went in the Service I got sent to Germany. That's where I met Eddie Harris and Leo Wright, Cedar Walton and Don Menza and Lanny Morgan, they were all in the 7th Army Jazz Band. I was in the Air Force – I wasn't part of their band but I'd meet them on the weekends and we'd play in the clubs in Heidelberg. When I left there I went to the Hartt College of Music (on the GI Bill) up in Hartford, Connecticut. Stayed there three years. (Bassist) Ron McClure and Dionne Warwick, we were classmates at Hartt College, that was a great experience. Then I went to New York City, to the Hartnett School for a while."

Person joined organist Johnny 'Hammond' Smith's popular touring group for three years playing the black club circuit. "That's where you got your skills together, learning about communicating with the audience," he said. The clubs were located in black neighbourhoods, mostly in industrial centres. "New York, Buffalo, Cleveland, Toronto, Pittsburgh, going out to Kansas City, St. Louis, Chicago, Detroit. Clubs ran mostly four to six nights. Names? There was the Bon-Ton in Buffalo, the Pine Grill in Buffalo; in New York you had Count Basie's and Small's Paradise, in Pittsburgh you had the Hurricane and Crawford's Grill, in Philadelphia you had Pep's, in Detroit you had Baker's Keyboard Lounge, in Chicago Talk of the Town and the Beehive." Something of a forgotten figure now (he died in 1997), Smith, according to Person, "was different than some of the other organists because he approached music for the organ group as more of an orchestra, by stressing arrangements and original compositions. Jimmy Smith was loose, McDuff was an orchestrator, Groove Holmes, he liked rhythm, he really stressed great bass lines; they all had something different." Smith's combo paired Person with Virgil Jones on trumpet, backed by Leo Stevens on drums, and the tenorist describes it as more of a Horace Silver-type band with organ instead of piano. "We recorded on Riverside."

Listening to Person expound his musical philosophy and career direction I detected a clarity of intention and a degree of business acumen that is unusual in a creative musician. So it was no surprise to hear that Person's next move after leaving Smith was to form his own group. He has been a bandleader ever since. A radical step for someone in the early stages of his career surely? "I just wanted to be in control of my own destiny," he stated flatly. "I didn't go through any bands. I started out on my own. In my first group I had Billy Kaye on drums and Jimmy Watson on organ. I was in Boston and then I moved to Newark, New Jersey, but I live in Westchester County (New York) now. We worked the same circuit (as Smith) but I broke out a little bit. I worked a lot of the other clubs because of my repertoire. I managed to take the organ group scene into new territory."

Mention the name Houston Person to a jazz follower and they'll usually bring up his long working association with the fine singer Etta Jones. Many assume, wrongly as

Houston Person–Etta Jones Quartet, unknown US location, c. December 1980. Etta Jones (voc); Houston Person (ts). Photo by Raymond Ross.

it happens, that the two were married. Person laughed and assured me that I wasn't the first to make that mistake, and then went on to mention his wife, his five daughters and similar number of grandchildren! "I added Etta Jones to my group just before I got Sonny Phillips, the great organ player out of Chicago. She and I got together in about 1967. She had a big hit on 'Don't Go to Strangers' on Prestige but when I met her she wasn't doing much. Then we just worked together and that was pretty good for us. I got her on the Muse label and I produced some records on her and kept her albums coming out. When I moved over to HighNote I took her over there."

Speaking of Jones, who died in 2001 of breast cancer, Person said, "She had no ego, she just sang. Her favourites were Thelma Carpenter and Billie Holiday and Ethel Waters. We were together 35 years. How come? I'm a nice guy. She did half the show and I did half. I had always designed it that way so if I left she had something to work with and I'd always make sure each one of us was established with recordings. It just so happened she went first but if it had been the other way she would have been in good hands and the group was intact." Was this format limiting to a player like Person I wondered? "No, I could always play as much as I wanted – I was the boss!"

Person has built up a parallel career as a record producer, working first on his own sessions and then with others. When I asked him to sum up the producer's role he laughed and said, "Mostly to stay out of the way. Let the guys play!" So why do it? "I wanted to be in charge of my destiny. When a record company wants to let somebody go they don't let the producer go, they let the musicians go. It's different with sports, when the players mess up they fire the coach but in music they fire the musician and the producer stays. I said, if I'm going to fail I'm going to fail with my own concepts so that's how it started. That was real early. I produced Etta's albums and then more musicians asked me to start doing theirs."

Person applauds producer Bob Weinstock of Prestige for his encouragement. "He was great to me, he hung in there with me, let me develop. He gave me the opportunity to find out where I was going to fit in as a player." Since then Person has built collaborative relationships with Bob Porter, also at Prestige and later "at Eastbound Records together, that's a Detroit label. I produced a couple of my own albums at Eastbound and I got Etta a date over there then we moved on to Muse Records and

Houston Person Quartet, HighNote recording session, Englewood NJ, 10 July 2001. *L-r*: Houston Person (ts); Grady Tate (d); Ray Drummond (b); Richard Wyands (p). Courtesy HighNote Records.

that's where I really started getting into producing." Person's ongoing association with Muse (and now HighNote) proprietor Joe Fields dates back some 20 years and is clearly based on mutual trust. "Joe gave me the opportunity to get involved in the business of music," Person said, adding that he has to persuade Fields to back him every time he has an idea for a session. "I'm spending his bucks so I have to go in and convince him. I wanted to bring some of these guys back, like Teddy Edwards and Ernie Andrews, like Dakota Staton, a lot of these people should have been recorded and weren't."

He's proud of a number of his productions, notably Etta's *Sings Lady Day* (HighNote) and *My Mother's Eyes* (Muse) and an album with (trumpeter) Bill Hardman also on Muse. Plus "some great Ernie Andrews things, the three albums with Teddy Edwards. I did a lot of good stuff. I'm working on *me* right now. Then I've got (guitarist) Randy Johnston, he's good and a good composer too. We've been working on some things together."

The Statesmen of Jazz, Brecon Jazz Festival, Market Hall, Brecon, Wales, August 2006. Kenny Davern (cl); Houston Person (ts); Warren Vaché (cnt); George Masso (tb). Photo by John Watson. Courtesy John Watson.

Houston Person (ts), 8th Annual Newport Beach Jazz Party, Newport Beach CA, 18 February 2008. Photo by Gordon Sapsed. Courtesy Gordon Sapsed.

Person clearly enjoys the camaraderie that characterises the all-star Statesmen of Jazz gigs. "Everybody gets along so well." He appears increasingly often at jazz parties – "they seem to have adopted me" – and pops up as a guest in many situations, while also working area clubs with his regular band. When I asked him for a final wish-list he smiled. "I'd like to see more intelligent booking: promoters giving the people the music they need to hear and presenting it right. Music with feeling, blues, swing, danceability. And dancing!" Cue some guffaws. "Jazz will always be around, it's just that we've got to get back to those elements. You sit the audience down and you play the blues, and everybody knows what it is. Like I say, it's so simple, it's difficult!"

With that, the ever-affable Person beamed and ushered me towards the door. It was show time!

First published as 'Houston Person: Don't Stop the Dance' in *Coda*, January–February 2006

Tom Artin

Tom Artin, JazzAscona, Switzerland, July 2004. Photo by Jonathan Farber. Courtesy Jonathan Farber.

Tom Artin is one of those American jazz musicians who grew to maturity just as the last generation of swing-era players was beginning to fade from view. He knew early on how he wanted to play and was fortunate enough to find companions who felt the same. They in turn were encouraged to perform by veteran players who felt that these young aspirants understood their values and could be counted on to keep the pre-bop style alive.

Unusually for a jazz musician, Tom was able to pursue his musical inclinations while holding down a series of important academic posts. It was through his association with his old friend, the cornetist Ed Polcer, that he travelled to Ascona in July 2004. Here were two men allied in their desire to foster the freewheeling Condon spirit, Artin also tackling the heady task of putting a big band together to celebrate Count Basie's centenary. Happily, he excelled in both situations.

Since then he has continued to play, sometimes with Polcer or with a new trio, We Three, completed by the pianist Conal Fowkes and bassist Frank Tate. He's especially pleased to have hooked up again with his boyhood friend, the opera composer John Harbison; the two men reunited in jazz at Harbison's Token Creek Chamber Music Festival where Artin has been the guest artist for the past five years. He has also held a number of exhibitions of his fine art photographs and has a website devoted to them: www.tomartinphotography.com. Tom says it's an honour for him to be included here; the pleasure's all mine, as they say.

Artin is tall, with an open personal style, and he laughs a lot. He's a thoughtful man who chooses his words carefully, like any good academic should, his eyes lighting up as he talks about his initial enthusiasms and influences. "My heroes when I was growing up were, first, Vic Dickenson, secondly, Cutty Cutshall, and third, Urbie Green. Three more different stylists it would be hard to come by but there's something in each of their styles and playing that I admired. I think that everyone begins by apeing somebody and then gradually, if you're lucky enough to get to that point of evolution, somehow you step over into an individual voice which you have found, which is no longer imitation."

When we settled down to looking at his career in detail, Artin surprised me by explaining that although he was born in Bloomington, Indiana, in November 1938, his family was originally from Germany. "My father was a professor of mathematics at the University in Hamburg," he said, adding that his mother was half-Jewish. "He had a job offer at Stanford (in California) but was not allowed to leave because he was declared 'indispensable' to the fatherland. Six months later he was fired, summarily, from his job

Tom Artin (tb), JazzAscona, Switzerland, 2 July 2004. Photo by Peter Vacher.

according to the racial laws of 1935 – I still have this official document with the raised seal and the swastika and the eagle – and they were lucky enough to get out in 1937. He got a job at the University of Indiana in Bloomington through the help of a very influential Jewish mathematician, who had already left, a guy named Richard Courant, who helped many scientific people to escape from Germany. We spoke German at home. My older brother and sister were born in Hamburg."

After spending his first eight years in Bloomington, Artin moved with his family to Princeton where his father had obtained a senior teaching position at the university. As so often happens, Tom's discovery of jazz was a matter of chance. "I had a radio and at first I was intrigued by country-and-western music. I used to listen to Grand Old Opry which broadcast live on the radio on Saturday nights. Then, every once in a while when I was turning the dial I would hear this other kind of music. I didn't know what it was but I knew I really liked it. I went to John Harbison, my classmate, because he was knowledgeable about music, and I tried to describe this music as best I could. My description must have been fairly good because he said, 'Well, I think you're talking about jazz.' To test this hypothesis he took me to the local record store. This was the tail-end of the 78rpm era. We went in a booth and he took a 78rpm record and it happened to be – I blush to admit this on behalf of both myself and John – a Firehouse Plus Two record. I think it was something called 'The Lonesome Mama Blues'. It spun away and he put the needle on and within four bars, I said, 'That's it. That's what I'm talking about. That's the stuff.' It was that Dixieland ensemble sound that was just so wonderful."

So where did the trombone come in? "When I moved over to Princeton Junior High School, the band director came into the classroom with a student who was his flunkey, carrying all these instrument cases. He was going to demonstrate all the instruments and try to recruit musicians. So he laid them all out and he demonstrated every one. I looked at all these instruments and it was clear to me which was the most interesting one. I figured it would be just my luck that everybody else would want to play the trombone and get first dip. To my amazement, nobody else wanted to play it so I got the trombone. I bought it home that day, much to my father's horror. My father was a really serious amateur musician. He played keyboards and he played the flute. He had an organ, a clavichord, and he had a harpsichord and a piano. My siblings are both gifted amateur musicians, too, both classical. My brother is a violinist; my sister plays cello and piano. But I'm the only jazz musician, the black sheep of the family.

"John (Harbison) was a fine jazz pianist and he started a band when we were in the seventh grade, when we were about 12 or 13 years old so I was playing jazz from then on. He is now a very prominent American composer – he's probably best known internationally as the composer of the opera based on *The Great Gatsby* that was done at the Metropolitan Opera. He told me recently he started playing jazz piano again. We rehearsed religiously every Sunday at the Harbisons' house. The band was called the Edgehill Five – his father was also a professor at Princeton, a very renowned professor of history in fact, and they lived on Edgehill Street. We had that band throughout Junior High School and up through High School.

"There was a band at the University made up of undergraduates that had lost their trombone player to graduation. They heard that there was this kid over at the local High School who could play jazz trombone so I got this phone call at school one day

The Edgehill Five (aka Harbison's Heptet), Princeton NJ, c.1950. *L-r:* Alan Shephard (t); John Harbison (p); Peter Smyth (d); Tommy Shope (as); Tom Artin (tb). Courtesy Tom Artin.

asking me if I wanted to join their band. 'Would you like to play in our band?' I thought I'd died and gone to heaven so from then on I was in the band. This was in my second year of High School.

"Do you know the name John Dengler? He was originally a cornet player, really marvellous, very Bix-oriented and he'd had a band at Princeton, called the IVJB. That's an acronym for the Intensely Vigorous Jazz Band and the pun is on Ivy League. John had gone on to other things; like playing baritone sax with Bobby Hackett. The remnants of his band had reassembled under the name of the Roundhouse Eight and we wore railroad engineer's overalls. One of the guys in the band was the nephew or the grandson of the President of the Pennsylvania railroad. So he got us all engineer's caps. So I joined in, I think, 1952 or '53. I was in that band for a year and a little bit.

"Then this young kid who was a freshman came around to one of the outdoor gigs we were playing on campus at the beginning of the term. His name was Ed Polcer and he sat in, and the band was so enthralled with his playing that he became the trumpet player. That's how I know Ed. That was the fall of 1954. So he and I have been playing together for over 50 years. None of the rest of the guys in that band went on to become professional musicians. The other more famous band at Princeton in those days was Stan Rubin's Tigertown Five. Both Ed and I played to varying extents with Stan. In fact, Eddie ended up going to play Grace Kelly's wedding with Stan."

Artin nearly became a full-time member of Rubin's group. "A week after those Roundhouse guys called me, I got a call from Stan Rubin because he'd also lost his trombone player to graduation. He said, 'Do you want to join my band?' I said, 'Gee, Stan, gosh I'd love to, but I've already promised these other guys I would play on their band.' Looking back, what a wonderfully innocent response! Totally ridiculous for my career. I would have done much better to have told those Roundhouse guys to go screw themselves and join Stan's band but I didn't do it. In those days, in the fifties, the standard Dixieland ensemble was the popular band for college parties. Every college on the East Coast, every party weekend, every fraternity, had a Dixieland band. We used to travel every weekend all up and down the East Coast. At one point, the bass player in that Roundhouse band was the son of David Stone Martin, the illustrator. David, at that time, had this very fancy Chrysler convertible, a real slick, snazzy car. We had this weekend job at Colgate University in northern New York State in a town called Hamilton. Now this is long before any of the super highways and in those days Hamilton was about seven-and-a-half hours from Princeton on local roads and this was in the middle of winter. Tony Martin was able to talk David Stone Martin into letting us use the convertible. There were six of us. There's a bass fiddle, a set of drums, all of our luggage and our instruments and we're all packed in to this convertible for seven-and-a-half hours, going right through the middle of every town and city between Princeton and Hamilton. The only way we could get the bass in was to put it edgewise.

It was poking out the top; this wouldn't have worked if the car hadn't been a convertible. Good thing David didn't see this. We did that job and I think we got paid, like $20 a night. We got to get up there and we got to play jazz!

"There's one more element to the story. Stan Rubin's band was so popular and successful that he had offers for at least twice as much work than he could fill. So he made an agreement with us that he would send us out on his 'B' work – by that time, we'd changed our name to the Nassau Jazz Band – as Stan Rubin's Nassau Jazz Band. This way we were working every weekend and it meant we didn't have to find the work. It was a great opportunity for us. After this horrendous ride to Hamilton, we pile out of the car and it's snowing like hell, there's about two feet of snow on the ground and we see the entertainment chairman from the fraternity coming down the steps to greet us through the snow and the first words out of his mouth were, 'Where's Stan?' Now Stan always was selling us as 'Stan Rubin' and he would never specify that he wasn't going to be there. So 'Where's Stan?' became a touchstone for us."

"One of the wonderful things that came as a result of this wonderful connection with Stan was a chance to play on the Holland–America Line student ship that summer. I was sixteen years old, I was a junior in High School. The Holland–America Line had a fleet of three or four converted Victory ships and kids from college would go to Europe for the summer on these ships. The entertainment was a Dixieland band. The deal was that we got free passage – we didn't get paid – in the beginning of the summer on one of the ships and at the end of the summer on one of the ships coming home if you played every night and every afternoon. To this day, I find it hard to understand that my parents let me go. I had the time of my life that summer. We went to Germany, we went to Paris, and we played in Juan-Les-Pins. It was fantastic."

Artin's affiliation to the ebullient, go-for-broke Condon style dates back to his earliest awareness of jazz, aided and abetted by live radio. "I used to catch broadcasts from Nick's (in New York). I heard Kenny Davern almost from the beginning when he was 17 years old and he was playing with Billy Maxted's band at Nick's. I had no idea he was still just a kid at High School! I was taken by the sound of, primarily, the Eddie Condon band and the bands that I heard from Nick's, those live broadcasts. I was under age so I couldn't get into nightclubs but there was a huge, family restaurant on Times Square in the basement of the Paramount building called Child's Paramount where they used to bring in Wild Bill Davison. I used to go and hear Wild Bill because I could get in there because it was a restaurant. There were two major strands for me: one was the Condon band, the Nick's sound, the other was the records made by Sidney DeParis, Edmond Hall, Vic Dickenson and James P. Johnson on Blue Note. My Blue Notes were worn thin.

"My great jazz hero, this was apart from the trombone, was Sidney Bechet. It must have been 1952, '53 and he came for a visit and played the Central Plaza in New York.

My mother, bless her heart, took me to the Central Plaza, which was this great big hall with long tables and pitchers of beer. When Sidney walked in there and started playing I thought I had died and gone to heaven. It was just amazing. I saw him twice and then I saw him again in Juan-les-Pins in the summer of 1958. My very first jazz record was a Sidney Bechet record, with Wild Bill, under Art Hodes's name; a quintet with Pops Foster and (drummer) Freddie Moore, with whom, later in life, I played very frequently."

For all his commitment to jazz and photography, another enduring passion, there were more pressing expectations for Artin to satisfy when it came to choosing a career. "The ethos of my family was such that it was simply unthinkable not to become an academic. It wasn't even something that you discussed particularly. It was just there; it was in the air that you breathed. I continued to play jazz all the way through college but when it came to the end of my college years, there was no question that I would become a musician or a photographer. I was going to go to graduate school. So I got a PhD in comparative literature and a got a job at a pretty good college teaching mediaeval English literature. I worked at that for about fifteen years, playing on the side the whole time. In the US, there is a system in the academic world called tenure. Typically you get tenure after your seventh year. You are judged for seven years and you either get tenure, which means that you have that job for the rest of your life, or you get fired. So I got tenure at the college where I was teaching and the year I got tenure, I quit, because I realised, 'My God, this is a millstone; I'm going to be dying in this job if I don't get out.' Teaching is something I never loved, although I liked it sometimes. I had some wonderful experiences teaching; I had some awful experiences. In certain situations, I was good at it; in others, I wasn't so good at it but I never loved the activity the way I loved music and the way I loved photography. I liked the intellectual life, the scholarly life, but you know there's a big difference between the intellectual life and the academic life. Academic life is about teaching as an activity and it's about the politics, get some papers published, jockeying for position. It just so happened that around this time, the last incarnation of Eddie Condon's had opened."

Before moving on to talk Artin and Condon's, I was interested to hear more about his association with some of the old-timers he'd come to know. "My first teaching job was outside Philadelphia, at Swarthmore College, so I fell in with a whole bunch of Philadelphia people including (banjoist/guitarist) Elmer Snowden. I played in Elmer's band for the last several years of his life. He was in his late 70s and still a banjo playin' fool, he was great. It was really interesting, hanging out with Elmer. He still talked about Duke Ellington having stolen his band – he hadn't forgotten that. Elmer was a Philly guy, lived on Durard Avenue. There had been a fairly well-known Dixieland jazz club in Philadelphia called Billy Kretchmer's and the trumpet player who had been in the house band there was named Tommy Simms, black guy, and he was in Elmer's band. The guy who played reeds was British, his name was Ray Whittam, he was a pretty good clarinet and tenor saxophone man. He had emigrated and he lived somewhere in Philly. He was a part-timer. I think he was an engineer or something.

"Elmer was a very eclectic guy. I remember one night going over with Elmer and the rest of the guys in the band across the river from Philadelphia in southern New Jersey to a black organ club. I'd never had a chance to play with an organ trio before. We all played with them and I had the time of my life. These guys could play. That Hammond B-3 – there's nothing quite like it. Basically Elmer's band played the Dixieland repertoire because that's where Elmer came from and that's what people wanted to hear."

I asked Tom if he'd socialised much with Snowden. "I really didn't have the time to do much hanging out," he said. "I had two kids, a job, and I was writing a book (on mediaeval literature, on Arthurian romance). It was an academic book. That aspect of the job interested me more than the teaching anyway: I didn't resent the pressure to publish, I've been perfectly happy to publish."

Another veteran performer with whom Artin worked often was the eccentric drummer and vocalist Freddie Moore. Artin retains a considerable affection for a man who saw jazz strictly as just another branch of show business. "I was in a band that played regularly, every Monday night for years, in New York with Freddie and I played in other situations with him, too. A wonderful banjo player by the name of Eddy Davis was very close to Freddie and he explained Freddie to me better than anybody else by pointing out Freddie started his career in the circus. Freddie saw himself as an entertainer more than he was a jazz musician. By the time I played with him, he was not the greatest drummer in the world. We're not talking Gene Krupa or Buddy Rich here. His time wasn't great but that's not what it was about for Freddie. He had these vocal numbers that he lived for, like 'Bill Bailey'. He always had this comb in his shirt pocket and that was his prop for 'with nothing but a fine tooth comb' at which point he'd pull out this comb and wave it over his bald head. That was part of the act. 'Old Man Mose is Dead' was another one of his special things. He had routines that he did with every song. People loved it. Everybody who worked with him loved him. There was not a mean bone in his body. He was just a great guy.

"This Monday band started in a place on First Avenue that was called the Fugue and then we moved over to a building with a wonderful restaurant at 1 Fifth Avenue. We played there every Monday night for years. It was an all-amateur band. I was an amateur at that point before I had given up my day job and devoted myself to music full-time. Freddie was the only professional musician with the exception that whenever the leader, the trumpet player Lee Lorenz, who was the Art Director of the *New Yorker* magazine and a great cartoonist, couldn't make it, he would send in Herman Autrey who was then in his 70s. I would always take Herman home. He lived on 127th St. in a pretty dismal place, made me very sad. He was virtually crippled by that time. He had to walk with heavy use of a cane, really leaning on the cane but could still play. He was a wonderful guy, a sweetheart of a man. I lived just north of New York at that time so I was always heading that way after the gig and would take Herman home. This was during the years, from 1960 to about '75, when New York was a dangerous place. I'd pull up in front of his apartment building and he would ask me to wait until he'd gotten into the door because he was afraid of being mugged. I would wait and make sure he got into the building. He got mugged one night inside the building, in the hallway. New York is very different now.

"Then I lost that job at Swarthmore College (Swarthmore, Pennsylvania). I was there for four years and I had to look for something else. I found a job at a small college outside New York and that's where I was when I got tenure. It was just at the time when the last incarnation of Eddie Condon's had opened. Vic Dickenson was the house trombone player and he was already ill so in the late seventies, Eddie Polcer was calling me more and more often to fill in for Vic. Ed began simply as the cornet player in the band. Condon's had been closed for at least a dozen years when a guy named Red Balaban, a bass player and the son of the President of Warner Brothers, wanted to have a jazz club. He made an arrangement with the Condon heirs to use the name 'Eddie Condon's' and he opened this club on West 54th Street, just a couple of doors away from what was the final resting place of Jimmy Ryan's. What Red opened was just a quite magical and wonderful institution. I look back on those days as the last flowering of the jazz life in New York.

"I think Eddie was the very first house band cornet player and after two or three years of the club's existence, there was a managerial shake-up and Red asked Eddie to become the club's manager. It was then that Warren Vaché came in because Eddie felt he couldn't both manage the club and play trumpet with the band. He got it out of financial hot water because as well as being a great trumpet player, he has a very orderly and business-like mind.

"After a few years of managing it, Ed became half-owner of the club and was really running the business. Red just came in and played the bass – he was in the band, sometimes more often, sometimes less often. Around 1979, I started playing more and more often. By about 1980 or so, Vic was getting really quite ill and I was playing three nights a week, then four nights a week. I gradually took over that chair. Vic had cancer. You wouldn't particularly know that he was dying of cancer but it certainly slowed him down. With me, Vic was just very kind and warm. The wonderful serendipity of this was that he was my childhood idol and I ended up, not replacing him because you don't replace Vic Dickenson, but assuming that chair.

"By the time I was working full-time at Condon's, it was late in my teaching career at Swarthmore. There were times when I had to bring stacks of papers that needed to be graded, so I would go downstairs at Condon's into the area where the toilets were and sit down there and grade these papers. When I had an eight o'clock class in the morning, it was really awful. But I had an amazing amount of energy at that point in my life. This was a period where I was working about three nights a week in Condon's – I still had my full-time job at the college – I was building a sailboat from scratch, a 19-foot sailboat. That alone seemed like a full-time job. I was writing a book on Wagner and I was a parent and a husband. I look back on that time and I think, 'Where the hell did I get the time, let alone the energy to do all those things?' But somehow I did them. Wow!

Wild Bill Davison Band, first jazz cruise on SS *Norway*, early 1980s. *L-r:* Tom Artin (tb); Eddie Higgins (p); Wild Bill Davison (cnt); unk (b); Chuck Hedges (cl); unk (d). Courtesy Tom Artin.

"About 1980, Vic left and I went in full-time. I'd quit my college job by then. For a little while it was Bobby Gordon on clarinet and then Jack Maheu came in. he was the leader of the Salt City Five. I'll tell you, two of the most thrilling drummers I've ever worked with were both house drummers at Condon's. One was Connie Kay, the other was Danny D'Imperio who replaced Connie. Two more different drummers you can't imagine. Sometimes the rhythm section would be John Bunch on piano, Connie Kay, and maybe Major Holley on bass. I can walk in a room if there's a record playing and I can hear Connie's beat within two bars. It can be with Paul Desmond, it can be with the Modern Jazz Quartet, it doesn't matter. His time is unmistakeable. It swings!"

When I suggested that Condon's was an odd haven for a modern drummer like Kay, Artin mentioned that D'Imperio, also better known as a bebop player, once listed all the musicians who had played there during his two-and-a-half years at the club. "It was like a who's who of jazz in that period; it spanned Warne Marsh and Lew Tabackin. One of the eclectic things at Condon's was that every Sunday night when the house band was off, they would bring in a guest band which was either a swing band, often it was Scott Hamilton and the quintet, or a more modern group, which is when Warne Marsh played there. Sometimes Danny would lead a band. For a while there was a Friday cocktail hour thing that would be led by Danny and the bass player Jay Leonhart and they would bring in various guys."

Eddie Condon's Hot Lunch Band, Eddie Condon's, New York, 1980. *L-r:* Pee Wee Erwin (t); Bobby Pratt (p); Dick Waldburger (b); Jack Maheu (cl); Tom Artin (tb, ldr); Ernie Hackett (d). Courtesy Tom Artin.

Tom himself led a Condon's Hot Lunch band on Fridays at noon for a while. "We had a loyal following of mostly businessmen (and women) who came in for lunch on a Friday and pretty much reckoned on hanging it up for the week by the time they left Condon's. It was great fun. We made an album in 1980." It's clear that Artin looks back on the Condon years as a kind of halcyon period. He remembered that, "Jo Jones used to hang out there. Roy Eldridge worked next door at Jimmy Ryan's and between sets he often came in. Tony Bennett lived around the corner and he used to hang out there. Joe Williams often sat-in with the band. He always sang 'Rosetta'. It was a magic time. Every summer Wild Bill (Davison) would come in for two weeks and whoever was the house trumpeter, whether it was Eddie or Warren, would go away and have a vacation. They would try and get Cliff Leeman to play whenever Bill was there. One night Cliff was on drums and I was on trombone, I'd been a kid growing up with this music and these guys were my heroes so it was thrilling to be on the bandstand with them. After the warm-up set, we always finished the night with a flag-waver. We launched into the out chorus with Wild Bill at the top of his game, the drums set up right behind my right ear and we got into about two bars of the last chorus and the band was just screaming. I heard Cliff shout, 'Jesus Christ, it's just like Condon's' and I thought OK, it's not just my imagination. I'll never forget that moment!"

Seemingly all good things come to an end sooner or later. The club ceased to operate in 1985. "It didn't fold. Unfortunately, the building was sold to build a huge Prudential building. The terms of the lease couldn't be duplicated in midtown and Eddie felt the club couldn't succeed any place else in New York than midtown as it depended on the tourist trade economically. The really sad part of it is they didn't break ground on that new building for at least two years after they made us move out of the club so making the club close down was gratuitous. We could have been there for two years more. By the end the band was Ed Polcer on trumpet, the piano chair switched around a little bit but it was usually John Bunch and Danny D'Imperio on drums, either Red Balaban on bass or Dave Shapiro, wonderful bass player, Jack Maheu on clarinet and me on trombone."

Keith Smith's Wonderful World of Louis Armstrong, UK tour, October 1983. L-r: Johnny Guarnieri (p); Johnny Mince (cl); Arvell Shaw (b); Keith Smith (t); Barrett Deems (d); Tom Artin (tb). Photo: by Denis Williams. Courtesy Keith Smith.

In between his stints at Condon's Artin took time out to tour Britain with (trumpeter) Keith Smith's Wonderful World of Louis Armstrong package in 1983.

"Actually I was subbing for Eddie Hubble. He was supposed to have done the tour but Eddie had a terrible car accident and lost his leg. At that time his leg was giving him problems and he felt he couldn't do the tour so he asked me to do it in his place and I was glad to do it. It was booked as a Louis Armstrong Alumni concert. That's stretching a point! But I did brush shoulders with Louis one time. That very first year I was with the college band Louis came to give a concert at Princeton and we were asked to play the intermission. We were backstage with Louis before the concert and he was warming up and talking to us. Oh God! It was so thrilling and he was so nice. You'd think that he would be dismissive. Not at all. Have you ever heard anybody say anything other than that about him?

"The band was Barrett Deems, Arvell Shaw, Johnny Guarnieri, Johnny Mince, Keith Smith and me. I'd played with Arvell with Eddie Polcer back in the seventies, several times, here and there, on Long Island but I don't think I'd played with any of the other guys before. It was great fun. Barrett Deems was a bad boy; he was constantly making problems. I don't know what it was about my personality but somehow I got along with Barrett. Being near Barrett was to be enveloped in this terrible cloud of this pipe smoke, he was constantly smoking his pipe, and it was awful. I was, for whatever reason, able to tell him to stop doing something he shouldn't be doing. Barrett was always threatening to go home or moaning and groaning about the food. At one point, I said, 'Barrett, just either eat your food or don't eat it, but don't insult the people who have brought you the food.' Oh, he said, I didn't mean to insult them. So we found some common ground. Keith was a good player and it was a good band. We made a record. Keith and I got along very well. A year or two later, Keith came to New York and played for a week at Condon's and again, I was in the same position with Keith that I'd been with Barrett because everybody else in the band at Condon's was going crazy with Keith. They were just constantly annoyed with him so I was somehow the intermediary."

Two years later, Artin was back in Britain, this time with Ed Polcer and a version of the Condon band. "The club had folded but we came over with a Condon's band. Keith Ingham was on piano; he often played at the club. The drummer was Oliver Jackson and we had Kenny Davern on clarinet. About a year before we did a mini-tour of Britain. We went over on the SS *Norway*, it made a transatlantic crossing. We played the *Norway*, landed at Southampton and did a small tour. That one had Red on bass, and Danny was on drums."

Nowadays Artin combines music with photography and has exhibited a number of times, his (non-musical) fine art prints attracting considerable appreciation. His website is well worth a visit. He was with Bob Wilber in the Smithsonian Jazz Repertory Ensemble for a number of years and "travelled quite a bit with that band". He has also started bands of his own and is especially proud of his TomCats Jazz Aces big band. "It's so hard to run a big band," he says. "There are kicks bands, there are rehearsal bands and there are bands that work regularly by virtue of playing jobs every Monday night at some restaurant and everybody makes $25. Well, I decided not to do that because

Tom Artin (tb), Eddie Condon's Band, [leader Ed Polcer], UK tour, 1985. Southern Comfort promo.

you can't get the personnel you want. Every time you ask people to do that, you're asking them for a favour rather than giving them work. It's a subtle difference. Running a big band is so much effort: collecting the library (I have over a hundred arrangements now), schlepping the stuff to the gig, getting gigs. Nobody who doesn't do it can have the slightest idea how much work and aggravation is involved so there's no reason to do it except to please yourself. If I can't make up the band out of the guys I really want to have, there's no point in doing it. When I do have a gig, I have an A-list. Mark Lopeman is my favourite lead alto player, Tad Schull and Chris Byars play the tenors and the other alto player is often Mike Hashim and Dan Levinson plays baritone saxophone and clarinet. Randy Reinhart is usually with me on trumpet, John Colianni plays the piano generally. Danny sometimes plays drums, sometimes it's Jeff Brillinger. He's worked a lot with Jackie Cain & Roy Kral, and he's recorded with Stan Getz. I used to have Scott Whitfield play lead trombone, a fantastic player, but he's moved away. Now my regular guys are Mike Christianson and Harvey Tibbs, both fine, fine players."

As is the way with all freelance performers, Artin handles a variety of assignments. More to the point, he has sought to extend the range of his music activities. "In 1992, I decided to take the bull by the horns and start a little music booking business to eke out my slender income. Actually it's been very good for me as a trombone player. I book string quartets and other people than myself, but it's also brought me opportunities as a trombone player that I wouldn't have otherwise had. Like little trio gigs that come in, where I use just a guitar and bass, with James Chirillo and Bill Moring, as my regular jazz trio.

"I've also done quite a bit of writing. Somebody called, years ago, and said that the chairman of Union Carbide was having a Christmas party and he wanted a brass quintet, and could I do it? So I put together a brass quintet to play Christmas music and for this gig I just quickly dashed off an arrangement of 'I'll Be Home for Christmas' for the quintet. I liked it so much that I decided to write more arrangements for this quintet and it led to writing a book, and I've got over 50 arrangements written of jazz standards written for a brass quintet plus guitar and drums. The tuba plays a walking bass part. It's called Standard Brass and we have recorded. Yes, we do improvise, and

Tom Artin (tb), unk club, possibly O'Connor's, New Jersey, January 1995. Photo by Andrew Wittenborn. Courtesy Tom Artin.

we've done concerts. Leading out of that I've written another book just for a Christmas brass quintet called Pickwick Brass. Kinda jazzy arrangements of Christmas standards and I have a book of about 35 tunes. How do I write? By the seat of my pants! Sitting at a piano and picking things out, making a lot of mistakes, trial and error. I call guys and they are consistently very complimentary. 'Gee, this is really fun to play this stuff,' they say."

When I asked Artin about his remaining musical aspirations, he said, "I'll give you a perfect example of how simple my aspirations are. In 1985 I did this tour with Ed in England and I had arranged a week in Stockholm playing with a couple of bands there. Then I was going to spend the rest of the summer in Paris doing an odd little teaching job that had nothing to do with music. A wonderful guitar player had set this up for me and I was staying with him, playing these gigs and getting paid but he liked to play on the street in Stockholm with a bass player, and he often had a clarinet player. He really wanted me to play with him on the street. So we went and played on the street in downtown Stockholm and that was the most pleasing thing of the week.

"Music really needs to please me. That's why I do it. You never know when it's going to please you. It's not necessarily on a stage in front of a thousand people. It may be at a wedding, it may be on the street, it may be on a stage in front of a thousand people. Sometimes it's nothing more than playing a background to the clarinet player's solo and just hitting the notes absolutely perfectly. When he and I choose just the right notes and we know where each other is going, it's those things that give you pleasure."

Artin arrived on the New York scene when the great days of 52nd Street were coming to a close. "There were a few clubs still open in the 1950s on 52nd Street. I remember Jimmy Ryan's was there and the Hickory House, notably. Birdland was at the end of the street but that didn't really belong to the 52nd Street thing. It was around the corner and it was a later club anyway. I often heard Marian McPartland, Barbara Carroll and Billy Taylor at the Hickory House. It was always a piano trio at the Hickory House and the DeParis Brothers band was at Jimmy Ryan's. That was the last of those brownstones – the rest of them were all there, the Famous Door, the Three Deuces. Every one of them became a strip club. I look at the older pictures where you see Nat King Cole, Art Tatum, Charlie Parker, on the marquees and I drool. It kills me that I missed it.

"Oddly enough, Princeton was really my 52nd Street because the student clubs and the class reunions held early in June every year always hired jazz bands. I heard the most amazing jazz groups as a kid by sneaking into the tents for the reunions and sneaking into the clubs. Lester Lanin, who was a society bandleader, he always had one of the bands there. I remember seeing Charlie Shavers in Lester Lanin's band, Big Chief Russell Moore, Bud Freeman, Pee Wee Russell. I mentioned that my other real love at the time was photography – it still is – I think the earliest photograph of my own that I still have is a photograph of Jonah Jones and Pee Wee Russell taken in a tent at a Princeton Reunion. One of the guys who was often down there in one of the tents was Urbie Green and he saw me standing there and kinda took me under his wing, let me play his trombone, gave me tips. I would see him occasionally after that and he would always have me come up and play. A marvellous guy. That kind of mentoring is missing now.

"I think the trombone is an intrinsically warm instrument. They say that it is like a cello, close to the human voice. Evocative. But it's a stern mistress – you have to practise it every day. Other instruments are different. I fool around a little bit on the flute. The flute is amazing. I can pick it up and not play well but play respectably. A trombone player of a more traditional persuasion once said and I don't think this is sour grapes, after he listened to one of the hot-shot players, he said, 'Well, he has defeated the instrument once again.' There's an aspect to modern trombone where the trombone is seen as an obstacle to be overcome."

Benny Powell and Tom Artin (tb), memorial service for Jane Jarvis, St. Peter's Church, 619 Lexington Avenue @ 54th St., New York, 10 May 2010. Photo by Fred Sater. Courtesy Fred Sater.

That was never Vic Dickenson's stance and it's not the way Artin approaches the trombone either. He dislikes some 'tricky' modern players or overly earthy traditionalists, and regrets that Americans, black and white, seem to care so little about jazz now. He feels that the music is in a precarious state and talks nostalgically about visits uptown in 1959 or 1960 when the Harlem joints had jukeboxes with Horace Silver or Count Basie records on them. "Now," he says, "it's all so dreadful, I refuse to even call it music."

When I asked him if he has any regrets, he said, "I often have wondered, gee, would I have gotten a lot further in my career as a music artist if I really had focused on being a musician right from the beginning or even if I had majored in music in college and gotten a better theoretical foundation. Yeah, probably is the answer, but I can't change it now because my life has taken a different course.

"It's been incredibly rich and full of all kinds of things. I'm just happy to find myself in situations where good music happens. When I play a solo that I know just nailed it, now that's the best."

Published as 'The Tom Artin Story' in *Jazz Journal International*, October 2005

John Eckert

John Eckert, Northolt, Middlesex, October 2002. Photo by Peter Vacher.

A phone call from US saxophonist Frank Griffith, who works as Director of Performance at Brunel University in Uxbridge, alerted me to the presence in Britain of trumpeter John Eckert. The two men knew each in New York and Eckert was staying with Griffith in nearby Northolt and that's where we met in October 2002 to talk about his career. Since then, I've had the pleasure of hearing John play with the excellent Howard Williams big band at the Garage in Greenwich Village in New York on a couple of occasions; we've shared a drink and kept in touch via e-mail. As this piece makes clear, John is unlikely to button-hole a journalist and demand coverage so it was a delight to try and present his story in some detail. Even the most cursory consultation of Tom Lord's jazz discography is enough to demonstrate just how valuable a player he is. He is also gracious and modest, and highly rated by his peers.

The chance to sit down with Eckert and talk about his musical activities came when he stepped off a cruise ship at Southampton (he was on board as part of Larry Elgart's orchestra) and made for London to stay with saxophonist Frank Griffith, an old bandmate from New York. Griffith got some gigs going for Eckert and it was at Frank's house that John and I met to tape his story. John is short, quite reticent and self-deprecatory, certainly thoughtful, sometimes laconic, and like many musicians, plays down his own prowess. He makes very little effort to publicise himself and is clearly far too shy to do much drum-banging on his own behalf. You'll look in vain for the John Eckert website and he doesn't travel with a ready-made press pack. On the other hand, he works a lot and everyone in New York seems to know and value his skills as a soloist and section man.

Before we started to tackle his career and musical origins, the modern-minded Eckert surprised me by talking about his first realisation that Louis Armstrong's performances held genuine validity for a younger player. "I didn't appreciate Louis Armstrong until I played a concert with Maynard Ferguson's band, when I was, maybe, 26 years old. A lot of big acts were there, including Maynard, Dave Brubeck with Paul Desmond, and three or four other modern groups. Louis ended the concert. I'd always seen him as this old guy, with the big smile, saying negative things about bebop, but I was just thunderstruck at how he sounded. I couldn't believe how powerful he was, his timing, just the authority he played with – his group wasn't really that impressive – but he was the king. All the demographics were there, the audience filled this football field, sitting on folding chairs, some liking Maynard, others going for Brubeck, but *everybody* knew exactly what Louis Armstrong was doing. They all loved him."

Eckert is from Leonia, in suburban New York, "a bedroom community about a mile from the George Washington Bridge" and was born there on 13 March 1939. Although his people were cultivated professionals, he attributes his musical awakening and first awareness of modern jazz to his older sister, or more accurately to her boyfriend, who was a trumpet player. "He was pretty much my hero. I probably wanted to emulate him so I started playing the trumpet when I was ten," he explained. "He was a Stan Kenton fan, and liked Shorty Rogers and Maynard Ferguson, and Chet Baker and Gerry Mulligan, so she had their records." Eckert listened to earlier jazz on the radio, bought an Eddie Condon record but found that "it didn't do it for me at all" and still laughs at the recollection.

"The suburb I lived in was upper-middle-class and we had a blue-collar town next door, Palisades Park, where their kids would come to our High School as sophomores. In came a drummer named John Bergamo and an accordion player, and a kid from Leonia learned to play bass so we started our little jazz group. I was studying with Ed Treutel, he taught at Juilliard and had a music school in the next town, and he had studied with Max Schlossberg, the great symphonic trumpet guru. But I had no guidance as far as jazz was concerned.

"Leonia was a stone's throw from Manhattan and we'd take the subway, go into Town Hall in New York and hear concerts. I heard Charlie Parker, I heard Miles and John Coltrane, and Duke Ellington with Sam Woodyard, while I was still in High School. My parents saw to it that I went to the University of Rochester, which is a liberal arts college, where I majored in music and that meant I could study at the Eastman School of Music. Kids that showed any talent in Rochester would come under the view of professional players and be told stuff and given records to listen to, but in Leonia there were no musicians, so there was nothing like that for us. It was like living a million miles away from anything.

"Eastman had no jazz whatsoever then – now they have a pretty extensive programme. There were some (jazz) players at the university, and I met some players at Eastman, and there was also an active local scene. There was a club in Rochester called the Pythodd Hall – it was just a bar where they had an organ and a little stage, and bands used to come in on the weekend. Ray Bryant used to come in, and when I worked there, tenorist Pee Wee Ellis and trumpeter Waymon Reed were there. They both went with James Brown later on. Chuck Mangione and his brother Gap, and Sal Nistico, they called themselves the Jazz Brothers, they played there later. Chuck and Gap were writing pop jazz tunes, they were in the jukeboxes all over upper New York State. In my last year in school (college), I worked at Pythodd Hall with a sextet, with Larry Covelli, a good tenor player, and Larry Combs on alto – he later became first clarinet in the Chicago Symphony. We had a great piano player named Paul Tardif – he's a classical professor now, and Clarence Beckton, a beautiful drummer from Buffalo, and Tommie Azarello on bass. We played all the current tunes, Gigi Gryce's compositions, stuff like that, as they came out. We had a great time."

Eckert attended John Lewis's legendary Lenox School of Jazz at Music Inn in Lenox, Massachusetts, in August 1959, the year that 'free-jazz' pioneers Ornette Coleman and Don Cherry, also participated. "They had a grant from Schaeffer Beer," he recalled. "The first time I saw Ornette, we were having a jazz session in the theatre, and he just came in and played, like 12 or 13 choruses of blues, and sounded great. Real Charlie Parker-based blues, completely straight-ahead. Don Cherry had this piccolo trumpet – it was the strangest instrument. Don wasn't a strong player but I was very impressed by his originality and the things he could do. Still, I guess the rest of us didn't really understand why they were evading the changes. That was the most common reaction of everybody."

He treasures his brief association with trumpet master Kenny Dorham, who was a member of the Lenox teaching faculty. "He was just a very nice, warm and encouraging person. Kenny was very understated about his playing but very intellectually in charge of it. I took a few lessons from him while I was there and a couple of lessons when we were both in New York. I think I learned most from just listening to his records. Kenny would tell me about things I could do, but I had a hard time soaking it up. What he wanted seemed very humble: he said he just wanted to be playing this tempo (a medium groove) and be saying something. That's what he could do and nobody could do it like him. He was very under-appreciated because he wasn't a picture painter like Miles. Kenny was much more of a contained player, with the ability to be lyrical while playing technical stuff."

Armed with his Bachelor's degree from Rochester, Eckert made for New York but took time out to learn more about big-band playing. "I went to a Kenton clinic in Indiana that summer. Don Jacoby (former Les Brown and Sam Donahue trumpeter) was there and the North Texas State band was there, too. Marvin Stamm was playing lead trumpet for them – he had just finished his last year and was about to go out with Kenton. I was impressed with the band and Don recommended that I go to North Texas State. So I went there, and worked towards a trumpet Master's, played in the lab bands but didn't take the degree."

After leaving North Texas State, Eckert emulated Stamm and toured for a few weeks with Stan Kenton – 'the mellophonium band' – but found it an unsatisfactory experience. "He used to play César Franck over the sound system in the bus, and French Impressionist music. The band wasn't exciting and it was all college kids, and he'd get drunk and tell us how much better we sounded than the Mel Lewis era. I thought it was all pretty corny," he said with a grimace.

Eckert's next stint was with a band led by trombone stylist Si Zentner. "Bob Florence was his major writer and it was like a little Basie band. Gene Goe was playing lead trumpet – he went with Basie after that and there was a fantastic lead alto player, Jerry Arrico. One-nighters for four months. We played country clubs and dance gigs. Si was not really a jazz player but played the instrument beautifully, with an old-style shimmering vibrato. He liked to hear the band crank it up. Everything swung, even the ballads. The drummer was Eddie Caccavale – a good swinging drummer who's played since with a lot of singers. I would have stayed on that band or maybe gone on other bands had it not been for the (Vietnam) war. I was about to be drafted: I'd joined a National Guard band in New York so I was sorta trapped. I had to be at a rehearsal every Thursday night or else! This was from '64 until '69. I did six months of basic training and then I stayed in New York all that time. I couldn't go on the road. I went to some rehearsals and somebody asked me to do some gigs with Buddy Morrow so I played lead trumpet for him for about three or four years. We'd travel on the weekends. There was a network of bands: Buddy Morrow, the Billy May band led by a singer named Frankie Lester, who was excellent, who had the franchise for the Billy May book, and Larry Elgart. I was in the little group of guys that would do all these things so I was able to live pretty decently."

During his enforced stay in New York and eager to accept new challenges, Eckert pursued a parallel career in the classical field. He played first trumpet in concerts for the National Orchestra Association and gained a scholarship to study with the legendary William Vacchiano, the first trumpet in the New York Philharmonic, who "farmed me out to Harry Glantz when he saw that I didn't want to be a symphonic player. Glantz was about 80 but I had a great time studying with him. Vacchiano had told me about a vacancy in the American Brass Quintet and I joined them. We'd go play a couple of college concerts on the weekend and every once in a while we'd get a library concert. Then it just started to take off. There was an educational grant whereby we were doing two concerts in the morning, and two concerts in the afternoon at grade schools, and High Schools, five days a week, and I was making a living doing that. We played a few concerts in Britain, in '68, on a State Department tour. Did two weeks in Europe, and two weeks in Japan."

Soon after settling in New York, Eckert had also started to play dates with Maynard Ferguson's band. "After a year or so, I was playing lead trumpet for him and he came back one time and played one of the lead parts, this was at the Showcase in Philadelphia, and I couldn't get over it. It was obvious he had energy when he played those double Cs in his solos, but to hear to him playing lead trumpet, boy, I never played with anyone like that. It's not normal!" he added ruefully. "Then he came to town less and less often – he was here in Britain a lot of the time – plus he was in Millbrook, New York, with the Timothy Leary people." It's clear that many of these associations ran in parallel; a date with the brass quintet might mean that a call from someone like Ferguson could not be fulfilled. Eckert then mentioned a rehearsal band led by writer Chris Swanson.

"He was a very tight friend with (saxophonist) Steve Marcus. They were on Kenton's band when I was on it, and then they both came to New York. Chris was a wonderful writer, and he had a great band, with players like Stu Martin, Bobby Porcelli, Phil Woods, and Jiggs Whigham. We just rehearsed every week but not too much ever happened. We played the Village Gate one time but he couldn't get anything else going. Chris later became involved with Moog on their synthesisers and he just gave up on the band."

Newly released from his National Guard commitments in 1969, Eckert took to the road to play lead with Ten Wheel Drive, a jazz-rock outfit on the lines of Blood, Sweat and Tears. He says he enjoyed the music, took plenty of solos, and relished the chance to travel. Having spent six years keeping his hair short according to Army dictats, he now had to grow it long to get the gig. "They *made* me grow my hair," he laughed. The band was "musically good", with saxophonist Dave Liebman among the personnel, but there were too many internal dissensions – "cat-fighting between the leaders and the singer" – and Eckert left after a year or so. His next move was to help start up a new band with his old Rochester associates, saxophonist Pee Wee Ellis and John Gatchell, New York's first-call jingle trumpeter, who had also played with Ten Wheel Drive. This group made an album in California, with "a guy named Linc Chamberlain, great guitar player, he played in a pretty prominent rock and roll group called the Orchids, and drummer Jimmy Strassburg, who was with Freddie (Hubbard) for a little while. It was a really interesting group, but like a lot of co-op groups, it sorta destroyed itself. Somebody has got to *do* everything, and a lot of times there's too many things that are left undone."

John Eckert (t), personal promo, New York, c. 2003. Courtesy John Eckert.

Eckert's first real glimpse of jazz fame came with an invitation to join alto star Lee Konitz's Nonet. How had that come about? "We had done a date for a record company and they provided him with a nine-piece group, and paid for the arrangements. We made the record and Lee kept the music, and he was working at Stryker's with a small group, so he decided to use these charts and form the nine-piece. So he put it together, and we had Jimmy Knepper on trombone, who was writing for the group, and for a while Sy Johnson played keyboards, and he was writing too. There were two trumpets, Burt Collins and myself, Ronnie Cuber on baritone, and different guys on bass and drums; it wasn't very consistent, it changed a lot. Eliott Zigman did it for a while, Jimmy Madison did for a while, Billy Hart did three of the records and a few of the gigs, and Knobby Totah was on bass for quite a time. The Nonet played for two or three years, and the group got sorta popular. For a while, we had, maybe, two or three nights per week, including festivals. We made four records and they all did well, with four-star ratings, but Lee didn't have the determination or the inclination to push the band. He had been in a real slump, playing once a week at Stryker's and at La Boheme, and these were $15 jobs. Plus he was teaching. He'd lost his audience but the Nonet attracted attention and he started really working again. And then the band broke up."

Eckert was enthusiastic about what he calls Konitz's child-like view of music and his openness to experiment. It's obvious that he retains huge respect for the saxophonist both as man and musician, even if he's critical of his business drive. "An inspiring and original musician who loved to play," he said of Konitz, adding, "One of the essentials of a good bandleader is that he goes out and forces people to hire the band – in that respect, Lee wasn't very good. He didn't want to hustle. Like we did one date in Holland, for a festival, we flew over for a one-nighter, and flew back. That's crazy. He would let things happen – you can't just let a nine-piece *happen,* it won't happen! But it was great while it lasted."

It was good, too, to talk with Eckert about trombonist Jimmy Knepper, another original and stimulating player, who died in June 2003. "I played with Jimmy a lot, in that (Konitz) group and we also had a gig at a Playboy Club up in New Jersey – I was living in that area at that time – and he used to come up and do that with me. A totally unique individual, in every way, but he was very earth-bound, he had a beautiful house and two apartment buildings that he maintained. He was very strong yet you would think he could barely stand up, as his (physical) demeanour was sorta like suspended animation," he said, smiling at the thought. "Jimmy's musical integrity was so deep, he had every conceivable music to play, like cello things, and things that he'd transcribed from chamber music for brass instruments, exercises in developing scales, so his trombone technique was just fantastic. He purposely played down so that the slide would fall so all he had to do was pull it. And he could play so fast. We were on this show gig that we did up at the Playboy Club – we used to get to play a lot, the leader,

Billy Dennison, was a great musician – and I remember being half-drunk. Jimmy was playing a solo and I had gone into sort of a trance there – we were in for a long gig – and I looked up at him playing the trombone on this up-tempo tune and I was so shocked to see him playing it on a trombone. It could have been a trumpet player! You didn't hear any characteristic slides or smears – he had alternate slide positions for every note. It seemed like he didn't move a muscle, his embouchure was so perfect.

"I called him for a wedding, and Jimmy had been sick and very depressed, playing maybe four times a year. See, he would not practise, and then he would go play and get very depressed because he felt like he was losing his chops. A couple of years before he died a doctor wanted to remove a wart or something with a laser, and it burnt his bone, so he had big problems with that. But I had him come on this club date and he hadn't played for probably a month or two but after a set he sounded great. His tunes were so interesting, especially the things he wrote for the Nonet. I made an album with him called *I Dream Too Much*, a sextet with trombone, trumpet, French horn, and Billy Hart playing drums. Jimmy had so much knowledge of music in general, the great tunes, the mechanics of bebop, and he would always play anything that had to do with jazz."

Toshiko Akiyoshi's Jazz Orchestra, unknown US concert location, 1998. *Rear L-r:* Andy Gravish, Mike Ponella, John Eckert, Joe Magnarelli (t). *Middle:* Doug Weiss (b); Terry Clarke (d); Luis Bonilla, Scott Whitfield, Pat Hallaran, Tim Newman (tb). *Front:* Lew Tabackin (ts); Jim Snidero (as); Dave Pietro (as); Tom Christensen (ts); Scott Robinson (bs); Toshiko Akiyoshi (p, cond). Courtesy Toshiko Akiyoshi.

When Toshiko Akiyoshi and her husband, the tenor saxophonist Lew Tabackin returned to New York in 1982, they set about re-forming Toshiko's big band. Eckert joined straight away. "We used to play every Monday night at Birdland but Toshiko has retired the band now. Also I play every once in a while in another band, called the Howard Williams band, that's a full bebop band, with eight brass. It's had a Monday-night gig for five or six years, at a place called the Garage in Greenwich Village. Howard is a piano player, he actually made a record with 'Trane in the fifties. He's a white guy, works at the union now, and he loves all the old bebop things. It doesn't matter whether it's a trio, or a quintet, or a big band, he just reorchestrates his favourite bebop tunes. He's written about 80 arrangements now. He uses mostly really young players, but he has a few pros like Danny Hayes, a great jazz trumpet player who played with Buddy (Rich) for a while."

Howard Williams Orchestra, the Garage, Greenwich Village, New York, 31 March 2008. John Eckert (t, *rear row, middle*). Photo by Ian Powell. Courtesy Ian Powell.

Essentially a jobbing jazz musician, Eckert has responded to calls from any number of important leaders, including Gerry Mulligan and on one occasion, Wynton Marsalis, to sub with the Lincoln Center Orchestra. He was with the late Grover Mitchell's big band for four or five years, and was featured on Mitchell's splendid *Hip-Shakin'* album. I asked him to talk about Mitchell, who died a while back in harness as Director of the Basie band. "I loved him," the trumpeter said. "He was a really personable guy, very friendly, very encouraging and he had great taste in music. His book was really beautiful – all great arrangements. Later he asked me to do a few things with the Basie band that I couldn't do. I had a great time playing with Grover. See, it was an area I hadn't been in that much: not playing in a totally white band. It wasn't all black, of course, and he had guys like Frank Wess, Billy Mitchell, what an inspirational guy *he* was, Norris Turney, Jerry Dodgion – he played in Toshiko's band a lot – and trumpeter Virgil Jones, who wound up playing with me in Bobby Short's band."

Buck Clayton Orchestra, New York, 1989–91. *Rear*, l-r: Dick Katz (p); Jerry Dodgion (as); Byron Stripling (t); James Chirillo (g). *Front*: Joe Temperley (bs); Lew Tabackin (ts); Buck Clayton (ldr, arr); John Eckert (t); Dennis Mackrel (d); Doug Lawrence (ts). Photo by Nancy Miller Elliott. Courtesy John Eckert.

Explaining the New York freelance life (and much the same might apply in London), Eckert said, "You get in different little pools around town, sometimes you cross over from one to the other, but the American Jazz Orchestra, Benny Goodman, Benny Carter, Buck Clayton and Bobby Short jobs all came through being tied in with one milieu. Now, the AJO was great, it's too bad it didn't last. It was a repertory band, Loren Schoenberg was involved as the straw boss, and John Lewis was the Director and (writer) Gary Giddins was the adviser. The only thing they didn't have was someone to look upon it, not as an institution, but as a band that had to get itself across. I don't think the publicity was good enough. It wasn't projected as well as it should have been but the format was great. We did really interesting concerts – everything was based on the composer, like Benny Carter would come in, sounding wonderful, and we'd rehearse all week and do a concert with him on Thursday night. We did the same with Gerald Wilson, David Murray, Muhal Abrams, Jimmy Heath, and we made albums with Jimmy and Benny Carter. We also made a Lunceford record, had Snooky Young in it.

Some of these were very well reviewed. The performances were good but after two or three years, the AJO ran out of steam."

Loren Schoenberg Band, New York, 1985. *Standing L-r:* Ken Peplowski (ts); John Eckert (t); Scott Peebles (t); Danny Bank (bs); Mel Lewis (d); Buck Clayton (arr); Paul Cohen (t); Matt Finders (tb); Bobby Pring (tb); Doug Lawrence (ts); Dick Sudhalter (t); Jack Stuckey (as). *Front L-r:* Eddie Bert (tb); Loren Schoenberg (ts); Howard Alden (g); Phil Flanagan (b). Photo by Nancy Miller Elliott. Courtesy Jean-Pierre Battestini.

At the time of this interview, Eckert was working regularly with the veteran singer-pianist Bobby Short (who died in March 2005) at the Café Carlyle in New York, Eckert's involvement coming through Short's MD Loren Schoenberg with whose big band Eckert had also performed and recorded. "Bobby just put on a show and the band was an integral part of it and he loved it. He was a very intense performer. After about eleven weeks into the Café Carlyle season, he'd start to break down, but the performance was always the same. You might have to carry him out on a stretcher but it would be exactly 100 per cent. The band was Virgil Jones and myself, trumpets, two trombone players who split the one trombone part, Bobby Pring, who was just unbelievable, and Eddie Bert. There was a place in Boston that we'd been playing before the season started for a couple of years, called Sculler's, and somebody walked up to Eddie Bert, and asked, 'Was that your father on the Woody Herman band?' Eddie looks so young and he's very vigorous, plays great. The sax section was a little less set because they moved around a lot, but Loren Schoenberg was always there, Patience Higgins played, Joe Temperley did some stuff at first, Scott Robinson did the first year, and there was Jack Stuckey, he was on Buddy's band, and Jay Brandford, excellent alto, played all the reeds. As for rhythm, Klaus Suonsaari, he'd been with Bobby for years, he's from Finland and plays drums. He's made quite a few albums on his own, with Tom Harrell and Bob Berg, then there was Frank Tate on bass, they were Bobby's regulars." It was Tate who told me, "I just look forward to hearing John's solos every night. He'll always surprise you."

When we talked about the precariousness of the freelance life, Eckert laughed and said, "It hasn't been a goldmine for me but I'm pretty happy about what I've done and what I'm doing now. As long as my playing is improving, I've got a future. Ambitions? I look forward to playing more small-group jazz and to playing the trumpet better. I've been selective because of my embouchure change, I wasn't really fit to do the most sought-after commercial work as I wasn't the kind of trumpet machine that you knew that whatever was on the paper would come out of the horn. There were just so many great trumpet players in New York that did all the recordings, from the big bands, people like Bernie Glow, Al DeRisi, Joe Ferrante, Marvin Stamm, and Burt Collins. I've been able to do enough that pays that I've been able to make a living and pretty much exclusively play what I want. I did do some jingles in the heyday of jingles. Now, there's so few. I don't think anybody's making a living doing that. There's some swing bands that play for dancing, and there's a couple of piano players that call me, that do weddings under a jazz format and I'm happy to do that," he explained.

Eckert spoke with some animation about the younger trumpet players who have emerged in recent years. "Most of the people that I'm inspired by are much younger than I am and they swim in a different sea of influence and skills and sensitivities than I do because they were born 30 years later than me. Joe Magnarelli, he's a wonderful player, he's made two or three albums on Criss Cross, Scott Wendholt, Roy Hargrove, Nicholas Payton, there's so many wonderful players. Everything I hear by Roy Hargrove and Nicholas Payton I like."

As we came to the end of our conversation, I asked Eckert if he had any regrets. "I regret that when I came to New York, there was no on-the-street jazz scene," he said. "It was very dry, there weren't any clubs that you could sit-in. I paid my five dollars once to go to a jam session in a loft, with Reggie Workman playing bass, it was a great group but there were 15 horn players in a line and each one could only play a chorus. It was ridiculous, and the ambience between black and white players at the club level was not too happy. This is as opposed to the past five years or ten years. Now there's all these little clubs where you don't make a lot of money, but they're jazz gigs. Guys like Joe Magnarelli and Jim Rotondi, a whole bunch of players, have had this great opportunity where they could be working as jazz players, three, four, five nights a week. Between blacks and whites, well, it's not as separate, it's not the Promised Land, but when everybody gets to play, the differences become much less, in both opportunity and respect. After the period where there was nothing going on, then there was the loft scene, but that was all 'free' jazz. I was hanging with Dave Liebman from Ten Wheel Drive then and I'd go round to places where they were playing 'free' jazz, and all these guys were great musicians but I just couldn't get with the free-form thing at all. Nobody was playing bebop."

For Eckert, performance is all. "You can talk about it, think about it, practise on a piano, practise your instrument from now until eternity but you're not playing a gig. Everybody's saying, what was with those guys in the fifties, what was it with Sonny Rollins, Hank Mobley, Kenny Dorham, they were just like unreal, inhuman giants. It's simple. They played five hours a night, six nights a week, for ten years, all over the place. Even when I was getting through college, there were still bands travelling all over the country, Pittsburgh, Cincinnati, Columbus, there was a circuit, and these guys were working all the time. That way you become a musical person.

"Like Lee Morgan. I heard him when he was on Dizzy's band. He sounded just like Dizzy. He was like a beanpole, 17 years old, phenomenal. Next time I heard him, he was 19, with Blakey, and he sounded like Lee Morgan. He just played, like, 35 hours a week and started sounding like himself. Guys like Lee wouldn't sit in front of a record player. They would go out and hear somebody and be impressed, or sit in the section and play with them for a year. You'd be influenced but it's a different kind of influence that way, you don't purposely copy it, but it starts to filter through without you even knowing it," he said.

Just as we were taking our leave, he had one more thing to add. "I would like to tout a great writer on one small-group project that I have been fortunate to get involved in, a guy named Tim Harrison. He's from England. He was at North Texas State: he's a great writer and we've made a record. His wife (Dee McMillen) is a beautiful singer – she's from the States – and he wrote five settings of poems by Emily Dickinson that she sang and they're very interesting. It's a quintet record, and the bass player is Tom Hubbard, who's played with Freddie Cole, and there's Grisha Alexiev, a drummer from New England, who was at Berklee and North Texas, who's doing a lot of work around town, a very imaginative drummer, Dave Rickenberg, tenor player, and Tim on piano. It's completely unique – to me, it sounds British. It's not straight-ahead jazz but it's not quasi-classical either. It has a very interesting flavour to it. You know," he added finally, "people like to hear beautiful music."

First published as 'John Eckert – A Sideman's Story' in *Jazz Journal*, February 2005

Rufus Reid

Rufus Reid, North Sea Jazz Festival, The Hague, Holland, 1993. Photo by Brian Foskett. Courtesy Brian Foskett.

The now-defunct specialist Double Bassist *magazine arranged for me to interview the distinguished bassist Rufus Reid while he was in London working with the Guildhall's jazz students in November 2005. Even though his schedule was already fully committed, Rufus agreed that we should meet at his City hotel and talk as he was preparing for the day's work ahead. Indeed, our conversation only concluded as we walked together to the nearby Underground station. Rufus and his wife Doris were wonderfully co-operative, happy to discuss music but equally excited by the impending arrival of their first grandchild. I was delighted when Rufus e-mailed his enjoyment at the "the wonderful response to the* Double Bassist *feature you wrote." He continues to perform at the highest level with the greatest players of the day and recently premièred his first symphonic composition.*

There's a celebrated story about a jazz musician who was called for an early photo shoot. It was the first time, he said, that he realised that there were two ten o'clocks in the same day. I began to understand how he felt when my appointment to see Rufus Reid was scheduled for 8.30am. Surely some mistake? Well, no, for Mr Reid was a busy man, who was shoehorning our conversation into a day already fully committed to rehearsals and performances.

Despite the early hour, Reid proved as amenable in conversation as he was gracious in demeanour. Irrefutably one of the outstanding jazz bassists of his generation, Reid is noted for 'his perfect sense of time' in the words of one commentator. He has played with a bevy of major jazz figures and is an educator whose pedigree is second to none. His discography is of encyclopaedic proportions and he is a leader and composer of consequence. No wonder Scott Stroman who ran the jazz course at the Guildhall School sought to invite Reid (for the third time, it turns out) to work with his students during the 2005 London Jazz Festival.

While in London, Reid conducted a bass master class and rehearsed the Guildhall's student big band in performances of his compositions before holding "an open session where I listened to several of the groups play and then I played with them. I talked a little bit about my history and musical things that either weren't happening or were happening. It was a good afternoon. My value to them? I guess I've been doing it longer than they have."

So how had his involvement with teaching come about, I wondered? "Well, people hear you play and they like what you play and then they ask, 'Do you teach?' And that's essentially how I got started. One on one. Initially, I didn't want to be a teacher but I found out that I actually enjoy teaching people who want to be taught. But I feel now that I don't want to just teach. I must play," he emphasised.

The pianist Junior Mance, another jazz musician who has taught, said that his job was to help students become effective performers. Reid concurred with this view, adding: "Well, that's basically what I did when I taught at William Paterson College in Wayne, New Jersey, where I was Director of Jazz Studies for 20 years (until 1999). I succeeded (trumpeter/composer) Thad Jones. I didn't teach bass: I developed a curriculum of study that prepared the student to perform." Reid knows that the great jazz masters in whose groups he worked were teachers too, if only by example. "There are a lot of pros and cons about whether this music can be taught. I believe it can be but it's only as a preparation for actual performing." It can be argued that a necessary aspect of teaching today is to help emerging players cope with quotidian realities. Reid agreed. "Quite a few of them are incredible musicians but they will have piss-poor lives because they don't know how to function in the real world. All these things are being addressed in the schools now. As you know, even here in the UK, the work isn't as prevalent, the network isn't like it used to be."

Reid has very clear ideas about the qualities he looks for when assessing a jazz bassist. "The sound and pulse," he says definitely. "If they don't have the pulse, then

Dizzy Gillespie group, TV rehearsal, with Rufus Reid (b), Wolf Trap Farm Park, Vienna VA, May 1987. AP Newsfeature photo.

forget it." Does the amplifier help? "If we don't have a good acoustic sound whatever comes through the amplifier is not going to be any good either. I use the amplifier but it can only amplify what's there. If you have a sloppy, crappy sound, then it's just louder (through the amplifier). The pulse is what the people remember. They don't remember all the notes you play. They just remember the feeling."

So, in a nutshell, what does Reid see as the bassist's role in the jazz group? "Well, you're the caretaker. You're there to be minding the store while everybody's out playing. I teach the bassists that if the piano player or the drummer don't make the gig, everything's all right because we can take care of it," he said, adding, "and we have the unique ability to sabotage every band in which we play if we hiccup and we don't know how to recover. You're going to play something you don't really intend and you have to rectify it really quick before someone realises that it did go awry."

Stan Getz Quartet, Italy, 1982. *L-r:* Kenny Barron (p); Stan Getz (ts); Rufus Reid (b); Victor Lewis (d). Photo by Pieroni Carlo. Courtesy Rufus Reid.

Reid was born in Atlanta, Georgia, in 1944, but moved as a youngster with his mother to Sacramento, California, when his parents split up. "We were always around music," he said. "My mother played piano well enough to play the hymns in the church and my father was an amateur pianist – after I got in the military we hooked up again – and he was very proud for me to be a musician." Reid's first instrument was the trumpet. "Why? That's what I wanted to play!" Intrigued by jazz he took every chance to hear visiting jazz stars. "I remember climbing over a fence to sneak in to see Cannonball Adderley's group. I didn't know what I was seeing but it was just fascinating to me.

"When I was in High School we had a group called the Saints, had sparkled shirts. The band was accordion, trumpet, saxophone, drums and bass. Every time we would take an intermission, I would go to the bass and fool around for the fun of it. Every chance I got. I was supposed to go to college but to my mother's dismay I passed the auditions as a trumpet player and joined the Air Force. I was 17."

Posted to Montgomery, Alabama, and with time on his hands, Reid began to teach himself the bass in earnest. "The love for the trumpet started to disintegrate," he recalled. "I began playing (bass) with the guys. They knew I didn't know much but my pulse was better than the (regular) bass player who was really a tuba player. As the years went on, I began to play more and more."

Al Stringer, a local musician, took Reid under his wing, one of a series of leaders whose help Reid remembers with genuine gratitude. "I didn't even own a bass: he had an electric bass. This was rhythm and blues. We had to learn things off the jukebox for dancing. He taught me a lot. I did that for a year and a half. This is where I first saw acts like Ike and Tina Turner, Bobby Blue Bland, and James Brown's band. Unbelievable. That was where my real education about what bass players did started. You were there to be the *rock*," he said.

Reid's next posting to Japan allowed him to hear Ray Brown in person for the first time, and suitably inspired, he persuaded his commanding officer to let him play string bass in the concert band, relegating the trumpet to morning formations. He also studied for a year with a retired bassist from the Tokyo Symphony, setting in train a process of serious musical education that culminated with a Bachelor's Degree in Music. After five years in the Air Force, Reid returned to Sacramento in 1966, played a successful two-week engagement with vibist Buddy Montgomery and then moved on to Seattle for yet more study, grateful for his brother's offer of rent-free accommodation. More lessons followed, this time from James Harnett, principal bass with the Seattle Symphony, Reid grabbing every opportunity he could to play with local musicians. "There was a lot of music going on. There was a guy named Joe Brazil, saxophone player from Detroit, very good friends with John Coltrane[1]. He had a sextet and he taught us all the Tadd Dameron music and we played a lot of Coltrane's music." Miles Davis, John Coltrane, (bassist) Andy Simpkins with The Three Sounds, and Stan Getz each played at a local club and Reid saw them all. "It was an amazing period. That was an incredible education, just seeing all those people."

Like many other jazz bassists, Reid pays homage to Ray Brown but selects the late Andy Simpkins for special mention. "He was the nicest man. He was an extension of Ray but he had his own power. I wanted to be like them both because they were nice and played the shit out of the bass. And they were having fun. You've got to have fun playing. It does bother me when I play and I see players who don't seem to be enjoying themselves. Not one bit! Even when they play an incredible improvisation."

Having completed his degree at Northwestern University in Evanston, Illinois in 1971, Reid opted to stay on in nearby Chicago as house bassist at Joe Segal's famous

Jazz Showcase club. This enabled him to work with an array of great soloists who came in to play short-term residencies. "Every week there was somebody that I had never played with before or even knew much about. Chicago is a swinging town; if you can't swing, you don't work and if you don't know any tunes, you don't work," he said.

The popular saxophonist Eddie Harris gave Reid his first taste of the big time. "I was going to quit school so I could go play with him. He told me to finish and I'm glad I did. He's the man who told me to write my own bass book (*The Evolving Bassist*, published in 1974). He told us about recording, the posture of going into the studio, of being on the road, looking out for one another, making sure people didn't steal our things, and the travelling, riding in the car."

Dexter Gordon Quartet, unknown US location, 1979. Dexter Gordon (ts); Rufus Reid (b). Courtesy Rufus Reid.

In a career packed with high-level associations, Reid attaches great importance and no little exasperation to his time with the legendary tenor saxophonist Dexter Gordon, saddened by this heavy drinker's lack of business sense. "A very imposing man," he says. "I did four years with him, travelling eight months out of the year. We were getting into the college circuits where you could make three times the money but he didn't know how to function, to abstain for an hour or two just so we could get in these situations. Dexter was never malicious. I loved being around him but he was so laid back that it began to take its toll. We had something that was just magnificent but after a while I just had enough." Reid went on to describe a concert in Poland where the band was topping the bill, with five thousand people waiting expectantly. "He got a bottle and cracked it on the bus before we even got to the hotel so that was that."

The trombone innovator Jay Jay Johnson was a favourite role model. "I was with him for about nine years but there was three years in the middle when nothing happened. That was when his wife died. It destroyed him. Then he remarried and rekindled his desire to play. He was so clear and so focused as to what he wanted. The way he presented it to us, it was exciting. He was an eloquent man."

Dexter Gordon Quartet, Cascais International Jazz Festival, Cascais, Portugal, November 1978. *L-r*: George Cables (p); Dexter Gordon (ts); Rufus Reid (b); Eddie Gladden (d). Courtesy Rufus Reid.

J.J. Johnson Quintet, Estoril Jazz Festival, Cascais, Portugal, 1993. *L-r:* Renée Rosnes (p); J.J. Johnson (tb); Rufus Reid (b); Ralph Moore (ts); Billy Drummond (d). Courtesy Rufus Reid.

With time slipping away, Reid was packed and ready to run – for the tube, as it happens. There were students waiting and music to play. One more question: who among the younger jazz bassists on the scene has earned his seal of approval? Reid reeled off a mini-catalogue of names: "Peter Washington is certainly a real strong player. Christian McBride is exceptional as is John Patitucci. Scott Colley is a wonderful young player and Larry Grenadier is a very good musician. There's a young lady from Australia I should mention, her name is Nicki Parrott. She came to the States and studied with me. She plays really well. She's got a good pulse too."

We exit, still talking, Rufus enthusing over Gary Karr's International Society of Bassists, marvelling at the numbers now involved, from both the classical and jazz fields. "I get inspired every time I go to the convention. Hearing those players just makes me think, 'Oh hell, I've got to go home and practise.'" Based in New York since 1976, Reid says he intends to play on as long as he can. He's composing more than ever before, has a new quintet staffed by fiery young players and was recently given the Mid-Western Arts Foundation's Living Legacy Award. "It's a very exciting period for me," he beamed.

Rufus Reid (b), personal promo, 2005. Photo by John Abbott. Courtesy Rufus Reid.

First published as 'Rufus Reid: Performer at Heart' in *Double Bassist*, Summer 2006

---

[1] Saxophonist Joe Brazil arrived in Seattle from Detroit in 1962. He established the Black Academy of Music to pass on African-American traditions to local youngsters, persuading artists like Dizzy Gillespie, Joe Henderson and Stanley Turrentine to talk to the children. Many Seattle players were given their start in music at Brazil's Academy.

John Stubblefield IV

John Stubblefield (1945–2005), personal promo, New York, 2000. Inscribed: *'To Peter. Best Always, John Stubblefield'*. Photo by Jimmy Katz. Courtesy John Stubblefield.

I first met saxophonist John Stubblefield at a press party when the McCoy Tyner big band played a London gig in 1994. I remarked on John's 'porkpie' hat and he told me he wore it in tribute to Lester Young, one of his all-time heroes. This promising start led to a series of contacts, culminating in this lengthy interview which took place in a London hotel in 2002 while John was appearing at Ronnie Scott's with the Mingus Big Band. As I've tried to convey in the piece, John was wonderfully open, ebullient and enthusiastic, and a keen student of his music's history. He supplied photographs, wrote often and was hugely pleased when Coda ran his story over three editions.

The sheer variety of John's accomplishments during these years was breathtaking. New compositions and arrangements flowed from him, he toured Japan regularly, appeared at concerts with academic ensembles, ran his own groups and played with others led by his peers, and performed whenever and wherever the Mingus band took the stand. All too soon, though, he was too ill to travel and was admitted to the DeWitt Rehabilitation Center in New York in April 2004 with prostate cancer. The letters still kept coming, mostly authored by his companion Katherine Gogel, and we spoke on the telephone and e-mailed regularly. If the messages were optimistic, the facts were against him: there was no hope of recovery.

Bill Cosby and President Clinton (they talked saxophones and he held John's hand for an hour) visited him in the Calvary Hospital where he spent his final days, as did his many friends. Rather touchingly, Pastor Lind of St. Peter's Church was on hand at John's hospital bedside to marry Katherine and John just weeks before he passed away on 4 July 2005. Looking back, John was great company, a true lover of life, always animated and invariably cheerful, and a wonderfully talented man. It's hard to lose people like him.

Some three decades ago, Sue Mingus created and has continued to maintain the Mingus Big Band to play her late husband's music. Along the way, she recruited a posse of players who knew Charles Mingus and worked with him, adding others who weren't even born when the great man was in his heyday. The result is a floating pool of musicians, established or emerging, able and willing to tackle the bassist's challenging musical legacy. Of these, none was more crucial than tenor saxophonist John Stubblefield whose talismanic presence on the bandstand was a vital factor in this band's success. John was ever mindful of the need to meet Mingus's exacting standards as well as the expectations of the band's audience. As a soloist he eschewed predictability, his playing fierce or tender as the occasion required, and he was hugely committed to his art.

The Mingus Big Band, Ronnie Scott's Club, Frith St., London, 2002. Mike Sim (bs), and John Stubblefield (ts). Photo by Berit Bolt. Courtesy Berit Bolt.

We arranged to meet up in a London hotel during the Mingus band's annual stopover at Ronnie Scott's club. John was blissfully articulate, had an encyclopaedic memory, was warm and friendly, smiled often, and frequently leant forward to emphasise a point. He had come to maturity at a time when American society was going through a painful process of change and his life experiences reflected this. John built his reminiscences like a jazzman's riff, and saw his pursuit of jazz expression as something of a spiritual quest. He was interested in the history of the music and its relevance to his people, read widely, and was optimistic about the future.

John Stubblefield IV was born in Little Rock, Arkansas, on 4 February 1945. His father, a skilled machinist, always enjoyed the work of Duke Ellington and Count Basie whereas John's mother had a stricter view, feeling that jazz was 'the devil's music'. She was employed as a domestic and served as secretary to her local Holiness Church. "As for yours truly, when I was in the fourth grade, I started studying keyboards. We had a wonderful pianist in the neighbourhood, Mrs. Douglas, and she taught me. Her husband was one of the Hellfighters, he came to Europe with James Reese Europe and he played the French horn in the band. As a kid, he would tell me about being here (in Europe) and what that band was like. Mrs. Douglas was a graduate of the University of Chicago and the two of them were Creoles from Louisiana. She trained a lot of students to become great pianists in the churches and that was her primary concern. She taught me piano from the fourth to the seventh grade but she was drug with me because I discontinued my studies when I got in junior High School and I fell in love with the saxophone," he remembered.

In 1957, Federal troops were despatched to Little Rock by President Eisenhower to enforce an order for the integration of black pupils into the city's Central High School, following the Supreme Court's decision that the nation's schools should be desegregated at 'all deliberate speed'. When I asked John to describe his experiences as a youngster growing up in this deeply divided city, he mentioned that some of the younger members of the Mingus band had quizzed him about this and then added, "I didn't find out about Jim Crow until I was in the fifth grade. I went to a water fountain to have a drink and one side had 'Colored' and the other side had 'White' but the two fountains were the same, made by the same company to the same design. I remember that so well. My dad said, 'You can't drink from that fountain, it's for whites only, you have to drink round here.' That's when I became aware of racism in this world."

John was brought up in an all-black neighbourhood in the city's South End. "When the de-segregation of schools started, I was in the seventh grade. The most important thing I remember was someone standing up, and that was Louis Armstrong. I read it in the paper. Louis Armstrong said to President Eisenhower, 'If you don't do something about this situation here and let those kids into those schools, I will not remain Ambassador of Music for this country.' From that moment on, President Eisenhower jumped to it and that's when Federal troops came in."

Although he played drums and piano for the Holiness Church, John's selection of the saxophone as his ultimate instrument of choice seems to have been fairly arbitrary. "I became in love with the saxophone because I felt sorry for it. There was a lady in my church that played the saxophone and, oh God, this woman was mean to us kids but she could *play* that saxophone. I'm not even ten years old yet but I see this woman play this horn that's bent, and I thought she was so mean she bent this horn like this, and made it play. Then around '54, I used to watch the Jimmy Dorsey show and I saw all of those guys sitting across in a row with these bent horns and I said, 'That woman went and bent up those guy's instruments, too.'"

Asked to talk about his formative influences, John recalled that, "In the Navy, my father was a jitter-bugger and he danced to Andy Kirk and the Clouds of Joy. Before he died he was so proud of his son because I was associated with Mary Lou Williams.

She recorded two of my songs and the record came out the year before he died. Other than my father, who was Baptist, my mother had records of Rosetta Tharpe, she had records of the Five Blind Boys of Alabama, a lot of gospel music – she was not into jazz or pop music. She had a friend, Sister Howard, who was the Musical Director of the church that we belonged to and she was sightless. They had the best Braille school in Little Rock for the whole country – Stevie Wonder went there – and Sister Howard was in that school with Al Hibbler. She would play the piano at our home, and when my mom was not around she would play me some Fats Waller, she'd play me some blues, but she wouldn't dare play that music when my mom was around. She helped me out a lot. I might add that her daughter was one of the first singers with Sly and the Family Stone."

When I suggested that his exposure to 'sanctified' church music still coloured his performances, John was quick to agree. "Oh yeah, it's a part of my delivery, although I love contemporary music too. I study all the time to play *all* of the music. I will not deny that I tried to run away from it for years but when I started acknowledging where my roots were, who I am, not trying to be somebody that I'm not, I began to re-melt into those situations." Music in the neighbourhood? "Oh, yeah, it was so beautiful. They would have musicians that would come through with livestock shows, and we would hear circus bands, and then there were ministers that would come through with their children, and serenade the neighbourhood. I thought that was so great. Blues guitarists that would come through with their cups, and just stand in front of your house and serenade you. As a kid, to hear the blues like that and to hear gospel music like that..., there was a sightless man that would be led around, sometimes he would come with his cane and his guitar and he would just serenade the neighbourhood. So I got a chance to hear that kind of thing very early.

"My first band director was Mr. Adams and then Miss Clay came. She was a graduate of Lincoln University and she had a little dance band that she put together for us. But what started the whole ball rolling in terms of jazz and the reason I'm playing the saxophone is because of Don Byas. He used to come into Little Rock with Count Basie and he married into a family there. They (Basie's band) were playing on Ninth Street and these two beautiful college girls would come to hear them all the time. Anyway he married one; she was my friend's aunt, from the Bush family, a very renowned African-American family. They built the ballroom where Duke would play. John Bush and I grew up together as kids, and all we did was look at these photographs from when Don Byas came to Little Rock before leaving for Europe with Don Redman's band in '46. The Bush family had a library of music covering a whole wall, and all of Don's recordings. So Bush and I are playing saxophone – he became a magistrate judge – and we're in the (school) band, and that started things. When Don Byas came back to America after being away for 25 years and I told him of this story, he let me

John Stubblefield and Don Byas (ts), Chicago IL, 1970. Photo taken during Byas's first and only return trip to the US from his home in Europe. Courtesy John Stubblefield.

hang with him every day and every night. I was married that year and my wife said, 'Are you going to leave that man alone?' and I said, 'I don't think so!' I was learning so much from Don Byas about sound and projection, about knowing what you're doing, being able to let your emotions flow, and being theoretically correct. In France they made a saxophone especially for him. It had the snake on the octave key, when you hit the octave key, the snake's mouth would open and it look like it was biting!"

It was peer group pressure that prompted John to play professionally. That and a busy club scene where younger musicians were welcome provided that they had the necessary talent. "Thomas East, we were in the same class, he used to come to school with his conk (processed hair), and the principal used to say, 'You gotta get rid of that conk' and he said, 'Man, I can't get rid of this, this is a part of what I am.' I'll never forget this! When the Soul Stirrers came through Little Rock, the last tour that Sam Cooke did with them, Thomas East played with them. He was a singer and he played bass. Those guys were out hitting at night in '57 and '58 while I couldn't get out of the house! Another guy, James Leary, bass player that's been playing recently with the Basie orchestra – he played with Basie in the eighties too – Leary was out there hitting too and he's a year younger than me. His father was a boogie-woogie piano player and he took over his father's gig at a club called the Brown Derby in Little Rock. We grew up together. In the ninth grade, we had a band called the Viceroys; we would play school functions and church socials. One day, Thomas East and Leary came to my home and said would I like to join Yorke Wilburn and the Thrillers, one of the baddest bands of that time. They were in residence at the Flamingo, one of the biggest clubs there in Little Rock.

"Yorke Wilburn was a tenor player and there was a great trumpeter, Teroy Betton, who played like Brownie, that man had perfect pitch, photographic memory, could arrange anything. Had he moved to New York, he would have been up there with Booker Little and Freddie Hubbard. He was of that quality. He's passed on now, but he has a younger brother who also played trumpet who was a few years behind yours truly, who's now a great physician. Then there was a saxophone player who became a great educator, Ben Pruitt. He was over the music department at Cass Tech in Detroit. Ben and I were in the same band with the Thrillers – that was a great band. It was much more than an r&b band. We'd play Top 40 things, jazz like 'Filthy McNasty', we were playing 'Drowning in My Own Tears', that hit Ray Charles had, we'd play pop, if you will, rhythm and blues – it was an eclectic show band that could play anything. Yorke needed another band so I played four nights a week, brought home some nice pay. My mom hated it, but my old man said, 'Hey, he's bringing home a pay check, let this man go.' That's how things started for me in the world of music. We backed anybody from Jackie Wilson, Al Hibbler; I played with so many people with the Thrillers. I did my first recording in Hot Springs, Arkansas, in '62 with that band. Al Bell, the Vice President of Stax Records, produced that record.

"They call Hot Springs a little New York because the guy that had the Cotton Club, Owney Madden, when he left New York he moved to Hot Springs. He also had two clubs in Little Rock. Walter Norris, the first pianist to record with Ornette Coleman, told me about the two clubs that Madden had, one set on the Hill, another set on Ninth Street. With the Thrillers we had a comedy act, dancers, the whole show, we took that out there and then they hooked us up into playing at Hot Springs. They had gambling there because they moved all the slot machines from Louisiana to Hot Springs. We used to play there a lot because Yorke Wilburn was a good bandleader and the gangsters liked him, so we worked all of the time."

John painted a fascinating picture of the Little Rock of his youth as a city with a thriving African-American entertainment quarter, with bands coming and going all the time. "On Ninth Street, I'm not exaggerating, there were at least 12 clubs, that's why Basie, and Duke, and Billie Holiday, they'd be playin' there. I met (pianist) Amina Myers when she was working on Ninth Street in '62. She, Oliver Nelson and Aretha Franklin attended Philander Smith College but I met her when she was working at the Bamboo Club. There was the Eldorado Club that was right down from the Flamingo where we worked, these were huge clubs. The former President Clinton loves the music and he knew the legacy of that street but I don't why, they tore that street down. It had so much history. Everyone played there."

It seems Little Rock was always a stopping-off point for territory bands. "All of the territorial bands that came out of Memphis, out of Oklahoma, out of Texas, would come through. In fact when Yorke Wilburn took over at the Flamingo Club, there was a big band there; cat named Classy Blue had 15 pieces. He was from Texas, had a *bad* band. I used to go there as a kid. On Sundays, the kids had to sit in a little booth, away from the adults and they serve you cherry cokes. I'd sneak away, man, and run down there and hear some great entertainers," he recalled.

Of course, there were pitfalls, too. "There were other bands around Little Rock that I worked with that Leary was in. I used to play the Chez Paree, the guy that owned the club, his family lived in our neighbourhood, my father thought it was cool, but one day we pick up the paper and see 'Club owner absconds with all the money and leaves the club' and my father looked at me and he says, 'So, that's what you want to do for a living?' and I says, 'I don't know if it's what I want to do for a living but I love playing music' and he says, 'You see this, this is what you gonna be seein'' for most of your life.'"

Casting around for early role models, John listened to the instrumentalists who were popular in the community. As if to emphasise his ignorance, he admitted, "When I started in '59 or '60, I was so green. I didn't even know who Bird was. I was intensely into people like Sil Austin, Eddie 'Lockjaw' Davis and Don Byas, and then one day, a guy said, 'You never heard of Bird?' He was a disc jockey and he was dating a girl in my neighbourhood. 'You a musician? Take these records.' He gave me, like, five Bird records. I went home, and I said, 'This is gonna be a hard journey, this is gonna be rough.' And that same year, *Giant Steps* came out and that made it even rougher. John Coltrane! Where did those notes come from? I'm discovering Bird, and I'm hearing John Coltrane so now I had to revamp a lot of things and start working on these different styles."

Like many musicians of his generation, John elected to go to college. He wanted to go to North Texas State, known countrywide for the excellence of its music programmes. "I was travelling in the early sixties with rhythm and blues bands, with Solomon Burke," he said, and added, "When I was with McCoy (Tyner) out on the road, I said to McCoy, 'I did a year with Solomon Burke.' He said, 'John, Solomon Burke and I were in the same class together. We grew up together.'" John continued: "His brother Jimmy was the Musical Director and we'd be travelling throughout the South and I would want to stop at North Texas State because my friend Leary was there at the time. That's when I met Billy Harper, he and Leary were roommates. The school that I did attend, at the time I matriculated there, it was called A&MN College, now it's the University of Arkansas at Pine Bluff. Jamil Nasser went to school there, Garnett Brown went to school there, and they won the first *Pittsburgh Courier* poll, they had the baddest big band in America in '52.

"So I wound up at the last minute getting a scholarship to go to A&MN and while I was there I toured throughout, from Florida to New Mexico. There was a guy that was an industrial arts teacher but he was also a booking agent. His name was C. Wood. He was too much, when the bands would leave the North or the West, they would come and work his circuit. I got in with him and I became one of his musicians that toured with different bands. I played with everybody. One of my favourites was

A&MN College/University of Arkansas **New Directions Quintet** prior to their European tour, Pine Bluff AK, 1967. *L-r:* John Stubblefield (ts); Sonelius Smith (p); James Leary (b); Benjamin Jones (t); Rev. Larry Ross (d). Courtesy James Leary.

O.V. Wright, one of the most soulful guys I worked with. After Sam Cooke left the Soul Stirrers, then there was Johnny Taylor, and then there was O.V. Wright. He was a wonderful singer – when I was there he also had James Carr in the band who is probably the godfather of soul, not to take anything away from James Brown! 'As We Walked Down the Street' was his big hit.

"My friend Joe Gardner from Memphis, he and I were in school together. That's how I actually got in Mingus's band later on when I came to New York. Joe had already moved there because Garnett Brown had cooked him up there and Joe was with Mingus. Great trumpet player, we lost him in 2002, 25 February. Mingus was crazy about him because he could play lead, he could play high, he could read anything you put in front of him, and he could solo. He was a virtuoso.

"We had dance bands there, we had all kinds of bands, I played in the Collegians there, I played with Booker T. and the Magnificent Seven, I played with the Tasty Bagful, I played in a lot of different bands, and then before I left I put a band together, the Leary-Stubblefield Quintet and we played the Collegiate Jazz Festival. We didn't win that year but we came in second place. John Hammond liked the band and the trumpet player Ben Jones. He really loved Ben, he got him with Count Basie and also with Ellington for a while. Great trumpet player. Pianist Sonelius Smith was in that band, he played later with Rahsaan Roland Kirk, did a record with him. I graduated in '67, with a Bachelor's in Music – majored in woodwinds, had to play piano, too," he recalled.

"I came to Chicago; I was on my way to New York, to tell you the truth. I'll never forget seeing Louis Armstrong on some TV show and he was talking about how all of

John Stubblefield (ts) **and Duke Ellington**, High Chapparal, Chicago IL, 1969. Courtesy John Stubblefield.

the great musicians come to New York because you get your training there and hear the best there. That stuck in my brain. Anyway, I have family in Chicago on my mother's side and my father had family there too. From '52 we would go to Chicago every summer. I arrived a few days before John Coltrane passed. Pharoah Sanders had already called me to say he had talked to John about me and he wanted me to come and hear them. They were going to play the Plugged Nickel and I was really looking forward to meeting the master. I was at Pharoah Sanders's home in Little Rock when he first got the call from John to join his band. He had no idea that John was going to call. It was a very powerful moment. I remember the aura in that room," he said.

"It was 17 July 1967 and I picked up the *Sun-Times* and I see at the bottom, 'Jazz star John Coltrane dies'. I was completely wiped. I just walked and walked, my eyes were like a sea. It was too much. I called Pharoah that night and it was unexpected for the whole band and everybody. I was just looking forward to meeting John Coltrane and to talking with him. I had scales that John had written out because Pharoah had given them to me. It would have helped a lot to meet him. So that just stopped me from moving to New York right away. Through rhythm and blues, I had a lot of contacts and I got calls to do record sessions at Chess. I did a few but I stopped. I was tired of r&b," John said, emphasising that he had no regrets about playing r&b but needed a change.

"I had heard about the AACM (Association for the Advancement of Creative Musicians) because Amina Myers was a member and then I ran into Lester Bowie at a session one day and he invited me to hear the Art Ensemble. From that, I became a

The Art Ensemble of Chicago, Meridian MS, 1968. L-r: John Stubblefield (sop); Malachi Favors (b); Alvin Fielder (d); Roscoe Mitchell (reeds). Courtesy Alvin Fielder.

member of the AACM in '67. That was a real turning point in my life because I had never met a person like Richard Abrams who not only knew so much about music but also had his own way of doing things with music. I studied the Schillinger System with him for a year. There was Roscoe Mitchell, Threadgill, myself, and a lady pianist, can't think of her name, and Lester Bowie's brother Byron Bowie in this class. We also taught students in the inner city in the South Side every weekend. The AACM had a school there and Douglas Ewart was in that school. We're proud of him – he's become some artist! That was an alternative for me, being around people like that. Also I met Anthony Braxton at that time too, in '67. In fact, I just saw a solo concert of his in New York. My God, it was an amazing concert."

I was intrigued to establish whether John Stubblefield's participation in AACM was sufficient to enable him to survive financially. He was quick to answer. "There wasn't a living in it for me. There was for some of the guys and I can name those that did nothing but music. I was not only part of the AACM, I had my eye on what Phil Cohran was doing, I had my eye on what the Pharoahs were doing, I had my eye on the whole black community on the South Side. I would go to the Pershing Room and jam with (organist) Baby Face Willette who was my third cousin. His father was a minister, Reverend Willette in Little Rock, and my mom knew the Willettes well. When I got to Chicago, Baby Face would let me sit-in because I was family. He was something, man.

"Then I would play with organ groups at the Coral Club, I would be at jam sessions wherever they would go. I would be trying to learn as much as I could. Eddie Harris was very nice to me and we became very good friends. There was an arranger, Prince

Sheils that arranged for Operation Breadbasket. He was very good to me, taught me a lot about arranging. He had this great way of arranging music through the overtone system. He also wrote for Ben Branch, great saxophone player out of Memphis who was the Musical Director for Martin Luther King. Then Phil Cohran, he had a thing called the Afro-Arts Theater and all of the horn players that came out of that became the horn section to Earth, Wind and Fire. There was about five or six people on the original charter for the AACM and Phil was one of them, but he parted company with Richard Abrams and Steve McCall and started his own entity.

The Phil Cohran Band, TV show, Chicago IL, 1970. *L-r:* Master Henry Gibson (cga); Henry Threadgill (as); Pete Cosey (b-gtr); John Stubblefield (ts); Steve McCall (d). Courtesy John Stubblefield.

"My aunt lived on the North Side and my other aunt sold things every Sunday on Maxwell Street. Now you could walk down Maxwell Street and it was a whole block, blues bands on one side, blues bands on the other. It was so regional you could hear Delta blues right here on this corner. Come in the middle of that block and you might hear a band playing the blues like people play them in Alabama. Then you come down here and you might hear some Texas stuff. All of these blues people from all over the different parts of the South had moved and migrated to Chicago. I used to go to Peppers to hear Howlin' Wolf, Muddy Waters, Little Walter; I used to hear all of these people. People loved their blues. I was very impressed by that.

"At 63rd and Cottage Grove was where I met the great bass player Wilbur Ware. I would never have believed it was him. He kept following me across the street, begging me for a quarter. A couple of days later they had a tribute to John Coltrane and someone got on stage and said, 'Ladies and gentlemen, I'd like to introduce one of the finest bass players, Wilbur Ware.' This guy went up on the stage and I said, 'Man, that's the guy that harassed me at 63rd and Cottage Grove!' When I moved to New York, Wilbur was very nice to me. He wasn't really strung out, he just loved his grapes. He was a real genius at music. Died far too young.

"I'll never forget seeing Mingus's band play in '72. Joe Gardner asked me to come and hear the band. They were getting ready to play and my man (Ware) walked in. Mingus introduced him and said, 'Ladies and gentlemen, one of the finest bass players in the world. I'm going to get him to come up if he wants and play one for you.' Wilbur Ware came up on that stage, didn't even look at the music that Mingus had in front of him. That band started playing, that man played so much bass, he was a natural, and when he finished Mingus was sitting on the side just smiling, just happy. That was the kind of love that musicians once had for each other.

"I did a lot of concerts with the AACM under my own name and I had a band with Edward Doherty, a straight-ahead jazz band. I also met Pete Cosey through Phil Cohran; he was my contact with Miles Davis later because of my knowing him in Chicago. See, Pete was a studio musician, one of those guys that did sessions for Cadet and Chess Records. They turned out hits from Howlin' Wolf to Little Milton, you name it, they did it. Those guys used to have Mercedes cars, they used to come five deep and when they finished doing sessions, they'd come down to the South Side of Chicago, driving their Mercedes and pull up in front of a club and just come in and tear the club up. And that's when I met Pete Cosey. His Mercedes was longer than the other ones. He had a hearse!"

John moved to New York in July 1971. "I was up to here with Chicago. Someone came into my home and took all of my instruments and took all of the pants to my clothes. My wife and I were newly-weds, we were married in '70 and I just had enough. Bowie and everybody had moved to Europe – they came over in '69 – and Leo Smith had moved there for a while."

I asked John to sum up the playing ethos of the AACM collective. "It was a communal thing where people got together to control their destinies, musically, and to control how they wanted to present their music. There was the whole rekindling of black awareness too. Mayor Daley used to come through and tear our posters off the street corners there and we would just put them back up. I was trying to keep up with everything that was going on musically in that town, to advance myself as a composer and arranger. I wrote for my small band and I was able to write for the big band and hear what I wrote back right away. When Lester Bowie took over the AACM, (Henry) Threadgill and I could write more and we wrote music that was not terribly orchestrated, there was a lot of space for creativity. We went that way for a while and then Richard (Abrams) took the band back over."

John said that his intention was "to find a way where I could play vertically and horizontal at the same time. Coleman Hawkins loved a guy named Prince Robinson – I met Coleman Hawkins a month before he passed away, got his autograph, too! – and he loved Stomp Evans who had come out of Kansas City. When he was in Chicago, Stomp was the guy that everybody was coming out of, Coleman Hawkins included. Hawk found a way to play vertically on chords where, if there was a C7th chord, he would start the melody maybe on the dominant seventh and make a melody out of it, or he would start it at the tonic and make some kind of a melody out of it. Then Lester Young came and he was, like, playing horizontally in a linear way, with melodies that floated over, that didn't spell the chord up and down. He played the right note of the chord that implied the whole chord. That's my man! To this day.

"I thought if I could find a way to fuse those two styles then maybe that would be my trademark. John Coltrane and Ornette Coleman and Warne Marsh, these people found ways, as did many other people we could name. I was trying to find my fingerprint. I always loved the mannerisms of the great saxophonists, but I was more akin to the saxophonists that were orchestrators and writers, people like Budd Johnson, Frank Foster, Al Cohn, Wayne Shorter, Benny Carter, Henry Threadgill, Bobby Watson. That's what I married myself to, those kind of guys. You look at Frank Foster, we taught together at Jazzmobile for a number of years; he had a whole system and once you learned his system, then when you heard him play, you could hear those systems through the melodies and the way he developed things. I also wanted to be a great sax player that could touch people. I hoped through my Master that I could express myself and people could hear some part of my life, some part of my feelings. My religion is very important to me; I'm a believer."

John had bittersweet memories of his arrival in New York in July 1971: "Didn't have a job, didn't have anything. My former wife and I came to New York at a telephone strike. We couldn't get a telephone until March of '72. Ornette Coleman was very nice to me. I used to hang at his place on Prince Street. He had like a performance space below and his home above. He was working on *Skies of America* there and he was happy, and he said, 'I live in SoHo, you want to try and move here?' For a loft, you could pay something like four grand for the fixtures and my wife, she said, 'No, we don't want to spend that money.' Man, we could have bought a place there, would be worth probably half a million right now. See, Ornette was going to hook us up to some lofts there. Anyway, we chose to find a place on the East Side of town and we lived on 89th Street between First and Second Avenues.

"All we had was a new car, some savings and faith. My wife went and found a job. I've been blessed in not working other than at music but twice in my life, I took a job for a while just to please her. I'm practising every day and she's looking at me, I can see it in her eye, 'That ain't paying any rent.' So I said, 'I told you when I came here, it was to do nothing but play this music.' Anyway, I became a messenger; I did that for a minute until I ran into Elvin Jones one day. He and Keiko were walking down the street and he said, 'John, why don't you come down to Slugs and play?' Shoot, man, I wasn't practising, didn't feel like going and exposing myself. I ran away from that opportunity and then I said, 'Man, I'm not messengering any more.' I did it for about a month and I said, later for that. So I started working with the Collective Black Artists (CBA) – it was a wonderful organisation and I got a chance to play with some great musicians, like one of my favourites, Kenny Dorham. Oh man, I pinched myself when playing with that man. I played with him twice. Then, Jimmy Owens, Reggie Workman, Stanley Cowell, Charles Tolliver, they had a big band. They were musicians that I got a chance to meet and play with. I'll never forget it."

How had John connected with the CBA? "At that particular time in the sixties, we [the AACM] were in contact with different organisations so the CBA wrote to the AACM and we would write back. We would let them know what kind of programmes we were doing. Did the same thing in Detroit and we were in contact with the people in California like Horace Tapscott, the guy that had the big band, so when I came to New York they knew me because I had served as the treasurer of the AACM." He already had friends in New York. "Like Reggie Workman, from when he came and played with Miles Davis at the Plugged Nickel in '66 as cover for Ron Carter. He was nervous, didn't know what the hell he was goin' to play. We got out of the taxi at the same time, he was just comin' in and I said, 'Reggie Workman, have you played with Miles before?' So different musicians that came to Chicago, they remembered me. CBA rehearsed maybe three times a week and we did jobs so that was some kind of work for me. I still couldn't get a phone call and a bass player named Milton Suggs who had played in my rehearsal band in Chicago told Mary Lou Williams about me and that I was a writer, an arranger. She sent me a Western Union – I still have it in my scrapbook – she hired me through Western Union! I played the flute for her, I arranged, I played a lot of my compositions for her. She found them interesting and in '72 when she premièred her Mass with the Alvin Ailey dancers I was in the pit with her band along with Julius Watkins. Those were my two primary sources of work."

John looked back in awe at his association with Mary Lou Williams, moved by his memories of her exceptional spirituality. "It was unbelievable. I saw what musicians got from her. I was a recipient once of her Bel Canto Foundation – she had set up a foundation to help struggling musicians. Eric Dolphy was a recipient too. They didn't call her the first lady of music for nothing. She said, 'John, you need to meet some real good people. I'm going to take you to meet Lorraine and Dizzy. You gotta meet people like that.' She was that kind of a person. When it came down to music, you sat at her piano and you played something, you were transparent when you played before her 'cos anything you did she could hear. 'John, why don't you take that C and put it down in the bass?' and I'm saying, 'Wait a minute, you in the other room, how can you just hear everything in this chord like this?' I didn't know the woman had perfect pitch. When Duke Ellington said she had soul on top of soul, he knew what he was talking about. If she loved you she gave to you, if she didn't love you, she (still) gave to you. A very religious woman. When she walked away from the music she told me the love had gone out of it and when you don't have the love, regardless of what band you're in and whomever you're playing with, it's no good. She left and came to Europe. Didn't play music for seven years and when she came back she had her own record label, Mary Records. She was an enterprising woman.

"She had this working five-piece group. We would accompany her with the Mass; we would accompany her for various concerts and all. I never played tenor with her, I played only flute. She wanted a flautist and I said, 'You got it. I need the work. I'm right in.' Then Milton Suggs told her I was a composer and she wanted to hear my compositions. She loved my pieces right away. I tell you something that's really beautiful. Hilton Ruiz was her student when I moved to New York, he was like a teenager then, and she used to tell me about this guy she was teachin' that had perfect pitch like her, and how much of a trip it was teaching him. In '96 Hilton Ruiz called me to do a record with him and he said, 'John, I remember one of those pieces Mary Lou Williams showed me of yours and I'd like to record that.' It was like Mary Lou Williams speaking through him to get to me. And we did his record, I think it was called *Island Eyes* and he started playing some of those Mary Lou Williams chords on that song and that really touched me. If she touched your life in any way it didn't remain for that year, it remained for years after. My father was so proud – just to be around a person like that that had so much love, had so much feeling. When a person says 'Well I love your music enough I'm gonna record it,' that's a great honour and she did that. She did a programme with Marian McPartland and they did a duet on the song I wrote called 'Baby Man'. It came out on Concord Records. The title of Mary Lou's album was a song I wrote called 'Free Spirits'."

It was the connections with his music's history that fascinated John Stubblefield. He remembered Mary Lou telling him how "she sat on Jelly Roll Morton's lap and what he imparted to her", adding that, "I put a lot of research into all that, into musicians and talking to historians and reading. One of my greatest joys has been to talk to people older than myself over the years and to see the linkages. It started with me as a kid. As a child I knew of (black) composer William Grant Still because his mother taught school on the site that my mom's church was on. Our pastor used to talk about this man so I knew about him but I never heard his music. Now I'm a member of the William Grant Still Society and I'm in touch with his daughter in Flagstaff, Arizona, to get as much research on what this man gave to the world. So it started very early for me to talk to people."

Rather to my surprise John mentioned that he'd been part of the New York Jazz Repertory ensemble alongside such luminaries as The Judge – bassist Milt Hinton – and pianist-historian Dick Hyman. "That was a great forum for me. I got a chance to meet a melange of people that were in the swing era, like Joe Newman, and to hear (trumpeters) Taft Jordan and Doc Cheatham. They were beautiful. I did Carnegie Hall with them; I did the Bi-Centennial tour – *The History of Jazz* – with them. We did some stuff with the organist Larry Young and with Joe Farrell. I think I did maybe five or six concerts in all."

Max Roach (d) **and John Stubblefield** (ts), unknown studio, New York, c.1980s.

Like so many freelance musicians of the time John turned his hand to a variety of musical work. "I played with Frank Foster's band at Club Baron in Harlem once a week for a year. That was some band. People like Thad Jones would come in, all the Basie alumni would come in, everybody would be at the bar. Then the Latin scene opened up to me. Pat Patrick who had played with Sun Ra but also with Mongo Santamaria, he hooked me up in the Latin scene. I played with Billy Hart, I played with the great flautist Mauricio Smith, I met Jerry Gonzalez there. There was a lot of work because on a Saturday, there was like three gigs in the day, then on a Sunday you played in a church and you played in the Latin community. I played with Eddie Bastian, I played with Tito Puente and that started cooling things out for me.

"Pretty soon we moved from 89th Street to Brooklyn and that's where our son was born, John Stubblefield V. This was while I was in Mingus's band, the week we were performing at the Vanguard. I'll never forget that as long as I live. Joe Gardner is there, Mingus is here, Roy Brooks is over here and Don Pullen is at the piano and Sonny Rollins comes and sits at the edge, right near me. I said, 'Sonny I love you but please when you come in a club don't make me know you're there.'" John then imitates the high Rollins voice –'Oh I didn't know. I love Charles's music and I came to support you' – adding that the presence of a master like Rollins meant that he couldn't concentrate or "get my stuff together. I got a chance to see Sonny a little bit later because Leary had come to New York and he was staying with me. He was playing in Sonny's band so I would go to their rehearsals. He left Sonny's band and went with Earl 'Fatha' Hines. So I got a chance to meet Sonny on that level. George Coleman used to make me nervous like that, Hank Mobley too, but those people were also very supportive and would tell you if you were doing something incorrectly. They would say, 'the most important thing you can do is find you own style, your own way of doing things.'"

John Stubblefield (ts) **and Charles Mingus** (b). Charles Mingus Jazz Workshop, Boston MA, 1973. Courtesy John Stubblefield.

Characteristically John's connection with Charles Mingus came about through one of his network of friends and proved to be timely. "I played the last job at Slugs with trumpeter Charles McGhee – we closed Slugs out – because after Lee Morgan was shot there (in February 1972) the club just kinda folded. After that I was just praying I could get a break. In those days it was hard because all of the masters were still alive. Anyway Joe Gardner that I knew from school at AMN, he was with Mingus's band. They had already come to London in '72, they did a tour there with Cat Anderson and Hamiet Bluiett. Hamiet just left out of nowhere and went back to St. Louis so Joe recommended me. Mingus said he wanted an alto player so Joe says he has a guy that can play alto – I was a *tenor* player – and Mingus called me one day out of a clear blue sky. Here John went into Mingus's gruff voice: "'I hear you play alto.' I said, 'Yeah.' 'I hear you play oboe.' I said, 'Yeah, I play oboe.' 'You play bassoon?' I said 'Yeah but I don't own one though.' 'You play bass-clarinet?' I said 'Yeah.' 'You play soprano?' I said 'Yeah.' 'Tenor?' 'Yeah.' 'Well bring the bassoon, bring all of them and we open at the Jazz Workshop in Boston.' And that's how I joined the band. Never rehearsed anything. Never played an audition, never did nothing. Joe Gardner came and showed me some of the songs but that was just the songs.

McCoy Tyner Quintet, Lincoln Center, New York, 1991. *L-r:* McCoy Tyner (p); John Stubblefield (b-cl); Todd Williams (sop); Christian McBride (b); Roy Haynes (d). Photo by Susan C. Ragan. Courtesy John Stubblefield.

"I had my oboe, I had my bass clarinet, I had my tenor, I had the alto, I had the flute. I had this gold-plated alto, Buescher, it was a beautiful horn and on the second day or so Mingus said, 'Now I played with Bird. You can play alto but you no alto player.' I said, 'Well it's true. You told me you needed an alto player and I needed a job, I got a new kid on the way.' 'Well what you play?' 'I play tenor.' So I played the tenor book but that week he had me play something on oboe, on bass-clarinet, on flute. Then he says, 'I'm gonna feature John playing something by Duke Ellington. Ladies and gentlemen, he don't know nothing about Duke. You call yourself a musician, you don't know about Duke.' He was just trying to embarrass me, so I said, 'Let's play, "I Got It Bad and That Ain't Good" and I played that song with so much passion and feeling there was a lady and her daughter who came to New York to hear me, hoping that I might play that again. They said they just wanted to cry the way I played that song.

"That's the way Mingus was, he was so honest, he would put his music in jeopardy sometimes just for the creativity that he had. So I saw all of that. I was fired after five months. I got in a fight with Mingus and I shouldn't have done that. I went toe-to-toe with him verbally about another musician whose name I'll keep off the record. After

Charles Mingus Jazz Workshop, Cleveland OH, 1973. *Rear, l-r:* Charles Mingus (b); Roy Brooks (d); Sue Mingus; Don Pullen (p). *Front:* host; John Stubblefield (ts); Joe Gardner (t). Courtesy John Stubblefield.

getting fired out of a major band like Mingus's I couldn't get arrested in New York. Even though the band was really getting someplace. Mingus was tired of Joe Gardner because Joe wasn't playing high no more.

"He never did say I was fired. We came back to New York off a tour after a month and less than a week later Joe Gardner was injured. I'm driving down Seventh Avenue and look over to the Vanguard and I see Mingus's band is appearing there again. I get out of my car and I run down to the Vanguard. I'm with Mingus but I don't see my name nowhere and I'm saying, 'Man, I ain't got a call.' I was hurt. The man in the Vanguard says Mingus was just down here, he just did a TV show. It tore me up. I had a new kid just born. So I went down one night to sit-in with Mingus and I was so angry I played my soprano so hard I bent the B key. The guy that used to play saxophone in his band, Bobby Jones, he said, 'Man that happened to me too, once he fired me.' I was shakin'. Mingus was just sitting back there laughin'. The first people who came in after Joe and I left the band were Charles McGhee and George Adams.

"Then I asked the Mingus band if they would come and perform for a benefit we were doing at Ornette Coleman's place for Joe Gardner and he was too busy to do it. It wouldn't have been nice for Mingus and I to run into each other after that. But two years later the man came to me and asked me to rejoin his band. Wrote me a letter in '76 which I still have in my archives. Offered me nice money. Asked me to leave Nat Adderley and I told him I was not going to bother. I went home, I thought about it, talked to my wife and I decided to stay with Nat. With Nat we got songs on every album and I knew I was not going to get songs on Mingus's records. I called Mingus and he said 'Soon as you finished your business with Nat, you coming back with me!'"

John added that his involvement with the Mingus Big Band, which had begun in 1990, was partly due to Mingus's original faith in him. "That man gave me a chance when no one else would. He also broke down and came back to me, which Clifford Jordan told me he would do. Which is what he did over the years with most of the people that played with him, even Jimmy Knepper, Jackie McLean, Tommy Turrentine, all

The Mingus Big Band, band promo, New York, c.1994. *Standing, rear:* David Lee Jones (as); John Hicks (p); Adam Cruz (d); Craig Handy (ts); Andy McKee (b); Kenny Drew Jr. (p); Steve Slagle (as); unk; unk; John Stubblefield (ts); Sue Mingus (mgr). *Front:* Frank Lacey, Jamal Haynes (tb); Philip Harper, Ryan Kisor, Randy Brecker (t).

of whom he hit in the mouth. I learned so much more about the man's music, the forms that he was fooling around with. He was way ahead of a lot of people. Yes, I joined the band three weeks into its existence. Sue (Mingus) saw me playing at Lincoln Center with Randy Weston. In fact she asked me in '89 if I wanted to play oboe with *Epitaph* and I said, 'No thank you, I don't play the oboe any more,' but then she called me to play with the big band. I went down there, I said, 'I don't want to play with no more big bands,' but there's something about this big band where you can bring your personality and express yourself. That's the way the Mingus band was."

John was a potent contributor to the band as both soloist and cheerleader whenever and wherever the band appeared, whether in New York or around the world. He also prepared the occasional arrangement. For all that, he seemed reluctant to become one of the band's ever-changing roster of Musical Directors. Surely there was no one better qualified? "Sue asked me to be a Musical Director many times. I could not function in that because I played with Charles Mingus and I've found that most people, other than (trumpeter) Jack Walrath, even John Handy when he came back and played with us, we can't do that. We might get in the way and cloud things because we played with the man. It's best to be a liaison, if you will, or be a bridge, and to work with the management, to work with the musical directors, to work with the spirit of the band. I found that I worked better by making suggestions about how Mingus would approach things and put things together.

" A lot of people have worked at being a Musical Director of this band but I feel very comfortable in my role. Sue wanted me to do it but I said no. I thought about it and I said I can play in this band to support everybody and make sure we're playing some of the things like Mingus would do 'em. I learned from Mingus; he never counted

The Mingus Big Band, Time Café, The Fez, 380 Lafayette St., New York, c.1996. *L-r:* Andy McKee (b); Randy Brecker, Earl Gardner (t); Don Braden (ts); Dave Taylor (tb); Chris Potter (as); Steve Slagle (as); John Stubblefield (ts); Gary Smulyan (bs). Photo by Alice Arnold.

off anything, you just followed the bass; the bass led everything, and the way you hook that up with a big band to make it sound like an orchestra, we have our means to get to that. I discuss that with everyone that comes in as Musical Director."

The late trombonist Britt Woodman was a childhood friend of Mingus and an active member of the MBB until shortly before his death in October 2000. "In fact, before Britt died, this band was out in California and we went to his home. We took photographs the week before he died. While he was in the band, he was, like, his (Mingus's) spirit because he and Mingus grew up together. When Britt would come in, with just the solos he would play, they had the history of jazz written in them, from that year all the way back. We revived off of his spirit, and John Handy, when he goes with us, we revive off of his spirit, Randy Brecker, when he's with us, anybody that played with Mingus, we like to be in that middle ground and carry it with us. Let the men know how things were done and try to make sure that we can get it as close to the way Mingus would do things."

John made much of the band's value to emerging players. "We like to let our young, great musicians come through and get a hand at doing these things. This band has served as a training ground for many great young musicians; on this 2002 tour, the drummer (Tommy Crane) is 19, the alto saxophone player Jaleel Shaw is 24; the drummer Johnathan Blake, he joined when he was 22. Chris Potter was in the band when he was 20. (Trumpeter) Ryan Kisor was twenty, and Jamal Haynes, came in when he was young. Jamal is teaching at the New England Conservatory now; if there was anyone that could do something for that trombone, he is in that line. But he don't want to play the trombone, he's interested in playing the drums, yeah. He's interested in modelling, playing the drums, teaching, acting. Philip Harper, great trumpet player, one of the young lions, he was with us. He moved to Holland in '99. We've had so many talented, young, mature musicians come through this band."

As so often in our conversation, John's train of thought alighted, momentarily, on another topic, that of his association with sound master Gil Evans. "He was one of a kind, a magician. I found him to be an amazing human being. I played with Gil for a year or more, couldn't believe I was playing with his band, used to pinch myself just like when I was with Kenny Dorham. Gil really liked the way I played lead alto, called me up and told me, and this when David Sanborn was in the band, as a lead alto player, in '74. I remember being on tour with Gil Evans, and Mingus was on the tour with us and we were on a bill together. I'll never forget that night, never as long as I live: Keith Jarrett was playing solo piano, the Thad Jones–Mel Lewis big band was on it, Charles Mingus and the Gil Evans band, and we were without our music. The music went on the train to Italy and we were in some other place in Europe. Gil was so relaxed, he was so laid back, he said (John emulates Gil's whisper), 'Oh well, you know, we're just gonna play the music, whatever you do, play whatever you remember, we just gonna play like we've been playing.' It relaxed everybody, and man, oh man, when you got to playing his music, the parts would just start coming to you. The spirit of every note that he wrote and orchestrated came out of you. He didn't have to ask you to play your part out; your part came out of your soul because that note was like an organic thing. That was what was so amazing about Gil Evans.

"We did some dates at RCA and Gil was like Mingus, too, in the way he would change things around. I walked into the session he was doing – I'm playing soprano – with my part on soprano, and he moved me back with the trumpets. I had to stop right there because I know the man wants something, he wouldn't have moved me back there if not. He didn't change the orchestration, he just changed the colour. When I go back and listen to the great orchestrations that he did, not only for Miles but also for himself and many artists, he had mastered something that a lot of people had not mastered, that goes for the classical people, too, he had mastered his own style. I would go to his home and he would voice a chord a thousand ways before he'd decide how he was going to orchestrate it. That, right there, is magic. I loved Gil Evans."

Later in the 1970s, John was a member of Nat Adderley's popular quintet. "I've been very blessed. I give thanks all the time. See, I used to sub for Harold Vick, he was the next saxophone player (in the band) after Cannon (Cannonball Adderley) passed. I was in the house band at the Apollo (in Harlem) a few months before Cannon died, and I heard the band every night. This was (agent) John Levy's *Black Music '74*, he had everybody on his roster, he had Nancy Wilson, he had Stanley Turrentine, he had Cannonball, he had Les McCann, he had Joe Williams, he had Freddie Hubbard, all of this was on the show, every night for a month. Who contracted me on that was the bass player that plays with Sonny Rollins now, Bob Cranshaw.

"Man, Hal Galper was leaving the Adderley band because the band worked too much! He said they worked 300 days out of a year. I said, 'I ain't never heard nobody leaving a band because they worked too much.' I would sub for Harold Vick, and Nat liked me, then it was Alex Foster, he also did it, but Nat didn't want to hear the alto; Harold Vick stood like 6'2" or 6'3", and there's Nat down here (motions). Nat didn't care but Harold was very sensitive to that, and he just decided to bow out; he was very busy in the studios. I was in California and I get a call from Nat to come back and join the band.

"I learned so much from Nat Adderley, like how to relate to the people when you're performing to them. What Cannonball used to call 'getting the music across the stage lights'. How to programme your show, how to programme the solos, how to be on time with everything, I learned a lot of that from Nat Adderley. He was a great cornet player, he was never given credit of how great he was, but he was also a great comedian. I saw him wipe out a lot of comedians. A lot of great comedians came to just see him, from Redd Foxx to Richard Prior, they loved him. It didn't get no better in terms of fun than with him. I laughed so much, my neck used to hurt. He kept us laughing all the time. 'Nat, please, just give us a break,' we'd say. We worked like nine months out of a year in the States, didn't come to Europe at all, stayed right in Canada and the US. Jack Whittemore booked the band. I spent two years with Nat. I learned a lot, not only about leading the band, but about how a band should communicate, and how a leader can communicate with the audience."

In considering such a wide-ranging career, it's impossible to do justice to all of John's many musical affiliations and experiences. He agreed: "There's so many more things we could talk about, like when I was around Miles Davis." John worked briefly with Davis in 1973. "Of course, everybody plays licks, you have to have certain licks under your belt regardless to how far they go back but Miles Davis was more interested in those musicians that knew harmony and theory so well that they could play inside of a sound and tell a story inside of a sound. That's like an arranger, because when an arranger and an orchestrator put a sound together, if they have one particular sound that they're dealing with, they gonna take some other sounds and stack those sounds on top of those sounds. The way the colours are mixed inside of the primary colour is what I hold to high esteem. I hold also to a high esteem being a part of the legacy, if I am or if I'm not, I still hold to it because I've dedicated my life to it."

Jerry Gonzalez and the Fort Apache Band, Milestone promo, US, 1990s. *L-r:* Jerry Gonzalez (t, fgh, cga); Larry Willis (p); Andy Gonzalez (b); John Stubblefield (ts); Steve Berrios (d, Cuban perc); Joe Ford (as, sip, fl).

Given John's considerable prowess as an instrumentalist, it's all too easy to overlook his status as a composer, an impression he was anxious to correct. "I would like to leave something of beauty, and I have some 80 songs recorded, some of them recorded more than once. Oh yeah. 'Bushman's Song' has been recorded seven times. It was the last song that Stanley Turrentine recorded. I know I can never get close to a Duke Ellington or a William Grant Still or an Aaron Copland but if I could just leave one or two songs that would really be beautiful for centuries …

"A lot of people play the altissimo register of the saxophone like they play the other part: everything is correct. I don't play the altissimo register like that – I play the altissimo register like a lead singer in a church, like an Aretha Franklin, or Patti Labelle because when I come from the altissimo register of the saxophone, I'm coming from it like a singer in a church. I would like to leave that (as my personal legacy). My whole plan is to give some kind of a beautiful feeling to a person, who can say, 'Not only does he have feeling but he has knowledge about what he's doing.'

John Stubblefield (ts), Kenny Barron Quintet, Village Vanguard, New York, 1991. Photo by Susan C. Ragan. Courtesy John Stubblefield.

John went on to tell me that he had made over a hundred recordings and added, with a smile. "I could say that there are quite a few that I can live with. I like the Kenny Barron record, *What If* (Enja, 1986), it was done without any rehearsal, it's what Mingus was about, that warmness, that spontaneity. This music that they call jazz is supposed to be about where you compose on your feet right there at the moment. That's it. There is a record that I did with Larry Willis (*A Tribute to Someone,* Audio Quest, 1993) that is somewhat the same way, Pheeroan akLaff (*Sonogram,* MU, 1989), there's a record I did with him. Gil Evans told me once, he said, 'Man, I heard something you played on a Kip Hanrahan record, John, it was sheer beauty.' I said, 'Gil, please, what do you mean?' He said, 'It was just the moment, it was sheer beauty.'

"I never forget Rahsaan Roland Kirk told me he heard something that I played in the lower register on a Lester Bowie record (*Fast Last,* Muse, 1974) and he said, 'John, you should work on that, you can develop that into something.' I kept listening and trying to find out what he was talking about, then one day it hit me where it was in that section of a solo, and I started working on that and I found something new. A lot of my stuff (with the Mingus Big Band) Sue has canned – there are a lot of things I've done with the band that she just didn't release. It's the truth. Sue is beautiful, she knows what's going on but I think about Mingus all the time, like when I played with his band, he would say to me, 'Avant-garde, avant-garde!' and I would say, 'Man, I wanna play my lines, I wanna play my licks.' 'I don't want that, I want something new,' he'd say. So a lot of times when I play with this band I think I hear Mingus saying to me, 'Something new, man. Make a mistake, turn that into something.' Don't just sit and play something that you know that's gonna work. Take something and turn it upside down, take it outside and then bring it back inside. Take it in and out. He was into that and I was saying, 'Mingus, I'm with you now, man.'

"Being a soloist, with expression and with feeling, and with musical knowledge, is what I really strive to be. With the Mingus Big Band, we did 'Hog Callin' Blues' on *Gun Slinging Birds* (Dreyfus, 1994), and it's OK. It was a one-taker but the one that we did for the first record, it was out there, it was fired up, it had energy, everything, and it wasn't released. I can't remember some of the things that I have done with the Mingus Big Band but I do remember that 'Hog Callin' Blues', it was alright."

In among his many moments of triumph and elation, I asked John whether there had been any occasions for regret. He was quick to reply: "I regret very, very much that I listened to my wife back in '75 when Art Blakey called me to become a Messenger. I regret that I did what she asked me, to stay home. I regret that to this day because I trained myself to be a Messenger from the time I heard that band in '60, oh man, and then boop, boop, Art Blakey called me. I told my wife, 'I just got a call to join the Messengers.' She said, 'We got a son that's two years old, you're working with Gil Evans, you're working the Jazzmobile, you got this, you got that, I don't want you going out there with him.' So I wanted to be a good husband, I wanted to be a good father, so I called Bu and he never forgave me for that. You know what, it's been hard for me to forgive myself for that, too. Yes, that was with the first Mrs. Stubblefield. I haven't married (again) yet, I've been a bachelor since, God, '77, for my divorce. There's been a couple of times it's been close and I am getting to a place where that could happen for me again.

"My son was born in '73 when I was with Mingus. He played the clarinet for a few years and gave it up. I told him to send it to me and he did. I'm playing it now. John is a graphic artist and he's very good. Our relationship is not like I would really want it to be. I brought him to Paris with me in '95 so he could go check some of the schools out if he wanted to study there. He studied at Fort Lauderdale Art Institute and in Chicago at Columbia and I wanted him to check things out here in Europe, wanted him to see as much as he

Charles Davis Quintet, possibly Hartford CT, late 1980s/early 1990s, New York, 1990s. L-r: John Stubblefield (ts); Paul Brown (b); Al Harewood (d); Richard Wyands (p); Charles Davis (ts). Courtesy Charles Davis.

could see. We're cool, but I would have loved to have been closer with my son. I hated to lose my family but when I was with Nat, we were on the road all the time."

With time running short and in an attempt to bring John's story more or less up to date, I asked John about his bandleading activities. "For a long time, from '74 until 2000, I didn't perform in New York under my name. I was tired of playing New York. I go to Japan, like, three times a year now with the John Stubblefield Quartet. What happened recently is that I started a new band, this is the band I'm really off on. It's a band called Quiet Fire, it's six pieces. Been going since '99, we have over 50 songs in the book, half of them are by yours truly and then I have a lot of composers that I love, and we play some of their music, too. In the band now is (drummer) Victor Lewis, (bassist) Cecil McBee, (trumpeter) Virgil Jones, (trombonist) Frank Lacy's played with the band, but that band chair has been Clark Gayton's, and Jason Jackson, a wonderful trombonist, has also played with the band. Hubert Eaves who worked with Gary Bartz, had a band called D-Train, had a lot of hits, wrote for Luther Vandross, wrote that hit for Miles Davis, 'Something on Your Mind', he's been the pianist from the start. I got him back into playing, he's in the church now, a great piano player, lot of feeling. Just recently, Kenny Drew's played with the band, George Colligan, very wonderful player, he plays with Quiet Fire.

"I want the band to be an eclectic band, where we can go back in the last 50 or 60 years and touch on any of those periods but be moving forward, but not too much forward. I don't want to be playing cold jazz; I'd like to see jazz move back to the area where people can relate to instrumental music and their instrumental hits. If you see something now, it's all singers. I'd like to see young people enjoying instrumental music more. We want the band to not only relate to young people but to relate to people from their 70s on up. I haven't recorded here in nine years but I've been busy, like with Kenny Barron's band, Billy Hart's band, Louis Hayes's band.... did a TV show for four years with my friend James Mtume. He wrote 'New York Undercover'. Mtume and I were in Miles's

Kenny Barron Quintet, Village Vanguard, New York, 1991. L-r: Victor Lewis (d); John Stubblefield (ts); Kenny Barron (p); Cecil McBee (b); Eddie Henderson (t). Photo by Susan C. Ragan. Courtesy John Stubblefield.

band together. We just have a certain closeness. I work with him now on projects. I have produced with Teru Nakamura a lot of music that's only out in Japan. We've been involved with that for the last ten years, doing a lot of projects."

And there we halted the interview, conscious that there was still much more to tell. Something of John Stubblefield's breathless energy, his awareness of jazz past and present, and his willingness to place himself in challenging environments can be discerned from these words. Better still, there's his music, his instrumental prowess and his compositions, forever there to be valued and enjoyed.

John Stubblefield (ts), Fort Apache Band, Detroit Jazz Festival, Detroit MI, 1997. Courtesy John Stubblefield.

First published in three parts, as 'John Stubblefield'/'Onward and Upward'/'Composing on Your Feet' in *Coda*, November–December 2003/May–June 2004/September–October 2004

Judy Carmichael

Judy Carmichael, c. 2008. Photo by Gordon Sapsed. Courtesy Gordon Sapsed.

> *Judy Carmichael seems to be everywhere these days. Touring in Australia or Brazil, staging concerts in the Hamptons and then turning up in Ascona to play the festival before headlining at the Boisdale restaurant in London's Belgravia, something of a home from home for her, all while she works on her American weekly PBS radio series. As this piece tries to convey, Judy is something of an unstoppable force, as dynamic off stage as she is on stage. Hearing her play is always a joy and I'm glad that she continues to travel so widely and so regularly.*
>
> *As uninhibited in conversation as she is on the bandstand, Judy is a journalist's dream interviewee. I arranged to call on her at the Dolphin Square service flat she was using during her Boisdale engagement in August 2008. Fresh from playing tennis, she made me a cup of tea and the talk began ...*

Slim, lithe, vivacious, with a shock of frizzed blonde hair, the pianist Judy Carmichael looks like the kind of woman you'd expect to encounter working out at an Upper West Side health club or jogging through Central Park. "Chatty, droll and restless, she is everything a New Yorker ought to be," said Clive Davis in *The Times* (3 February 2009). In fact, she's only a New Yorker by adoption (she lives in the Hamptons now) but is certainly keen on fitness, happy to play tennis against (and beat) the likes of Harry Allen among many others.

That said, she's also an expert practitioner of that most masculine of art forms, Harlem stride piano, perfected in the first decades of the 20th century and usually seen as the preserve of powerful men. As she explained when we met to talk at her borrowed London apartment, she has had to face (and overcome) two drawbacks as she seeks to practise her craft. One, that she's a woman, and two, that she's white. Indeed, she recalls an early meeting with the celebrated talent-spotter and recording impresario John Hammond who was discomfited and quite put out when he realised that she was not African-American. Their putative relationship foundered on the spot.

Judy Carmichael (ɔ), personal promo, c. 2010. Photo by Michael Benabib. Courtesy Judy Carmichael.

At the time of our interview, Judy was in London for a two-week engagement at the swish Boisdale Restaurant in Belgravia with her guitarist friend David Blenkhorn, supported on the night we heard her play by Alan Barnes on alto and clarinet. Since then she's been back to play at Pizza on the Park and the Shaw Theatre, this time with Allen as her playing (and tennis?) companion. In between times, she's toured in Brazil, played in Australia, released a CD featuring Jon-Erik Kellso and Mike Hashim, and appeared at prestigious locations in New York including Hotel Carlyle and Lincoln Center.

Judy Carmichael (p) **and Michael Hashim** (as), possibly New York, c. 2008. Courtesy Judy Carmichael.

In effect, Judy is an 'independent contractor' in today's terminology. She has no agent, handles her own bookings, owns her own recordings and issues them, produces her own concerts and controls her own successful radio series. 'Jazz Inspired' on national public radio. If that makes her seem formidable, then so be it; on relatively brief acquaintance, she's enthusiastic, voluble, committed and pleasingly self-deprecating. She's in her 50s (born 1952), but looks decades younger, and is in demand around the world.

It's usual when talking to jazz musicians for them to look back to a childhood surrounded by music or to have had some sort of Damascean moment of discovery. Judy's beginnings were more prosaic. "I grew up in a place very few people have heard of called Pico Rivera," she said. "That's south-eastern Los Angeles County. When I was a kid it wasn't even a city yet. It was just a land grant. That makes it sound very rural which it wasn't. It was just a suburb of LA. I didn't like it. Even as a child I didn't want to be living in this place," she continued. "My parents were star-struck. They came from Illinois and both were extremely talented. They were the stars of their individual families. My mom wrote music and played piano, good living room piano, like ballads with pretty chords, and my dad sang beautifully, did civic light opera. They were accomplished amateurs. They were both attractive and energetic. They went to California for a better life. My dad worked for the phone company. They were not jazz fans, not at all. We didn't even listen to the radio. I don't think we had a record player."

Why be so negative about Pico Rivera? "I hated it because I was looking for something that was individual and had character. It didn't have either of those. I felt it all terribly depressing, even as a child. It became a family joke that I said to my dad, 'It's true, Los Angeles is culturally bereft.' My dad thought that was hilarious. Of course, it's not true now but it was then. You asked about black people? No, it was all Mexican. I was in the minority. It was fascinating in that way. We were all born in LA but 80 per cent of my High School graduating class was Mexican, the rest were Asian and there were a few like me. I feel very fortunate in that I grew up in a time and place that I can't imagine happening anywhere else."

Initially, it seems, Judy was known as a ragtime pianist, that is, before she discovered stride. "The reason I played ragtime was that my grandfather had offered all his grandchildren $50 to be the first one to learn 'Maple Leaf Rag'. Why? Just because he liked it. He wasn't hip. He just picked the most popular tune there was. He offered $50 for 'Maple Leaf' and $100 for 'Cannonball' so I immediately looked for 'Cannonball'. Couldn't find it, so I learned 'Maple Leaf Rag'. He never thought any of us would do it. On one of our trips to visit the relatives I played it and very, very grudgingly, he gave me that money. That was a huge amount of money for this man. He gave me the $50 and said, 'Don't learn "Cannonball" because I'm not giving you a hundred.' I like this story because I can say that I'm the first musician to say that I went into it for the money! I was only 11 but I had these big hands. I could already reach an octave. I was taking piano lessons and my teacher said I didn't have any real ability so I got the $50 and quit my lessons. After hearing 'Maple Leaf', I took to that rhythmic structure and I really liked it. I then wanted to play all that stuff and my mom got me 'Kitten on the Keys' and 'Dizzy Fingers' and I learned, probably, ten Zez Confrey things, and lots of ragtime. That really built up my chops and I found I had a knack for that kind of thing.

"I went in and got my first job when I was 19. I was in California State College, and then I went to Long Beach as well. Mine was a German major, although I knew I wanted to perform in some way. I'd done a lot of comedic acting in High School and civic light opera and I'd started auditioning. I was either going to be a German scholar or a comedic actress. But not a jazz musician! So, on a bet, again, a friend said, 'There's a drunk playing at a place in Newport Beach and I bet you can play better than he does.' So I went down, really on a dare, and played one tune: 'Maple Leaf Rag'. The guy was not a drunk, just a sweetheart and he said, 'I can't play that tune, you've got the job.' He didn't know that I only had five tunes memorised. He said it pays $20, and I said 'I never work for less than $40.' Even though I'd never had a job! So I started at the top!"

Judy talked about a boyfriend who thought she had something pianistically and sought to introduce her to sterner stuff by taking her to the Lighthouse Club (in Hermosa Beach) to hear saxophonist Yusef Lateef. "I hated it, absolutely hated it," she laughed. "I hated the atmosphere. I hated how dark and smoky it was and I hated how depressing and how pretentiously cool everybody was. I said, 'I hate jazz and I will never go to another jazz club.' So I started working in nice restaurants, places where I felt more comfortable, and did that for a while before my transition into jazz."

That transition was furthered once Judy began working at Disneyland in Orange County, California. "I worked at Disneyland from the mid-to-late 1970s. For five years. It was a golden time at Disneyland. In a way, none of us liked it because you're wearing a costume. They were taking away all your personality. I'm the only woman (staff) musician they've ever had so they made my costume for me and it still looked horrible. I had to wear a high-collared turn-of-the-century outfit. Big puff sleeves and stripes. And a bustle!

"The reason Disneyland was so great was just for the amount of work there. They hired a lot of musicians then. Great musicians have worked there. It sounds like an unhip gig but it wasn't. I was the only one who was in a stationary spot so musicians used to come by and see me. People would say, 'You gotta hear this crazy girl playing stride.' I was hired to play ragtime but I spent most of the day sneaking in stride. If the supervisor came by, I'd play 'Maple Leaf Rag'. Then he'd leave and I'd play 'Carolina Shout'. The great thing is I got to meet these guys and they would come sit-in. We'd always get in trouble because they were in a different costume, from a different 'land' (area of

Disneyland) but that way I got to play with Jack McVea. That was a great thrill. He was playing clarinet then. (Bassist) Red Callender; he played there sometimes and became a great friend. Jackie Coon was a big influence on me too. He was the first person to make me play a ballad and let me see what could happen playing with a beautiful horn player. I'm so fortunate I played with these people."

Another seminal encounter at Disneyland was with Harold Jones, the former Basie drummer. "He heard me playing. He was subbing on a band there. Ironically it was an all-white marching band that was all freaking out that they had Harold Jones with them. I didn't know who he was. He said, 'Did I hear stride?' So he came over and introduced himself. He'd just left Nancy Wilson and this was right before he joined Sarah (Vaughan). It was just a great meeting. I owe a lot to him. He really convinced me to be a jazz musician. I didn't think I was particularly gifted and I knew I'd started so much later than everybody else. I hadn't been a music major and I wasn't facile in terms of harmonic things. We had a lot of conversations with him saying, 'You have a real gift. You have to do this. You have a specific approach. There's a million guys out there that can be copyists. You've got a voice.'

"One of the other great things about Disneyland at that time was that in the summer they'd feature different big bands. Basie came in for a week and Harold came out. He says, 'Freddie (Green) and Basie have to hear you. They're just gonna go nuts.' Just over the fact that I existed. So one time, Basie and I, we were talking, and I said something about hating jazz as opposed to loving it and he said, 'You're a jazz pianist. Hasn't anyone told you that yet?' I was that naïve. I can't emphasise enough that being a jazz musician is just not something a middle-class white girl from California ever fathomed.

"How did someone like me become comfortable enough to be able to have a dialogue with Freddie Green or with Count Basie? The first black person I ever met was (drummer) Harold Jones. I'd never met a black person before. I was the only one of my friends who knew anybody black. And then I met Basie and then I met Freddie Green. So I asked Freddie, 'Why do all these black musicians support me so much when I haven't had as much support from white musicians?' He said, 'Everybody romanticises it but when *we* started we didn't have a lot of choices. We could either be criminals or we could be jazz musicians, which wasn't much better than being a criminal. We look at you, you could be a doctor, a lawyer or marry a rich guy yet you have chosen not only to be a jazz musician but a stride player. You had options.'

Sarah Vaughan (voc); **Freddie Green** (g); **Judy Carmichael** (p), private party, Los Angeles CA, c.1976. Courtesy Judy Carmichael.

I was just a 24-year-old girl playing at Disneyland who liked the music. I'm not being noble about it. I had not seen the future yet. My dad told me he was disappointed. He thought I'd be an actress. I liked the honesty with jazz – it's just you and the piano and you either played it or you didn't. That's what drew it to me. That and the fact that I loved the music."

Naïve or not, Judy made sure to organise her first album recording, knowing that she needed a calling card, but not without some difficulty. One again, Harold Jones played his part. "I put this record out; it was called *Two-Handed Stride* (recorded in April 1980 and released on Progressive), now it's called *And Basie Calls It Stride* and it's reissued on CD. Harold said 'You really should record with a group. We'll do it this way; you're going to have to ask everybody. Let Freddie hear you and see what happens.' Freddie was not recording with many people besides Basie then. 'Ask Freddie and say I'll (Harold Jones) do it and then ask Red Callender – you know his first gig was with Fats Waller so he's gonna go crazy about you – if Freddie says yes and I say yes, he'll say yes if I talk to him.'

"Then he suggested Marshal Royal. Marshal could be very intimidating, very grousy. Harold said, 'You're actually who Marshal should be playing with but Marshal would never hire a stride pianist because he would feel it's not hip enough but he's gonna be in his element. He's gonna like it but he won't be able to act like it. He's gonna look at you and think, 'These other guys said yes, she must have something, so I've gotta say yes.' We walked into the studio and I was the leader all the way. I sat down – it was the first time I was ever in a studio – I was sick to my stomach – I thought I was going to pass out all the time. Freddie said, 'Let's all wear headphones but not Judy, because she's never done this before.' So we all sat around so we were very close to each other so I could hear it acoustically. We finished the first tune and Red said, 'I knew my music would come back,' so he was into it.

"Marshal was really fantastic. It was all first takes because I was too nervous to do anything else. After the first take and this is revealing of Marshal, I went back in the booth and we all listened to it. It was great and I couldn't believe it because it was me on piano with my heroes. They all walked out to do the next tune and I couldn't move. I just kept sitting there. Marshal came back, very sweet, patted my hand, and leaned down and whispered, 'We're lucky to get one that good on the first take' and took my hand and led me back in and we did the rest of it. He was in *Ain't Misbehavin'* (musical show) at the time and I went to see a recording with him and he got up and came out and gave me a kiss. He was an absolute pussycat after that. He was really good to me." Reflecting on Marshal's known liking for the ladies, Judy laughed, "I was a bit young for him at that time. I got a Grammy nomination out of that."

Eventually Judy took the plunge and moved to New York City. "I first went to New York with my father during the telephone company strike when I was 17. He was a supervisor so he had to be there. I swear I stepped off the plane, my foot touched the tarmac, and I thought I'm going to live here. I loved it so much. I've always had a lot of energy and I grew up with people saying that I was intense, which was always irritating to me, so when I got to New York it actually relaxed me. I finally felt I was in my element. I knew then I wanted to live in New York.

"Originally I was living in both places. I was going back and forth. I had bought a house when I was very young. I was 22 and single. I sold that and bought a place, actually in New York. This was 1985. Everybody except the old guys thought I was crazy because I was giving up a steady gig at Disneyland with 'retirement', 100 per cent dental care, 100 per cent medical cover, something that doesn't exist anywhere else in the States. That was really something.

"When John Hammond turned me down, he said, 'Well, nobody knows who you are – who have you played with?' It was true, I hadn't done any sideman work. I left devastated but thought, 'people are going to know who I am, so I've got to just go sit-in.' I looked at the paper and there was Roy Eldridge at Jimmy Ryan's so I got in a cab and went over and listened to him play. He came over to the bar and kinda looked at me because I was pretty conspicuous. I said, 'Hello, Mr. Eldridge, my name's Judy Carmichael and I play stride piano' and he started laughing. To him, I looked like a surfer girl. I had this long blonde hair, tanned, wearing a little sun dress and Roy said, 'Oh, really, play "Handful of Keys" and called the band because he was getting a drink and he said, 'Get off the stand, this chick thinks she plays stride.' I did it and the crowd went wild – people jumped and screamed. It was a real Hollywood moment. One of the great moments of my life and everyone was saying, 'play more.' Roy was pushing people away, saying, 'She proved her point' and pulled me off the stage, sat me down and said, 'What's your name again? Why are you here?' I said I've got this record, I'm trying to get somebody to buy it. He said, 'I want you to do two things. I want you to go to a place called Bradley's and introduce yourself to Tommy Flanagan and I want you to play "Handful of Keys" for him, that's downtown, and then I want you to go uptown to a guy called Dick Wellstood at Hanratty's.'

"So I went the next night to Wellstood. It was funny because only Dick and the owner were there and Dick was hilarious, really funny. So I played and he was really cute. He put his head down, and said, 'Oh, she's cut me on my own gig.' The next night I went to see Tommy and Roy had already called him so when I went in, Tommy walked right over and said, 'The word's so hot on you, I know who you are, I know what you're gonna play.' He was so generous. He played 'Lush Life' and I was going to slit my wrists, and he then played this beautiful oral sorbet that made the juxtaposition to 'Handful of Keys' extremely hip and set it up beautifully. He introduced me and made a big deal about it. He said, 'She's new in town, we're going to welcome her from LA.' Whenever he'd see me after that, he and Basie would always go like this (stride hand movement) and that was their hello."

After Judy debuted officially at Hanratty's, bolstered by a half-page press feature authored by John Wilson, her relationship with Wellstood foundered, as this extract from his biography indicates.

> *From time to time Dick (Wellstood) complained that artists he had brought into Hanratty's drew larger crowds than he did. He was particularly troubled by the success of Judy Carmichael, a young, attractive pianist of decidedly modest skills who also affected a stride style of piano. She had attracted some attention in the media (primarily because she was a woman playing what was perceived as a 'man's' style of piano) and Dick booked her into Hanratty's. She packed the place with a coterie of her fans.*
>
> From *Giant Strides – The Legacy of Dick Wellstood* by Edward N. Meyer, Scarecrow Pres, Lanham, Maryland, and London, 1999

When I asked Judy to elaborate on this breakdown of regard, she said, "He alternated, frankly, between being an absolute pussycat and lovely with me, to being enormously threatened and extremely mean and cruel. It was alcohol, and everybody thinks that's really cool after drugs but it's not. He bad-mouthed me, told his musician friends not to play with me. He drew a line in the sand. See, I was getting all this attention. I think Dick genuinely liked me but when he had a lot to drink, it wasn't about me, I think it was his bitterness, understandably, about the business. I went to hear him one time and the people were talking and being rude, and it hurt me more to see it happening to him than it did to me. I wanted to stand up and scream, 'Don't you realise who this man is?'

"His behaviour was so different from the treatment I'd gotten with Basie and Sarah. She would have me over to a party at her house in LA. I'd be the only white person there and at some significant moment, she'd say, 'Judy, play a tune' and everybody would growl. I remember Freddie Hubbard just looked at me and probably thought, 'Oh God, it's going to be "Claire de Lune" or something.' She would just giggle like mad and watch these people being surprised. She was actually setting up these situations to show me off. How did this come about? Harold was with her then and we had just done our record and Harold kept playing Sarah's own stuff when they were on the band bus. She said, 'I'm sick of me, don't you have anything else?' He says, 'I've got this thing we did with Judy Carmichael.' He put it on and Sarah started dancing on the bus. Harold called me and told me all about it and after that Sarah sorta requested a meeting."

Judy told me how older musicians might be encouraging but also quite intimidating. After all, Roy hadn't given her time to warm up at Ryan's. "It could be very threatening and difficult but you'd have to rise to it," she said, citing other occasions when stride veteran Joe Turner threw her in the deep end. "Like he'd start 'Handful of Keys' and then he'd say 'I don't want to do this ... oh, look, Judy Carmichael's in the audience. Come up here, sweetie' and then not give me a choice about what I was going to play, with my hands still cold. One time, I went to a party that Harold invited me to that was given by one of the members of the Tonight Show band so it was all musicians, the cream of the Los Angeles guys. Sarah was there with her band, different people were sitting-in, Leonard Feather played piano, different people did stuff and they asked Sarah to sing. She only sang because she had her trio with her, that's Mike Wofford, Andy Simpkins and Harold. Then they all said, 'Sing another' but she goes, 'I don't feel like it but Judy will play a tune.' I'm thinking, what? I've got to follow Sarah but nobody knew who I was but they all had to listen because Sarah said I was going to play. And I played and that was a huge gift and it was also her perverse way, because I think she thought I'd chicken out because it was too threatening but I did it. It's a metaphor for all of us. We get these opportunities to do whatever it is so we have to jump on them.

"So then I went to New York and started getting some attention. That's also when I started to form ideas about how I'd pursue the rest of my career. I did a bit of sideman work and it was OK but I was certainly not mad about it." There's a view that men seldom hire women in the jazz business, I suggested. "Absolutely," she concurred. "Marian (McPartland) said that too. We talked about it. In fairness to men, if you're out on the road, you have to have an extra room for the woman. Also you're not one of the 'boys'. I'm very comfortable with men but a lot of women aren't and it changes things. When I was at Disneyland I was in a dressing room with ten men and I knew when to leave, what to do. Soon as they brought in a girlfriend, everything changed. People got cranky. I'm not blaming the men. It's a very testosterone-filled business and you're either a woman who gets that and adapts or you don't."

This brought up the wider issue of Judy's single status. "I'm not married. I've dated musicians. I've always been a great observer and I do think things through. For my entire 20s I said if this music thing doesn't work out, I'll do something else. A friend took me out for lunch on my 30th birthday and said, 'Judy, if you're going to do something else, now's the time.' She was right and to my horror I realised I wasn't going to do anything else and that wasn't good news. I realised, 'Oh God, I really love this.' I'll probably never make even enough money to support myself. I probably can't have a family. I was hyper-aware of the vagaries of this business. I knew a lot of people were doing a lot of drugs and drinking. So I made real conscious choices." One of those choices was to eschew sideman jobs. "I thought, 'Well, I'm not going to be a great sideman'. Men have been good to me. Warren Vaché, bless him, tried to have me as a sideman. I'm just not a particularly good sideman. I don't have those skills. I realised that when he hired me once. I'm not going to play a million tunes, like a super-sideman; I'm going to play two hundred, perfectly. So that was the career choice. That's when I started producing my own concerts and my own records."

Let's go back to John Hammond's expectations. What's it like being female and white in the jazz business? "There isn't anybody who hasn't made it an issue," she stated, firmly. "I've had enormous prejudice against me. The only people who weren't prejudiced were the blacks. I've had people tell me they came to hear me when I first came to New York, saw me and turned around and walked out because they just assumed I couldn't play. Other people told me that they'd hear me on radio, then see my picture and think it was faked.

"I've made my living by being very entrepreneurial. I had day jobs before I played piano. I had a couple of jobs in college but since then I've never done anything but play piano. I haven't taught, except those rare occasions when I give piano lessons. I either charge an obscene amount of money for someone to have that time or if some kid who's serious and wants to do it, I give it to 'em free. I was fortunate in that I connected with people in other areas of the arts, that's people who don't consider themselves jazz fans. For instance, I play the Aspen Design Conference rather than the Aspen Music festival. It was actually something that Phil Schaap, the writer and producer, said to me early on and it was a great piece of advice. 'Your focus, your goal, is to have people want to come and hear "Judy Carmichael", not to hear a jazz pianist or a stride pianist. You want to be known for being "Judy Carmichael".

Isn't 'stride pianist' too limiting a description, inevitably self-defining? "I've never seen myself as just a stride pianist. I've always seen myself as a jazz pianist. In the early years it was a thrill that I was carrying on this tradition. But I've always played what I liked. I love bebop and I see myself evolving more into the swing thing. One of the things about singing for me is that it's given me a key to a different way of playing that I want. It's not all stride.

'Joe Cohn (g) & Judy Carmichael (p), Judy Carmichael Group JazzAscona, Ascona, Switzerland, July 2007.
Courtesy Judy Carmichael

"By the time I got to New York the stride players that were around were a minimum 30 years older than me. There was Dick Hyman, Dick Wellstood, Jay McShann, and they had a very different approach to stride than I do. They had a different mind-set, a different rhythmic feel. Basie was my first stride player, I'm not all in to a million notes, not into that kind of bombast, dynamics are always important to me. It's significant that my supporters were Tommy Flanagan, Hank Jones, Sarah Vaughan, and Barry Harris, much later, they were all boppers. They would ask me to sit-in on a place like Bradley's, that was a bebop gig where you'd never have a stride player play so I think they were hearing something even before I knew it. A lot of stride players I hear, especially now, they're playing like 'Boy, this stuff is hard.' I always wanted it to be just something that I use as my vocabulary. I got to know Joe Turner and those guys. I feel fortunate to have known these older black people. It was a love-fest with these guys. If you played great, that's what counted. They weren't really trying to put somebody down.

"Am I re-creating an old style? That was never me. I was the opposite of that. I think this kind of music – stride – is timeless if you do it right. I think it's got an appeal and it doesn't seem necessarily like old music. I see myself as very contemporary," she affirmed. Judy's entrepreneurial streak has taken her well away from the usual round of clubs and one-off casual gigs. "I've really made my living for concert audiences. I don't do a lot of jazz clubs. I've created my own thing. I'm starting to do more jazz festivals now. The early part of my career, I did Nice and Breda but they always wanted you to play with lots of different people. I didn't enjoy that, didn't think that was what I was best at. To put me with a bebop band, I'm not gonna be their favourite piano player. I'm not Warren Vaché, who can play beautifully in every situation, and make it work. People were asking me for those gigs but it didn't pay very well and it wasn't a lifestyle I wanted. Jazz parties? I did one and wanted to kill myself afterwards. That was really bad. It's where I first met Harry Allen. A woman was sitting in the front row knitting, people were talking, that kind of thing, and yes, I know they're not all like that. If someone asked me now, I'm sure it would be really nice."

In this post-feminist world, a woman's appearance is still relevant, a point with which Judy concurs. "It's a case of assessing what you've got," she said, smiling. "I have

Judy Carmichael (p), with Harry Allen (ts), JazzAscona, Ascona, Switzerland, July 2008.
Photo by Chris Lee.
Courtesy Chris Lee.

an ability to be funny on stage and I sing now so these skills give me a much broader appeal. I have people come because they're enjoying that side of me. The days of the piano player sitting there not saying anything are gone; people don't have that kind of attention span. I don't have that kind of attention span."

Finally, we spoke about Judy's parallel career in radio and her weekly show. How had it come about, I wondered? "This was something I started 14 or 15 years ago. I raise all the money for it because it's for PBS. Radio people really liked my voice and I've done a bit of voice-over work. I did Marian McPartland's show and her producer said, 'You should have your own show,' so I gave it a lot of thought. I'm very interested in the creative process and got very tired of most American shows being about promoting things, so my fantasy was to have people talk about how much jazz has inspired them, to broaden the audience for the music. If people heard a Robert Redford or a Billy Joel talk about loving jazz, maybe a younger audience would get it." That said, Judy has succeeded in attracting the likes of the "extremely bright" Redford on to her show as well as classical musicians such as the pianists Simon Tedeschi and John Lythgoe, the

Judy Carmichael (p), UK 2008. Photo by Gordon Sapsed. Courtesy Gordon Sapsed.

production process controlled from the ever-present laptop.

"Things have been terrific but it's a huge burden. I'm working on my radio shows in the middle of this engagement. It's technology that makes this possible, of course. I've met people that have been great and inspired me but it's been a Herculean task getting things going. Now it is going and it is popular. People are coming to me now – they want to be on the show. Right now I'm launching on a project to do interviews on stage in front of an audience. It's going to be most likely a TV show as well. This is very exciting, I'm co-producing it. It's going to be at a little theatre in my town of Sag Harbor, called the Bay Street Theatre and we're going to continue the theme of bringing in unexpected people, to talk about ideas, and do some things that are really unusual."

Favourite players? "Bill Charlap, he's my kind of player. I'd go to hear Bill anywhere and I have. Same went for John Bunch. Brad Mehldau? No, too intellectual. Keith Jarrett? No, definitely not. All that standing up and sitting down, all that histrionics really bothers me. It's the opposite of what I'm about. Obviously he can play but I went to

Judy Carmichael (p) dancing with Alan Barnes, UK, c. 2005. Courtesy Judy Carmichael.

his Carnegie Hall concert and it felt like everybody thought they were having a religious experience. It was all tremendously pretentious to me. I didn't like it at all." Judy's tastes are nearer the mainstream, in fact. "I love Scott Hamilton. He's incapable of playing an insincere note. Just like Chris Flory, the guitar player. Chris and (saxophonist) Mike Hashim and I have played together for 20 years now, not every day obviously. Warren Vaché's one of the smartest people I know. I'm a big fan. And (UK saxophonist) Alan Barnes, who I don't get to see often enough. I tell Alan I take the gigs with him just for the car ride, just to spend time with him. My fantasy is to have a TV series with Alan. He's a fabulous musician and a fascinating man."

Judy Carmichael is a one-woman whirlwind, multi-tasking madly, juggling her roles as pianist, singer, bandleader, recording artist, radio producer, TV show host, label boss, and concert promoter, and is seemingly possessed of boundless energy. More to the point, she's an engaging companion and "a polished exponent of stride" (Clive Davis again) who, as I can confirm having heard her perform a number of times, never fails to captivate audiences and produce music of genuine worth.

First published as 'Judy Carmichael in Her Stride' in *Jazz Journal International* in April 2010

Judy Carmichael, Australian tour, c. 2007. Photo by Jill Duhon. Courtesy Judy Carmichael.

Tardo Hammer

Tardo Hammer, Vaché Brothers Quintet, JazzAscona, Switzerland, July 2008. Photo by Chris Lee. Courtesy Chris Lee.

Although I was already familiar with his recordings on the Sharp Nine label, my first in-person encounter with the pianist Tardo Hammer was at the Marbella Jazz Festival in May 2005. He was working with Annie Ross as her Musical Director (a role that he continues to fulfil) and also played a trio concert with Len Skeat on bass and drummer Bobby Worth. What I heard I liked and we arranged the interview from which this piece developed during his Marbella stay. Since then I've been fortunate enough to observe him performing with cornetist Warren Vaché's stirring quintet at the JazzAscona Festival and again with Annie during appearances in New York and here in the UK. We've kept in contact by e-mail and I've been impressed with his thoughtful, clear-eyed comments. Even more happily, I was able to arrange for him to play a well-received trio concert in my local parish church in Pinner where I live. Now married with a little boy, Tardo stays busy around New York, and is slowly building an international reputation, touring regularly with Ms Ross or with Warren Vaché's fine quintet.

New York pianist Tardo Hammer may be one of that city's better-kept jazz secrets, to coin a cliché, yet those in the know have few doubts about his qualities. "He's just a gem of a player," said cornetist Warren Vaché. Listen to his recordings, hear him in action, most often with singer Annie Ross ("We work when she wants to work") or multi-reed specialist Charles Davis, and you'll soon understand Vaché's enthusiasm.

In person, Hammer is likeable yet laconic, his playing sure-footed and incisive, with a refined harmonic sense and in-built propensity for swing. What's more he has eschewed the temptation to emulate McCoy Tyner or Herbie Hancock, leaning less fashionably towards the great bebop maestros for inspiration while remaining quite definitely his own man. "The kind of music I like to play, and the musicians I like to play with are always changing things and finding new, surprising and unexpected sounds. Perhaps the form is old but we expect the content to be new," he explained.

When we sat down to consider his career, it seemed sensible to settle the origins of Hammer's distinctive first name. Was it redolent of some far-flung Middle Eastern connection, I wondered? "No," said Hammer, "it's a derivative of Richard. It started about the seventh grade, in the Spanish class. For that I became 'Ricardo' and after a while that morphed into Tardo." That's that, then. As we meandered through the meat and bones of his jazz life, it became clear that Hammer has no grand career plan, more that he's typical of many of today's jazz musicians in responding to short-term opportunities – "bits and pieces", in his words – in the absence of long-term affiliations.

Tardo Hammer (p), Hotel Guadalpin, Marbella, Spain, 13 May 2005. Interview during the Marbella Jazz Festival. Photo by Peter Vacher.

Tardo Hammer (p) with Len Skeat (b), Marbella Jazz Festival concert, Conservatory, Marbella, Spain, 12 May 2005. Photo by Peter Vacher.

Hammer is a New Yorker through and through, born in Queens in February 1958, and now living in Upper Manhattan. As we talked, he alluded often to a lost period when 'giants walked abroad' in and around New York and tyro musicians could 'hang out' and learn the jazz lexicon by osmosis. "I guess the most famous guy that I met earliest was (pianist) Duke Jordan," he recalled. "This would have been when I was about 16 or 17 years old. Duke was playing in little clubs and there'd be, like, four or five people in the

Tardo Hammer (p) and **Grant Stewart** (ts), Grant Stewart band, Soka University of America, Aliso Viejo, CA, 2008. Courtesy Tardo Hammer.

place. I was probably the only one listening to every single note so he learned to recognise me. He'd always come and sit and drink his vodka. One day, he said, 'Can you play the next set? I've got to make a phone call.' I said, 'No, I don't know what I'm doing.' Duke said, 'Last week you told me you played some piano, now this week I'm asking you to play piano and you say no. Let me tell you something, from now on if anyone asks you to play, get up and play. I'm gonna ask you again – will you play the next set for me?' I said, 'Sure.' John Ore was the bass player. He was scary. I'd learned to play maybe three songs but I think it was OK. Nobody said anything afterwards. I figured they hated me but looking back, for 16, it was passable."

Tardo was given piano lessons as a youngster, took against them and changed to clarinet before dabbling with guitar. When his schoolmates all adopted guitars and began to play as a group, he was reassigned to the piano, having already begun to explore his father's jazz record collection. Other friends came to listen: "We'd put on records, play them and then we'd pick up the thing and play it again. I don't think people do that now. We started a little band. There was an older kid, Rick Hupp, played trombone and guitar. He was the best one of us. He had charts of Charlie Parker tunes, bebop things. A friend sent us on a New Year's gig, which was a big mistake. We didn't know one song that people knew. They just hated us and they fired us *before* midnight. It was wild."

After a short spell in Akron, Ohio, and by now mad for jazz, Hammer left High School to enter the early admissions programme at Purchase College, part of the State University of New York. "I just wanted to get to New York, and Purchase is in Westchester County, about 20 miles from New York. I went there for about a year and a half. Ten hours a day of sonatas and no jazz," he said. Anxious to get among the action, "I took a leave of absence, which I'm still on, and moved to town to a loft. I was barely 18."

While studying at Purchase, Hammer hooked up with Tristano disciple and pianist, Sal Mosca. "I went with Sal for about three years. Sal was a mini-Lennie." Hammer recalled meeting Tristano at concerts when, "he was starting to get a little crazy; he had all these women students that just idolised him. They all believed and said the same things. Very culty. He was hell-bent on getting a teaching system where everybody would do their own thing because that's what the great musicians do. It must have driven him a little nuts as these people all started coming out the same. He and Sal would show you the raw materials and say put it together your way," he said. "You learn to understand the things you prepare may not be the things that work when you get into a situation. Jazz is an improvised music. Sometimes you surprise yourself. That's the best."

In 1980, these Tristano connections landed him a gig with tenorist Warne Marsh. Looking back, he said, "I wish I knew then what I know now. Marsh was intimidating and not rhythmically helpful to play with. He was kinda odd – it was like the drummer was your slave. 'I can go any way I want, how come you weren't a metronome?' I had heard recordings of him when he had been out in California where he was really firing. We never got to that. Great player, though."

Another interesting association was triggered when Hammer ventured down to the Surf Maid on Bleecker Street. "That was a little thing with a bass player named Ted Wald. He played with Bird. White guy, shaved head. I played in there sometimes; it paid about $8 or $13. One time, (alto-saxophonist) C. Sharpe wandered in, played three tunes and walked out. I was, like, 'Wow, that's the best guy I ever played with in real life.' Later I spent a lot of time playing with him. Recordings? This is another mentality. C. said, 'This guy from Japan wants to record me and I said you gotta bring a wheelbarrow full of money.' He's just about on the street and when the break comes, it's not enough money! I think he had a habit and didn't want to get away from his stuff but that doesn't explain the record thing. He finally went to France just before he died (in 1990) and played on a big alto summit with Jackie McLean and had a great time. He was completely uncorrupted. A true artist."

Hammer reserved his greatest appreciation for trumpeter Bill Hardman and tenorist Junior Cook. "In the late eighties, I got some calls from them to play with their quintet. In contrast to Tristano, these guys were funny, funny people and they hung out.

Tardo Hammer (p), Grant Stewart band, Dusseldorf, Germany, c. 2009. Courtesy Tardo Hammer.

We just played places in town, a lot of times at the Flamingo Lounge in Brooklyn. That was a black club, really something. It was supposed to be a 10pm to 3am gig. Junior was always late. In fact I thought you were supposed to be late, that's what the cool guys do. Junior would come in at 11, we'd go 'til four. He was great, and really accessible. Him and C. Sharpe both. They would be out every night playing somewhere; if they weren't working, they were looking to play. Junior and I had a Thursday-night gig together for about six months at a little club. People would come up and play. Junior would keep it going and when it was time to get everybody off, he'd pull something out that was too hard and too fast. They'd kinda slink away. He had the power and presence to do that. Junior was able to establish enough real swing, a real groove with complexity combined."

Hardman was another of those senior musicians who encouraged younger players. "One of the nicest people I ever met," said Hammer firmly. "No airs, he was completely unpretentious. He really looked after people. I met him first at the Star Café, a place on 23rd Street, where I met Junior too. There'd be a jam session until all hours. I was playing and I didn't know who Bill was, and he just gave me a nod. 'How you doin'?' He'd have everyone over to his house, guys like Jim Rotondi and Eric Alexander, Joe Farnsworth. They couldn't even play yet, hope they won't mind me saying that. They were fresh in town. He didn't do lessons for pay but he'd be practising, and there'd be trumpet players there and they'd be practising together. He just wanted to see the music continue and thrive. A rare person."

Another association, briefer but no less memorable, was with Johnny Griffin, the little giant of the tenor, in 1986. "This was a last-minute booking. They put a rhythm section together for him in upstate Rochester. He would swing the band

Johnny Griffin (ts); **Tardo Hammer** (p); **Keith Copeland** (d), unknown location, Rochester, New York, 1987. Courtesy Tardo Hammer.

harder than the bass player or the drummer and make it easy for you to be in time, and just ride on that. Junior Cook had the same thing, he could swing the whole band.

"Around 1989, I started working with Art Farmer and Clifford Jordan. You know the singer Marilyn Moore? She asked Art if I could sit in and he said, 'Have him send me a tape.' I got this cruddy cassette, put about three tunes on it and put it in the mail. I got a handwritten letter back: 'I will be calling you when I come to New York. I really enjoyed the tape.' I was with Art for many of his stateside gigs between 1989 and 1992. We always played at Sweet Basil and occasionally out of town. Usually with Clifford Jordan, later on Jerome Richardson. Drummers were Smitty Smith or Carl Allen. I'd be sitting with Art, not knowing what to say, and he certainly wouldn't lubricate the conversation any. He'd just be happy to sit there and not say a word." Perhaps surprisingly, given its personnel, Hammer says the Farmer-Jordan group failed to swing. "Really didn't swing like Bill and Junior's, not even close." Why not? "That was a paper-laden band. (Bassist) Vinnie Burke came down and he went into a rant about how you can't have improvisation if you've got paper in front of you … I never would have said that to those guys but he was right. When you engage with your eyes that way, there's a bit of oral detachment that goes with that."

If we liken Hammer's career to a relay race, then the next giant to grab the baton

Tardo Hammer Trio, Village Gate, Greenwich Village, New York, 1989. *L-r:* Tardo Hammer (p); Dennis Irwin (b); Leroy Williams (d). Courtesy Tardo Hammer.

was Ahmad Jamal's former drummer Vernel Fournier. "Vernel hired me to go to Japan, with Victor Sproles on bass, in 1990. We played the same club for eight weeks. He's another guy that was really nice and regular. He'd been in Chicago but I think he'd been working at a Sears store or something. He came to New York, and wandered in where I was playing, and started calling me up with work. I think he felt that Ahmad Jamal's sound was his as well. It was a different way of playing the piano than I was used to but it was very educational. He'd say playing in two would be freer than playing in four. For him, it really was – he'd play the most beautiful two. If you went into four from those vamps, it would be like going up a gear."

In between times, the pianist was a member of drummer Danny D'Imperio's Metropolitan Bopera House. "That was a good band," he said, before telling me that they were collectively sued by the Metropolitan Opera. "They got a new exec and he was from advertising so he said there might be some confusion there (over the similarity in the names) so we all got served papers. Must have been 11 or 12 of us. Anybody that ever recorded or was advertised as appearing with the band. I woke up, some retired guy served me papers. Then the phone started ringing. First it was (trumpeter) John Marshall, then it was people from the newspapers. I think we made a few funny quotes. Next day we actually made the front page. John and I showed up in court; the other guys defaulted. They were intimidated so they signed things saying, 'we promise never to do it again and we're sorry'. The judge didn't like the Met's very high-powered, high-price attorneys, and threw it out. I think we're sworn not to reveal the terms of our settlement. It wasn't great but we made a few dollars …"

Hammer is pretty hard on "career musicians who come out of schools with briefcases

The Metropolitan Bopera House, Saratoga NY, early 1990s. *L-r:* Tom Melito (d); John Webber (b); John Marshall (t); Ralph Lalama (ts); Tardo Hammer (p). Courtesy Tardo Hammer.

John Marshall Quintet, Obing, Germany, August 2001. *L-r*: John Marshall (t); Doug Sides (d); John Goldsby (b); Tardo Hammer (p); Ferdinand Povel (ts). Courtesy Tardo Hammer.

and suits – and press kits!" and expresses his disbelief that they should have been awarded record dates. "Why would they need those guys when they could have got Charlie Rouse (who was playing $60 gigs up in Jersey when I worked with him), or Junior Cook?" he said. "Those guys were not exploited as well as they could have been at the prices they were working for. There's a lot less of them to work with now. Maybe Charles Davis is the last adult saxophone player in New York!

"He's playing tenor and some soprano these days, and we play together a bunch now. He's straight-ahead but he's always got something new. We had a quintet thing on Sundays at a little space called The Zipper on West 37th St. Jimmy Wormworth was our drummer, Lee Hudson on bass, and the trumpeter was Duane Clements. He's from Texas, very spicy. I think he was a mentor to Roy Hargrove at one time."

What with the Charles Davis connection which runs to occasional European tours and engagements at clubs like Smoke and Small's, his work with Annie Ross, continuing involvement with Bopera trumpeter John Marshall, solo forays into Europe, teaching at the Lucy Moses School on West 67th Street and a flurry of trio albums on Sharp Nine, Tardo Hammer seems about as well set as any freelance can expect to be these days.

"Ideally, I should do more trio tours but it's just a little more agitation to have to deal with the external stuff so the lazy me would rather be the piano player in a good quartet or quintet," he said, smiling. Thinking back to his early experience with the simpler modal structures prevalent in the seventies, he reflected, "For some of us moving forward meant developing the ability to deal with more complex musical language than that, so if we looked up and saw Charlie Parker or Art Tatum, I don't think of that as backward-looking." For now, "I'm just trying to get better at playing the piano. That's my major ambition. Sometimes just what you want to hear comes out. But that's not often, for anybody. We're all trying to be able to speak in our own voices. It's hard to do."

Tardo Hammer (p), JazzAscona, Switzerland, July 2005. Photo by Jonathan Farber. Courtesy Jonathan Farber.

First published as
'Tardo Hammer: Boppin' Among Giants' in
Coda, September–October 2006

Byron Stripling

Byron Stripling, personal promo, USA, 2006. Courtesy Byron Stripling.

Byron Stripling was a featured performer at JazzAscona in June 2007 and proved to be a rewarding interviewee when we met at his hotel overlooking Lake Maggiore. Since then, he has continued in his role as the Artistic Director of the Columbus Jazz Orchestra, creating broadly based musical programmes and often appearing as a much-lauded guest artist with other well-known orchestras. After we had spoken, he provided photographs to Coda where this interview appeared but sadly we have failed to keep in contact in more recent times. His Executive Director at CJO described Byron as 'one of the greats of the trumpet and a versatile entertainer' and that seems about right to me.

You sense that Byron Stripling has all his ducks in a row, as we say over here in England. Blessed with a sure technique on his instrument and a restless creative spirit, he has a plum job and a balanced home life. This is a trumpet player who travels with his laptop and his mobile phone: in touch at all times, and seemingly at ease with himself and his situation. Quite the contrast to the usual stereotype of the struggling jazz musician, wouldn't you say?

We talked in the spacious hotel room assigned to him by the authorities in Ascona, Switzerland, on the morning following his performance at the festival. Stripling was heading a quartet and impressed everyone with the intensity of his improvisations, the sure-footed way he shaped his set, and lastly but not least, for me, anyway, the leavening of humour that coloured his presentation. His blues lyrics are just plain funny. Stripling likes to communicate, and seems to enjoy exchanging banter with members of the audience. He's relaxed and outgoing, quick to spot what works and happy to adapt.

Closer to, he exudes physical well-being: he's a powerful, healthy figure who you suspect likes to work out at the gym and keeps a bowl of fruit on the table for more than mere decoration. He's also thoughtful, articulate, and expressive in conversation, his stories carrying an actor's flair for mimicking the voices of others. He talks about his responsibilities with some pride. Before we settled down to consider his career at large, Stripling handed me a brochure for the upcoming season of concerts by the Columbus Jazz Orchestra and explained that he's the Artistic Director of the Orchestra, based happily in Columbus, Ohio. The guest artists already set ranged from soul diva Mavis Staples, via ragtimer Terry Waldo, to trumpeters Roy Hargrove and Terrence Blanchard, and on to reedman Ken Peplowski and Peter Appleyard who were to celebrate Basie, Benny and the Duke. Phew!

Apart from envying the citizens of Columbus their musical good fortune and deducing that the CJO must be pretty versatile if it is to properly support such a wide variety of musical presentations, it's easy to see how Stripling's own varied experience

Byron Stripling, CJO Artistic Director, with the Columbus Jazz Orchestra, Columbus OH, c. mid-2000s. Courtesy Byron Stripling.

must have informed these choices. The briefest of glances at his CV reveals a career that has embraced academic study, work with touring big bands, theatre pit jobs, studio sessions, stage appearances and small-group jazz, with a plethora of recordings along the way.

A number of themes emerged as our conversation developed. First, that Stripling's parents had aspirations for him to become a professional music educator rather than a 'feckless' jobbing trumpeter; second, that key individuals, notably Clark Terry, interceded beneficially on his behalf and finally, that each phase of his career has provided what he calls 'learning experiences'. In other words, Stripling sees his career to date as a journey, with diversions here and there, the sum of his experiences helping to prepare him for his present role. "They did a search for an Artistic Director and a lot of people auditioned to be the conductor of the Columbus Jazz Orchestra. It's an organisation that's been around for over 30 years. I won the audition," he said. "I knew I wanted to be part of a community that supports a big band and says yes to jazz. There's (state) government support, there's business support and all kinds of sponsor support. I tell them who I want to hire and the theme of the shows we want to do, and I get to shape things the way I want. That's my responsibility. I design the season with my Executive Director. I usually try to get something written for most concerts, rather than just offer a throwback. Our programme is put together like a symphony series – we have 2,500 subscribers."

Stripling moved with his wife and two young daughters to Columbus, Ohio's biggest city, although initially reluctant to leave New York. "The whole scene has changed," he explained, and went on to describe the ways in which freelance session work in the Big Apple had dwindled with the advent of electronics. "Don't get me wrong. New York is the greatest city in the world. It still has an incredible energy but you don't *have* to be there to be a jazz musician."

He said he's happy to embrace his family responsibilities but cautioned, "I had to find models of musicians that live the kind of life I want to live. People who have families, who have a house and are responsible. Like Jon Faddis or Dick Hyman, for example. I'm the breadwinner and I have a responsibility not to get drunk or stay out until four in the morning." He smiled, and then confided, looking back to the earlier part of his career, "I loved being on the road. I still love it – don't tell my wife – what better life could I have? I love being out." Given the circumstances that surrounded our interview, with Stripling hired to play with a compatible all-star group over a week-long period in a lovely location, five-star accommodation thrown in, and an appreciative public on hand, it's easy to understand that view.

Stripling's personal journey began in Atlanta in April 1961, this early location succeeded by others in Kentucky, Colorado, Minnesota, St. Louis and finally, Texas. The explanation for all this movement? "My father was a classical singer who wanted a Master's in Voice so he went where the scholarships were, first to the University of Kentucky, then for his Doctorate to the University of Colorado, before taking a series of college jobs, the third in Texas where he retired."

Stripling senior "had an intense love of all kinds of music so I'd hear classical during the day and jazz at night. To relax he'd always play Miles, Count Basie, and Duke Ellington, they were like his big three. He loved the Sarah Vaughan record with Basie; I knew all the solos because he played that constantly. Also he had Louis's 'Hello Dolly' which I heard a lot. So I said I want to play trumpet and he went out and bought a trumpet for $200 which was a lot of money for a college professor. I was 12." For his parents there was a kind of race pride in supporting the great black artists of the day so "we went as a family to see Sarah Vaughan, we saw Duke Ellington three or four times, I saw Count Basie often, as well as opera singer Leontyne Price. We went to Ella (Fitzgerald) one time which was great, saw her with Keter Betts, Tommy Flanagan and Bobby Durham on drums, Al Grey on trombone, this is the opening set, and then Roy Eldridge walks out. I didn't even know he was on the bill. I'll never forget he played 'Stardust' that night. It gave me chills."

Once their son had become set on music as a career and gained a place at the prestigious Eastman College of Music, the pressure was on Stripling to conform to his parents' aspirational stereotype. "My father really wanted me to be a doctor. He didn't know what a musician could do besides *teach*. He paid for me to be at Eastman, worked his butt off and wanted me to finish school. I never finished school! I did three years. When you come up as a musician you can't tell your parents what it is you're going to do. You just know you want to do it. My parents were constantly saying, 'What are you going to do with your life? We're glad you're playing with Woody Herman – we love that band – but you're (only) making $325 a week. We think you should leave the band and go back to Eastman, get your degree and go teach in a college.'

"My parents were very supportive, but they worried for me. Like once I got to New York, I called up my mom and told her, 'I just played Carnegie Hall last night with this new band (Carnegie Hall Jazz Band), made a ton of money' then I called her up another time, 'Mom, I just *soloed* at Carnegie Hall with the New York Pops Orchestra; I was the featured soloist!' So after five minutes of accolades, she goes, 'But what are you doing tomorrow?' 'Nothing,' I said. 'And the next day?' 'Still, nothing – actually I don't have anything for a couple of weeks, I'll be home practising.' They just didn't understand the concept of a freelance. You have to have something to fall back on, they said. I said I'd rather fall back on a sword! I changed my major at Eastman to performance, which is a worthless degree: I wanted to have no (safety) net. It's like jumping off a building and building your wings on the way down. I knew that would be best for me and inspire me to work harder. That's the way I had to do it."

It was Clark Terry who encouraged Stripling to escape the classroom for the first time. How come? "The Eastman Jazz Ensemble was run by a guy named Raeburn

Trumpeters **Red Rodney**, **Claudio Roditi**, **Byron Stripling**, **Clark Terry**, **Roy Hargrove**, probably New York, c.1980s. Courtesy Byron Stripling.

Wright. He was the former Director of Radio City Music Hall. He was incredible for the school, a great arranger, and he had high expectations of us. He said, 'When you come to rehearsal, on time is late, and early is on time.' So you went there five to ten minutes early, in your seat, tuned ready to go. That helped me later in life. You could arrange whatever you wanted, from jazz to pop, but it had to be good. Clark came as a guest soloist and he heard me play. I was a freshman. He heard something there. He said, 'I'm putting together a band. I want you to play.'

"To be in a band and hear him every night, that was a treat. (Alto saxophonist) Chris Woods was our manager; he and Clark would play three or four tunes together. Branford Marsalis was in the band – he became my best buddy – and Tony Lujan on trumpet, Conrad Herwig, incredible trombone player, John Campbell, great piano player, he went with Mel Tormé for a while, and Michael Baker on drums. He went pop later on and I played for him many times with people like Whitney Houston, and Al Jarreau. That's the kind of gigs I did in New York. I did a lot with Aretha Franklin; I used to contract all her bands.

"What did I learn from Clark? The desire to have an individual sound, being able to affect people with the sound of your instrument. As an encore, he used to play 'When I Fall in Love' on flugel, all by himself. It was like a piece of lush velvet that was rubbing up against your face – it immediately gave you comfort. I learned you can affect people emotionally, not with technique but just with the sound of your instrument. Plus, he's the most fun to be with. It's a case of 'let's have fun and let the audience in on it'. He rode the bus with us and loved to hang out. Me, too."

Back at Eastman and contemplating graduation, Stripling got scared. What to do next? Well, obviously, he contacted Clark again. Rather mysteriously, Terry said, 'Somebody will call you in a couple of days.' "Next thing I know, Lionel Hampton calls me up and says, 'Clark Terry tells me you can play higher than Cat Anderson.' I lied and said, 'Yessir.' He says, 'I'm going to Europe and I want to take you. Clark says you're the man. Let's go.' I call Clark up and say, 'Why are you telling Hamp that I can play higher than Cat?', so Clark says, 'Hamp loves high notes. When you get on the gig play a bunch of high notes, he'll love it.'

"The musical experience was great with Hamp, although the business relationship was not good but that was with his manager Bill Titone. I saw a situation where a lot of guys were really getting screwed financially and otherwise. That's why it was only a year for me. The learning experience was, one, get everything in writing, and two, respect yourself. I think Hamp liked the way I played. After two months, he said, 'I want you to play "When You're Smiling" with me. Have you heard Louis play that?' I hadn't but I said I had, because I wanted to play with Hamp! He said, 'When you make that last note I want you to make it seem like the highest note in the world because that's what Louis would do.' So we did that every night as my feature, just in a small group. I was, maybe, 22 years old.

"As soon as Hamp walked on stage, he brought the people in, gave them a big musical hug. He's playing for *you*, generating excitement and giving out energy. You know what, Hamp could have closed for the Rolling Stones," he laughed. "He'd come out and he'd better them! The band never left the stage until Hamp had the audience in the palm of his hand. The same smile that he'd give, he'd get back. Same with Clark, when he walked out on stage, he was already swinging – that walk of his had a kinda bounce to it. Gates (Hampton) was the same, he never gave less than 100 per cent and he demanded the same of you. That made sense to me. OK, there was too much music and it was too loud but that's cool. Hamp used to tell the audience, right at the beginning, 'We're here for you and we're going to play until five o'clock tomorrow morning.' He meant it."

The next step for Stripling was a year-long sojourn with Woody Herman's band – as the only black member – playing lead trumpet. Once again, Clark Terry played his part. "Clark and Woody were very good friends so I got a bunch of references from him. I got along great with Woody, learned a lot about programming and announcing. He couldn't ride on the bus, though, he was too old, he'd ridden it too much, so he would fly to the gigs. Musically, the book there was pretty incredible, from through the years, like those great arrangements by Ralph Burns. The band was all young guys, my age, my peers," he said, recalling their consternation if and when anyone made a mistake. "It was a big deal. We're all university educated, they'd say – they were mostly from North Texas and Eastman – and 'he made a mistake at letter B. That's horrible. How could he do that?'"

Stripling remembers a somewhat more relaxed response from Basie's musicians to an error of his own when the call came to join that band. On the first night, "I made a big clam in a rest and everybody turned round and laughed. 'Sounded good, kid. Keep going, we didn't care if you miss a note – just swing!'" He had joined the Count Basie Orchestra, the ultimate home for the proverbial road rat, forever on the move, its ranks still packed with Basie veterans, in 1984. "This was a whole different thing. Basie had passed away about a month before I got there. The band had these jobs, probably paying $100,000 because Basie could get whatever he wanted. Now the promoters are saying 'I'm not paying that because Basie is not there. Who's the leader?' We were just going to have (tenorist) Eric Dixon as leader. So we say, 'It's the exact same guys. We got a piano player who used to sub for Basie. We'll be fine.' The promoter says, 'Great, I'll have you but I'm not paying that money.' It goes down maybe from $100,000 to $10,000, which is a big thing. Nobody took a break in pay but what they quickly found was the band did need real leadership, not necessarily for the band but for the promoters.

"The first person they picked was Thad Jones. The decision was made by the office. I felt he was great for the band. I idolised him but he was maybe not a good fit for the

Count Basie Orchestra, directed by Frank Foster, agency promo, USA, 1988. *Standing, rear*: Robert Trowers (tb); Dave Gibson (d); Carl 'Ace' Carter (p); Bill Hughes (b-tb); Cleveland Eaton (b). *Middle*: Bob Ojeda, Byron Stripling, Mike Williams, Sonny Cohn (t); Mel Wanzo, Clarence Banks (tb); Danny House (as); Paul Weeden (g); Eric Dixon (ts); Carmen Bradford (voc); John Williams (bs). *Front*: Frank Foster (ts, arr, ldr); Kenny Hing (ts); Danny Turner (as).

guys. There was a tremendous amount of resentment – these were guys who had sat with Thad when he was in the band. I knew him as 'Thad Jones, the trumpet player and great arranger' from the Thad Jones–Mel Lewis band, who had left the Basie band and established his own style. They remembered him as 'a goof-off who drank too much'. They didn't care about him.

"The first thing Thad wanted to do was rehearse. They didn't like to rehearse. They said, 'Byron, you should have a feature. Bring something in.' I had a friend of mine write a feature: he put a 5/4 bar in it. We pass it out and the guys look at it. Somebody says, 'There's a 5/4 bar in here.' Danny Turner, the lead alto player, said, 'Pass it in.' They didn't even read it! When Thad came, he got some press, made the cover of *Down Beat*, and we had an incredible six-to-eight months with him. We did some great things like the album with the singer Caterina Valente, toured Europe, all Thad's arrangements. He wrote some good things for the band. I happen to have them in my library – I've actually been able to record them. I was around Thad like a puppy. I got to really know him. I saw how he led the band, tried to shape it and then he passed away (August 1986). So they got Frank Foster: a whole different style of leadership but still with a desire to move things forward. Actually the guys didn't like that – 'Wait a minute, he's writing

Thad Jones, **Byron Stripling**, **Snooky Young** (t), unknown New York studio, with Bob Ojeda (t, arr, *at right*), 1970s. Courtesy Byron Stripling.

these new arrangements and it's not Basie's style' – so there was that conflict again."

Stripling's analysis of this tricky situation yielded a series of fascinating questions. "This is the difficulty of having a band that outlives its leader. Where do you go with it? Do you only play 'Shiny Stockings' and about four other charts? Can you never write anything new? Who's going to be the judge? Is Frank Foster the one who makes the judgement or is it going to be the guys? Where's the cut-off? Should he not write certain harmonies when he writes a new chart? Should it be Danny Turner's decision or should they get together as a group? They didn't want to shake things up – so they wouldn't let Thad or Frank do that much.

"What did Frank give me? A looser sense of leadership. Thad was more contained, in a totally good way. He was also able to excite me with his conducting. In fact, the biggest thing the guys didn't like about Thad was that he *conducted*. When he pointed to me, I got total energy from it – it would be like a lightning bolt would go through me.

"I was playing lead and loving it. I worked my ass off. I'd studied classical trumpet and I had the stamina." Once again, Clark Terry enters the picture. "He saw me at Nice and pulled me aside. 'Man, you're doing great. You've been with Woody, got you with

Count Basie Orchestra, directed by Frank Foster, Northampton, UK, 1989. *Rear*: Bob Ojeda, Byron Stripling, Sonny Cohn, Mike Williams (t). *Middle*: Robert Trowers, Mel Wanzo, Clarence Banks (tb). *Front*: Kenny Hing (ts); David Glasser, Danny Turner (as); Eric Dixon (ts); Johnny Willliams (bs); Frank Foster (ts, standing). Photo by Brian Foskett. Courtesy Brian Foskett.

Basie. It's great but you need to start learning tunes. You know 155 is "Shiny Stockings", 139 is "Splanky" and 150 is "Li'l Darlin" but when you leave the band – and you should leave soon – you got to be able to fill up a four-hour gig as a soloist. Nobody's going to call 155, 139 or 150. They're gonna say "You'd Be So Nice to Come Home to" in Eb – let's go. While you're on the road here, you could rot. So keep working at it.' Yes, I'm playing the same charts every night. That's what the road does – it's kinda comfortable. The guys didn't want to play Thad's new charts and they barely wanted to play Frank's. You had to force them. That's cool if you're maybe 70 but I'm in my 20s – I gotta see something else.'

"I loved everybody in that band. They all had their own personalities and I wanted to be like them. I loved being on the road. On the Basie bus, we had the greatest fun ever. You'd talk about what happened on the gig; you talk about every chick in the audience. Talking about the bus, I'm told that Basie rode the bus everywhere with the guys. I'm also told he was on time which the Basie band had a thing about. Frank Foster was always late, he had trouble making time. Trumpeter Sonny Cohn, the band manager, said, 'Frank, if you're late, we'll leave you.' The next day he was late and Sonny said, 'Pull it' to the driver and here comes Frank to the gig, so mad because he had to spend $300 on a cab ride. Guess what, he was never late after that.

"I left the band after two years with Frank to do the show *Satchmo: America's Musical Legend*. It started in 1988. It was hopefully to go to Broadway. It never did. It was about a $10 million dollar production with tons of dancers and a band on stage. There was a world-wide search for the person to play Louis Armstrong. Because of the Lionel Hampton experience, I had always listened to Louis and I had learned a bunch of his solos. They wanted you to send in a tape – mine had 'Laughin' Louis', 'When You're Smiling' and 'I Can't Give You Anything but Love'. They loved it and I was one of the four finalists. I went to do the audition and they said OK. I did two months studying with an acting coach. I found out what music we were going to play and learned a lot of his solos from music. Maurice Hines was the choreographer and he was a great help to me in regard to being on stage. It was a great experience but the show did not do well. It was not a great show. It was not balanced in the right way. The Musical Director was a guy from the circus named Bill Prine. The producer was from Ringling Brothers and Barnum and Bailey so he used his circus guys but he loved Louis and hopefully, he liked my trumpet playing!

"We opened in New Orleans and toured for about six months, we did all great halls, we did the Kennedy Center in Washington, the Colonial in downtown Boston, where I could never get a cab afterwards but my girlfriend could. She was white. Jeff Clayton (alto) was in the band and Herlin Riley played the drums. He was a big plus; he knew how to do that strut they do, when the brothers get down and dance with the umbrellas in New Orleans. He showed Maurice Hines how to do that and he put that in the choreography. Talk about getting the girls – being the drummer helps!"

Trumpeters **Claudio Roditi**, **Byron Stripling**, **Freddie Hubbard**, unknown US concert location, c.1980s. Courtesy Byron Stripling.

After returning briefly to the Basie band, Stripling decided to make for New York and moved there permanently, "to become a musician who would do something". He then embarked on a heady round of playing shows, doing a lot of studio work, using his contacts. "I knew all the New York trumpet players from seeing them on the road so work was pretty easy. I'm still getting cheques from it today, especially from movies. If you do a lot of movies (soundtracks), once a year you'll get a good cheque. I feel bad that jazz musicians don't have that. It's a shame they only get paid when they work. The big deal for me was meeting all the New York musicians who all my life I had seen as names on the backs of albums. Guys like Randy Brecker, Jon Faddis, of course, and Jerome Richardson, just to be part of that. Then there were the big bands that were forming, Grover Mitchell had one, I got to be part of that. Buck Clayton had another. Someone said, 'Buck heard you once, he wants to have you in his band,' so I went to his apartment to hang out with him. He's getting up to 80 or something and he says (slowly), 'Yeah, Byron, we got a gig next week, you wanna do it?' I was always up at his place after that because he was a lovely man. Always wanted to drink Beaujolais and talk about Billie (Holiday). Then I was playing with bands like Loren Schoenberg and he's doing these Ellington tributes, with guests like Louie Bellson. In New York, they're always doing some kind of Ellington this or that! They needed people who could do it so I began getting those calls.

"There's no freelance world now. I had two years of playing these big sessions with guys like Lew Tabackin, Jerome Richardson, Jim Pugh on lead trombone, Faddis, reedman Danny Bank all the time, Ron Carter playing bass sometimes if they got a good band, and maybe Grady Tate on drums. Now it's done in somebody's little room. Sweetening a track they've done on a synthesiser thing. It sounds like it is actually a big band – 'put something on top of this' – I'm by myself with headphones, a little bit of music, one time through, then you play a little solo on top of it. That's it."

Stripling went on to tell me a tale about a call to growl like 'Cootie Williams' as the featured soloist on a 30-second perfume jingle written by Don Sebesky. The job done, to a round of applause from his fellow musicians including altoist Jerry Dodgion, there was silence from the suits in the sound booth. In the event, the client decided that he wanted his son, a novice amateur, to play instead. "That's the kind of crap you get," said Stripling, mentioning that a toothpaste client wanted the musicians on a jingle to 'play more orange'. All in a day's work, I guess.

There were some compensations, of course, as when Stripling played the show *Jelly's Last Jam* on Broadway. "Britt Woodman, Jerome Richardson and a bunch of New York guys were in there with me. I used to get to work an hour early to play cards with these guys. I just loved them. So much laughter. Sure, they were serious about music, but they weren't walking around with tight asses, nervous about everything. Magic

Trumpeters **Marcus Belgrave**, **Byron Stripling**, **Jon Faddis**, **Wynton Marsalis** with **Dizzy Gillespie** (*seated*), probably New York, c.1980s. Courtesy Byron Stripling.

Dave Brubeck (p); **Chris Brubeck** (b-gtr); **Clint Eastwood** (host); **Byron Stripling** (voc), US TV show, possibly Los Angeles CA, c. 2000. Courtesy Byron Stripling.

moments, like playing cards with Britt. He had narcolepsy, where you fall asleep, but he would always win. We didn't know if he was messing with us!"

After *Satchmo*, Stripling was called to play as a soloist on a TV show with the Boston Pops Orchestra. Using charts commissioned from star arranger Manny Albam, it seemed to go well but it was two more years before a similar opportunity presented itself. This type of featured speciality is now part of his regular pattern of work. I was intrigued to know how Stripling sees himself: which is the real person here, the star soloist in front of the Boston Pops Orchestra, the leader of the CJO or the guy that can play some blues and interact spontaneously with an audience? Byron's answer surprised me: "You're asking me to label myself. Nietzsche said, 'When you label me you negate me.' So the real Byron Stripling is in fact all of those things. My inspiration comes from so many great musicians who looked at themselves in that way, from Louis Armstrong to Leonard Bernstein. I think that great artists try to live in the field of infinite possibilities. So when you start to say I'm 'this' or 'that', it makes me nervous. I enjoy all of those things equally; they're all a part of who I am. I get fulfilled by doing all of those things and hopefully, do them all well."

Looking to the future, he said, "I have to continue developing the band and myself as a soloist. I'm still a trumpet player to be hired and I'm still trying to establish my voice on the instrument. I have some gigs with my small group, that's my guys in Columbus:

Byron Stripling (t), Joe Ascione group, JazzAscona, Ascona, Switzerland, June 2007. Photo by Peter Vacher.

Bobby Floyd plays B-3 organ as well as piano, we play a lot of gospel music in that group which I love doing too. We've got Bob Breithaupt who's this great drummer who also plays in the big band with me, Christian Berg on bass, and we'll play all kinds of stuff. So, there's plenty still to do.

"Do I have any regrets? That I didn't get more girls. I was too busy practising! For now, I love playing the trumpet and being in front of people performing. If people want to hear it, I'll play it."

First published as 'Byron Stripling:
Living in the Field of Infinite Possibilities' in
Coda, May–June 2008

Acknowledgements

My thanks go principally to the musicians themselves for willingly putting the time aside for these interviews and to the editors who published the outcomes. I'm perfectly well aware that there is often a quid pro quo in all this – time spent with a journalist discussing a new project or recording should result in welcome column inches for that musician in the trade press. Publicity, for good or ill, is the necessary oxygen of show business. Consider just how many interviews Wynton Marsalis gives in a year. Happily, for me, the type of career stories that I prefer to concentrate on do require the musician in question to suspend disbelief and spend time recalling a complete career (or something like it) without necessarily expecting to see the whole of their outpourings in print. This has happened with all of these individuals in this book. Even so, when a feature piece does appear, they're often pleasingly satisfied. Indeed, when my Benny Powell article appeared in *Jazz Journal*, he was so excited that he ordered 50 extra copies of the magazine to distribute to family and friends. How gratifying was that?

Some of these players have become friends and we continue to keep in contact. They have answered additional questions (the pleasures of e-mail!) and provided photographs, and often been at pains to act as their own fact-checkers. I'm grateful to them all. Sadly, I have also had the sad task of writing the *Guardian* obituaries of several musicians represented here including Benny Powell, John Stubblefield, Herman Riley, and Bill Berry.

When it comes to widening my search for appropriate photographs, my first port of call is always to my friend Theo Zwicky of Zurich. Theo operates his mr.jazz Photo Files and is renowned for his vast collection of jazz images and as a historian of jazz on film, presenting his popular jazz film recitals all over Switzerland. He has, as usual, been very helpful as have the photographers Ian Powell, Derek Drescher, Fred Sater of New York, Jonathan Farber, John Watson (who provided our cover), Gordon Sapsed, Val Wilmer and Brian Foskett, while many other collectors and researchers including Joe Mosbrook from Cincinnati, Jim Gallert in Detroit, Jean-François Villetard in Paris, Robert L. Campbell from Chicago, Armin Buttner in Zurich, Dave Bennett, Dave Clarke, Terry Dash, Chris Lee, Marty Morgan and Bruce Boyd Raeburn from the Tulane Jazz Archive, have all found images for this book, as has Bill Berry Jr., e-mailing from deepest Colorado. They are all credited – where they are not, the prints come from my own collection. I should also pay tribute to Peter Ryan, Mick Beazley and Anne Bennett who have expertly copied many of these photographs, allowing me to return the originals to their rightful owners.

I am particularly indebted to Mark Gilbert, the editor of *Jazz Journal* (www.jazzjournal.co.uk), the only journal still extant of those who originally published these pieces, for his agreement to the re-publication of those that first appeared in his magazine. I'm also very grateful to Ross Bradshaw of Five Leaves Publications who responded so positively when the idea for this book was first mooted, and to his designer Tony Marson for his elegant design work.

Finally, of course, it is to my wife Patricia that I owe the most, not only for her typing skills, but for her forbearance while I was compiling this book and for her support and enthusiasm over so many years.

Index

Aarons, Al 53
Abene, Mike 168
Abrams, Muhal Richard 221, 244, 245, 247
Adams, Adam (Shiny Goldmine) 11
Adams, George 253
Adams, Joe 42
Adams, Mr 238
Adams, Pepper 85, 97
Adderley, Cannonball 257
Adderley, Nat 257
Akiyoshi, Toshiko 220, 221,
akLaff, Pheeroan 259
Albam, Manny 303
Alexander, Adolphe 'Tats' 13
Alexander, Eric 285
Alexander, Tommy 162
Alexiev, Grisha 224
Allen, Carl 286
Allen, Charlie 52
Allen, Harry 265, 266, 275
Allen, Henry 'Red' 59, 146
Allston, Albert 23
Allston, Joe 22, 23
Ames, Nancy 29
Ammons, Gene 131, 145, 186
Anderson, Cat 93, 95, 251, 295
Anderson, Ernestine 185
Andrews Ernie 192
Anthony, Ray 164
Appleyard, Peter 291
Arlen, Harold 71
Arcaraz, Luis 162
Armstrong, Louis 14, 35, 59, 64, 69, 74, 75, 105, 108, 110, 112, 205, 206, 213, 237, 242, 300, 303,
Arnaz, Desi 112
Arnold, Eddy 30
Artin, Tom 108, 194–211,
Austin, Earl 15
Austin, Patti 121
Austin Sil 241

Bacon, Louis 26
Bailey, Buster 131
Bailey, Donald 150

Bailey, Pearl 154
Baker, Chet 165, 214
Baker, Josephine 85
Baker, Michael 295
Baker, Shorty 93
Balaban, Red 202, 205
Barrajanas, Danny 29
Barbarin, Louis 13
Barbarin, Paul 146
Barefield, Eddie 52
Barksdale, Don 42
Barnes, Alan 266, 278
Barnes, Harrison 146
Barnhart, Scotty 121
Bartholomew, Dave 147
Barnet, Charlie 160
Barron, Kenny 259, 262
Bartz, Gary 261
Basie, Count 7, 12, 20, 22, 30, 33, 34, 36, 38, 46, 47, 50, 52–55, 58, 85, 100, 106, 108–121, 138, 140,–145, 150, 153, 189, 195, 211, 215, 216, 220, 236, 238–242, 250, 269–272, 274, 291, 293, 296,–299, 301
Bastian, Eddie 250
Batiste, Alvin 181
Baxter, Les 134
Bazley, Tony 129
Beckett, Fred 85
Beiderbecke, Bix 104,
Belafonte, Harry 28, 29
Bell, Al 121
Bell, Warren Sr. 112, 148
Bellson, Louie 154, 301
Bennett, Dave 57, 305
Bennett, Tony 204
Benton, Walter 148, 149
Berg, Billy 41
Berg, Bob 223
Berg, Christian 304
Berghofer, Chuck 157
Berigan, Bunny 90
Bernhart, Milt 160
Bernstein, Leonard 303
Berry, Bill 83, 87, 89–106, 145, 171, 305
Bert, Eddie 222

Best, Skeeter 15
Betton, Teroy 239
Betts, Keter 293
Beutler, Allan 163
Blackwell, Eddie 181
Blake, Johnathan 256
Blakey, Art 224, 260
Blanchard, Osceola 13
Blanchard, Terence 177, 291
Bland, Bobby Blue 229
Blanton, Jimmy 20, 25
Blue, Classy 240
Bluiet, Hamiet 251
Bonnemere, Eddie 110
Boone, Richard 150
Booth, Chick 50
Bostic, Earl 13, 25, 130
Bowie, Byron 244
Bowie, Lester 243, 244, 246, 259
Bradford, Kirt 'Mustapha' 148
Bradshaw, Tiny 23, 25, 189
Braff, Ruby 8, 56–77
Brandford, Jay 223
Braud, Wellman 179
Braxton, Anthony 244
Brazil, Joe 229
Brecker, Randy 255, 301
Breithaupt, Bob 304
Brice, Percy 27
Bridgewater, Cecil 123
Brigham, Froebel 148, 149
Brignola, Mike 157
Brillinger Jeff 207
Brooks, Nell 146
Brooks, Roy 250
Brooks, Tina 148
Brown, Boots 127
Brown, Charles 131, 132
Brown, Clifford 84, 85, 141, 187
Brown, Garnett 241, 242
Brown, James 132, 214, 229, 242
Brown, Jimmy 22, 23
Brown, Les 215
Brown, Pete 59
Brown, Ralph 26
Brown, Roy 147

Brown, Willard 52
Brubeck, Dave 160, 185, 213
Brunious, John 'Picket' 112
Bryant, Bobby 150
Bryant, Clora 103, 133
Bryant, Ray 214
Bryant, Rusty 141
Buckner, Milton 'Milt' 35, 115
Budwig, Monty 101
Bunch, John 203, 205, 277
Burke, Ed 26
Burke, Solomon 241
Burke, Vinnie 286
Burns, Ralph 296
Bush, John 238
Byard, Jaki 167
Byars, Chris 207
Byas, Don 131, 238, 239, 241
Byrne, Bobby 34
Byrne, Clarence 34

Caceres, Ernie 162
Cadena, Ozzie 157
Cain, Henry 150
Cain, Jackie 207
Caliman, Hadley 150
Callender, Red 269, 270
Campbell, John 295
Candido (Camero) 145
Candoli, Conte 170
Capp, Frankie 87, 101, 152, 157, 171, 172
Carle, Frankie 162, 163
Carmichael, Judy 264–278
Carney, Harry 95
Carpenter, Ike 161
Carpenter, Thelma 190
Carr, James 242
Carroll, Barbara 209
Carson, Tee 142
Carter, Benny 41, 50, 70, 79, 103, 106, 116, 152, 221, 247
Carter, Betty 'Betty Bebop' 114
Carter, Carl 'Ace' 137–143
Carter, Chic 38
Carter, Ron 248, 301
Cash, Johnny 30
Cato, Adam 149
Cavanaugh, Dave 134
Celestin, Oscar 'Papa' 13, 14, 178
Chaloff, Serge 61
Chambers, Henderson 23

Chamberlain, Linc 217
Chamblee, Eddie 51
Charlap, Bill 71, 277
Charles, Ray 33, 127, 148, 240
Chase, 'Dooky' Sr. 111, 112, 130
Chase, Edgar Lawrence 'Dooky' Jr. 111
Cheatham, Doc 250
Cheatham, Jeannie 152
Cheatham, Jimmy 152
Chirillo, James 207
Christian, Charlie 25
Christianson, Mike 207
Christlieb, Pete 159
Christy, June 145
Church, Eugene 134
Clay, Miss 238
Clayton, Buck 66, 67, 221, 301
Clayton, Jeff 300
Cleveland, Jimmy 84, 115, 169
Clinton, President Bill 235, 240
Cobb, Arnett 23, 43
Cobb, Junie 54
Coe, Jimmy 141
Cohn, Al 166, 247
Cohn, George 'Sonny' 46, 47, 50, 52, 299
Cohran, Phil 244–246
Coker, Dolo 150
Coker, Henry 120
Cole, Freddie 224
Cole, Nat King 131, 134, 161, 209
Cole, Natalie 171
Cole, Walter 'Chippy' 55
Coleman, George 251
Coleman, Ornette 215, 240, 247, 253
Colianni, John 207
Collier, Joe 140
Collette, Buddy 151, 164
Colley, Scott 232
Colligan, George 261
Collins, Burt 218, 223
Coltrane, John 120, 151, 186, 214, 229, 241, 243, 246, 247
Condon, Eddie 63, 195, 199, 200, 202–206, 214,
Confrey, Zez 268
Connick, Harry Jr. 177
Cook, Junior 283, 286, 288
Cooke, Sam 239, 242

Coon, Jackie 269
Cooper, Bob 160
Cooper, George 'Buster' 78–88
Cooper, Joe 141
Cooper, Sarah 79
Cooper, Nick 50
Copland, Aaron 258
Corey, Shirley 176
Cosby, Bill 152, 235
Cosey, Pete 246
Cottrell, Louis 13
Courant, Richard 196
Cowell, Stanley 248
Crane, Tommy 256
Cranshaw, Bob 257
Crawford, Jimmy 62
Crawford, Joan 115
Crosby, Bob 58
Cross, Criss 223
Crump, Bill 52
Cuber, Ronnie 218
Current, Gloster 36
Cutshall, Cutty 195

Daley, Mayor 246
Dameron, Tadd 229
Dance, Stanley 79
Dankworth, John 185
Davern, Kenny 199, 206
Davis, Charles 51, 280, 288
Davis, Clive 265, 278
Davis, Eddie 'Lockjaw' 30, 151, 201, 241
Davis, Jesse 177, 178, 257
Davis, Miles 68, 185, 229, 246, 248, 261
Davis, Sammy Jr. 46, 152
Davison, Wild Bill 199, 204
Day, Bobby 134
Day, Mathew 23
DeCormier, Bob 28
Deems, Barrett 206
Dengler, John 198
Dennard, Oscar 83
Dennison, Billy 219
DeParis, brothers (Wilbur & Sidney) 199
DePass Jr., Arnold 112, 209
DeMichel, Rey 164
DeRisi, Al, 147
Desvignes, Sidney 111
Dickenson, Vic 59, 67, 195, 199, 202, 211

Index

Dickinson, Emily 224
D'Imperio, Danny 203, 204, 205, 287
Dixon, Eric 85, 296
Dixon, George 15
Dodgion, Jerry 43, 221, 301
Doherty, Edward 246
Dolphy, Eric 248
Domino, Fats 127
Dorham, Kenny 215, 224, 248, 256
Dorsey, Jimmy 237
Dorsey, Tommy 14, 67, 124
Douglas, Mrs 237
Downing, Ken 162
Drew, Kenny 261
Duca, Mayo 58
Durham, Bobby 293
Durham, Eddie 110
Duvivier, George 74

East, Thomas 239
Easton, McKinley 50
Eaton, Cleveland 138
Eaves, Hubert 261
Eckert, John 125, 212–224
Eckstine, Billy 36, 106, 113, 117
Edison, Harry 'Sweets' 38, 47, 54, 118
Edmondson, Bob 161
Edwards, Cecil 22, 23
Edwards, Teddy 42, 43, 132, 149, 151, 157, 164, 192
Eisenhower, President 237
Eldridge, Mr 48
Eldridge, Roy 49, 64, 204, 271, 293
Elgart, Larry 213, 216
Ellington, Duke 7, 23, 33, 34, 37, 39, 52, 69, 71, 75, 79, 83, 85, 90, 93, 94, 95, 96, 104, 105, 106, 110, 122, 130, 141, 145, 152, 187, 200, 214, 236, 242, 249, 252, 258, 293, 301,
Ellington, Mercer 95, 152
Ellis, Don 163
Ellis, Pee Wee 214, 217
Europe, James Reese 237
Evans, Gil 256, 259, 260
Evans, Stomp 247
Ewart, Douglas 244
Ewing, John 49

Faddis, Jon 293, 301
Farmer, Art 42, 84, 286
Farnsworth, Joe 285
Farrell, Earl Daniel 147
Farrell, Joe 250
Fazola, Irving 130
Feather, Leonard 273
Felice, Dee 90
Ferguson, Maynard 90, 156, 164, 166–168, 213, 214, 216
Ferrante, Joe 223
Fields, Ernie 113, 114
Fields, Ernie Jr. 114
Fields, Joe 192
Fernandez, John 148
Fitzgerald, Ella 26, 44, 138, 141, 293
Flanagan, Tommy 271, 274, 293
Fleming, Dan 156
Fleming, King 47–49
Florence, Bob 159, 162, 215
Flory, Chris 278
Flowers, Hamilton 188
Floyd, Bobby 304
Floyd, Harlan 'Booby' 55
Fontana, Carl 85
Ford, Jimmy 165
Forrest, Jimmy 49
Foster, Alex 257
Foster, Frank 53, 138, 247, 250, 297–299
Foster, Pops 200
Fournier, Vernel aka Amir Rushdan 112, 113, 146, 287
Fowkes, Conal 195
Fowlkes, Charlie 23, 53, 116
Foxx Redd 34, 257
French, Papa Albert 178
Frommer, Gary 161
Fuller, Walter 149
Francis, Willie 127
Franklin, Aretha 114, 240, 258, 295
Freeman, Bud 68, 70, 209
Frishberg, Dave 101
Fulham, Ray 140, 141

Gabriel, Joe 11
Gadd, Per-Ola 187
Gaffney, George 102
Galper, Hal 257
Gardner, Joe 242, 246, 250–253
Gardner, June 146

Gardner, Poison 133
Gatchell, John 217
Gayten, Paul 147
Gayton, Clark 261
Gensel, Reverend John 'the Night Shepherd' 108, 110
George, Karl 36
Getz, Stan 74, 91, 159, 207, 229
Gibbs, Terry 164
Giddins, Gary 221
Gillespie Dizzy 16, 41, 43, 54, 67, 90, 112, 130, 145, 185,
Gilliam, Richie 161
Giordano, George 28,
Glantz, Harry 216
Glow, Bernie 223
Godfrey, Arthur 27
Gogel, Katherine 235
Golson, Benny 166
Gonsalves, Paul 93
Gonzalez, Jerry 250
Goodman, Benny 35, 57, 61, 74, 85, 105, 159, 163, 221
Goodman, Herbie 25
Gordon, Bobby 203
Gordon, Dexter 231
Gordon, Max 28
Goto, Sayuri 109
Gowans, Brad 63
Grady, Eddie 162
Granz, Norman 41, 145
Grauso, Joe 63
Gray, Wardell 34
Green, Bennie, 47–49, 117
Green, Bill 145, 150, 151
Green, Freddie 38, 269
Green, Hal 35
Green, Thurman 79
Green, Nat 188
Green, Urbie 195, 209
Greene, Bobby 52
Greenlee, Charlie 169
Gregg, Ken 159
Grenadier, Larry 232
Grey, Al 115, 120, 293
Griffin, Johnny 85, 186, 285
Griffin, Merv 98, 100, 109, 136, 171
Griffith, Frank 213
Grimes, Tiny 141
Grissom, Dan 39
Gryce, Gigi 84, 215
Guarnieri, Johnny 206
Guy, Joe 25, 26

Hackley, Crackshot 23
Hackett, Bobby 62, 63, 68, 70, 198
Hall, Edmond 199
Hall, Harry 167
Hall, Lawrence 11
Hall, Solomon 52
Hamilton, Scott 278
Hammer, Tardo 279–289
Hammond, John 242, 265, 271, 274
Hampton, Gladys 115
Hampton, Lionel 'Hamp' 'Gates' 43, 60, 83–85, 109, 114—116, 131, 132, 140, 152, 295, 296, 300
Hampton, Slide 116, 166, 167
Hanna, Jake 104
Hancock, Herbie 280
Handy, John 132, 254, 255
Hanrahan, Kip 259
Harbison, John 195–197
Hardman, Bill 148, 192, 283, 285
Hargrove, Roy 223, 288, 291
Harnett, James 229
Harrell, Tom 71, 223
Harper, Billy 241
Harper, Philip 256
Harris, Barry 274
Harris, Bill 91
Harris, Eddie 163, 189, 230, 244
Harris, Kid 11, 14
Harrison, Donald 177
Harrison, Tim 224
Hart, Billy 218, 219, 250, 262
Hashim, Mike 207, 266, 278
Hawkins, Coleman 59, 64, 74, 85, 145, 247
Hawkins, Erskine 38, 52, 83, 112, 140
Hayes, Al 85
Hayes, Danny 220
Hayes, Edgar 41
Hayes, Louis 262
Hayes, Tubby 150
Haynes, Cyril 52
Haynes, Jamal 256
Haywood, Cedric 43, 83
Hearn, Larry 150
Heath, Jimmy 221
Henderson, Fletcher 9, 35, 69
Henderson, Horace 49, 50

Henderson, Roy 145, 147
Henry, Haywood 83
Henry, Pat 43
Herman, Woody 90, 91, 140, 160, 222, 294, 296
Herwig, Conrad 295
Hibbler, Al 238
Hicks, Robert 26
Higaki, Paul 115
Higgins, Patience 222
Hillery, Art 150
Hines, Earl 'Fatha' 15, 34, 49, 83, 178, 251
Hines, Maurice 300
Hinton, Milt 'The Judge' 250
Hirt, Al 179
Hite, Les 41
Hodges, Johnny 93, 104
Hogan, Wilbert 112
Holiday, Billie 64, 190, 240, 301,
Holman, Bill 157, 158, 172
Holmes, Groove 189
Hope, Stan 187
Hopkins, Linda 141
Horne, Lena 71
Horton, R.H. 26
Houston, William Sr. 147
Houston, William, Jr. 147, 184–193
Houston, Whitney 295
Howard, Camille 132, 141
Howard, Kid 14
Howard, Sister 238
Hubbard, Freddie 217, 240, 257, 272
Hubbard, Tom 224
Hubble, Eddie 205
Hudson, George 49
Hudson, Lee 288
Hughes, Bill 121
Humphrey, Emery 112
Humphrey, Willie 14
Hupp, Rick 282
Hyman, Dick 250, 274, 293

Inzalaco, Tony 168

Jackson, Duffy 138
Jackson, Harold 52
Jackson, Jason 261
Jackson, Oliver 206
Jackson, Quentin 118
Jacquet, Illinois 23, 43, 106, 117, 131, 145, 147, 186

Jamal, Ahmad 113, 146, 287
James, Harry 49, 161
Jarrett, Keith 256, 277
Jarreau, Al 295
Jefferson, Carl 105
Jenkins, George 133
Jenkins, Gordon 146
Jim Crow (Jim Robinson) 14, 237
Joel, Billy 276
Johnson, Budd 247
Johnson, Buddy 130, 140
Johnson, Bunk 14
Johnson, Charlton 138
Johnson, Gus 49
Johnson, James P. 199
Johnson, J.J. (Jay Jay) 79, 115, 152, 231
Johnson, Jimmy 85
Johnson, Keg 52
Johnson, Harold 'Money' 85
Johnson, Plas Jr. 126–136, 145, 151
Johnson, Son 130
Johnson, Sy 218
Johnson, Tuts 11
Johnston, Randy 192
Jolly, Pete 157
Jones, Ben 242
Jones, Bobby 253
Jones, Elvin 120, 248
Jones, Etta 27, 185, 189, 190
Jones, Hank 274
Jones, Harold 171, 269, 270
Jones, Herbie 52
Jones, Jack 157
Jones, Jo 204
Jones, Jonah 209
Jones, Mingo 141
Jones, Philly Joe 150
Jones, Quincy 152
Jones, Reunald 52
Jones, Roger 25
Jones, Rufus 166, 167
Jones, Sam 83
Jones, Spike 62
Jones, Thad 53, 96, 104, 106, 113, 122, 228, 250, 256, 296, 297
Jones, Virgil 189, 221, 222, 261
Jordan, Clifford 169, 253, 286
Jordan, Duke 281
Jordan, Kidd 177
Jordan, Louis 130, 140

Index

Jordan, Marlon 177
Jordan, Taft 188, 250

Kamuca, Richie 98, 104, 169
Karr, Gary 232
Kaye, Billy 189
Keenan, Norman
  'Dewey' 19–30
Keillor, Garrison 108
Kellso, Jon-Erik 266
Kelly, Grace 198
Kelso, Jackie 132, 145, 151
Kennedy, Charlie 164
Kenton, Stan 36, 96, 121, 140,
  145, 147, 160, 162, 214, 215
Kersey, Kenny 26, 59, 67
Kilbert, Porter 50, 51
Kimball, Jeanette 14, 178
Kimball, Narvin 'Bubba' 178
King, Martin Luther 245
Kirby, John 98
Kirk, Andy 23, 49, 140, 237
Kirk, Rahsaan Roland 151,
  242, 259
Knepper, Jimmy 218, 253
Knowling, Ransom 13
Kohlman, Freddie 146
Kolax, King 112–114
Konitz, Lee 145, 218
Kral, Roy 207

Labelle, Patti 258
LaBarbera, Joe 157
Laine, Cleo 185
Land, Harold 148, 149, 151
Lanin, Lester 209
Larkin, Milt 23, 43
Lateef, Yusef 268
Leary, Herb 14, 147
Leary, James 239, 241, 251
Leary, Timothy 216
Lee, Buddy 36
Lee, Cecil 36, 37
Lee, Chris 305
Lee, Peggy 134
Lee, Sam 147
Leeman, Cliff 204
Levinson, Dan 207
Levy, John 257
Lewis, George 14, 16
Lewis, Jerry 121
Lewis, John 215, 221
Lewis, Mel 96, 215, 256, 297
Lewis, Steve 14

Lewis, Victor 261
Liebman, Dave 217, 224
Liggins, Joe 132
Lind, Pastor Dale 108, 235
Little, Booker 240
Little Richard 127
Lockwood, Robert Jr. 138
Lopeman, Mark 207
Lord, Tom 213
Lovano, Joe 138
Love, John 147
Lowe, Curtis 43
Lowe, Sammy 38
Lujan, Tony 295
Lunceford, Jimmie 34, 35,
  38–40, 61, 62, 111, 116, 148
Lynch, Carl 27
Lynne, Gloria 54
Lythgoe, John 276

MacDonald, Al 141
Maddocks, Elvin 141
Maddocks, Max 25
Madden, Owney 240
Madison, Jimmy 218
Magnarelli, Joe 223
Maheu, Jack 203, 205
Maiden, Willie 165, 166, 168
Maini, Joe 164
Mance, Junior 227
Mancini, Henry 127
Marable, Fate 12, 15
Marchard, Harry 60
Marcus, Steve 217
Marsalis, Branford 175, 295
Marsalis, Delfeayo 175
Marsalis, Ellis 148, 175–183
Marsalis, Jason 175
Marsalis, Wynton 70, 175, 220,
  305
Marsh, Warne 204, 247, 283
Marshall, John 287, 288
Martin, Bill 54
Martin, David Stone 198
Martin, 'Little Willie' 38
Martin, Stu 217
Martin, Tony 198
Martyn, Barry 15
Matthews, Bill 14
Mathews, Happy 146
Maxted, Billy 199
May, Billy 216
May, Susan 90, 156
Mayers, Lloyd 85

McBee, Cecil 261
McBride, Christian 232
McCall, Steve 245
McCann, Les 257
McCarney, Eddie 25
McClure, Ronnie 168, 189
McDonald, Bob 159
McKibbon, Al 145
McCoy, Clyde 62, 75
McGhee, Charles 251, 253
McGhee, Howard 169
McLary, Rod 28
McLean, Jackie 253, 283
McMillen, Dee 224
McPartland, Marian 209, 249,
  273, 276
McShann, Jay 54, 274
McVea, Jack 269
Mehldau, Brad 277
Meissner, Zep 62
Menza, Don 101, 106, 166, 189
Messner, Eddie 134
Milburn, Amos 132
Miller, Doug 121
Miller, Glenn 40, 162
Miller, Jesse 47
Millinder, Lucky 25, 85, 130,
  140
Milton, Little 246
Milton, Roy 132
Mince, Johnny 206
Mingus, Charles 168, 235, 251,
  256
Mingus, Sue 235, 254
Minor, Orville 54
Mitchell, Billy 169, 221
Mitchell, Blue 100, 105
Mitchell, Cat 100
Mitchell, Grover 220, 301
Mitchell, Roscoe 244
Mobley, Hank 186, 187, 224,
  251
Montgomery, Buddy 229
Montgomery, Monk 152
Montgomery, Wes 151
Moore, Big Chief Russell 209
Moore, Freddie 200, 201
Moore, Marilyn 286
Moore, Melvin 47
Moore, Phil 41
Moret, Tony 148
Morgan, Harold 158
Morgan, Lanny 8, 100, 101,
  155–173, 189

Morgan, Lee 224, 251
Morgan, Marty 305
Morgan, Sam 14
Moring, Bill 207
Morrow, Buddy 216
Morrow, George 150
Mosbrook, Joe 138, 305
Mosca, Sal 283
Morton, Jelly Roll 71, 249
Moss, Elwood 140
Mtume, James 262
Mulligan, Gerry 214, 220
Murray, David 221
Myers, Amina 240, 243
Myerson, Don 160

Nance, Ray 93
Nakamura, Teru 262
Nasser, Jamil 241
Nelson, Ellington 141
Nelson, Louis 10–18,
Nelson, Oliver 83, 166, 240
Nesbitt, Joe 140
Neumann, Roger 152
Newman, Joe 250
Newton, Frankie 59, 60, 63
Niehaus, Lennie 162
Nimitz, Jack 100
Norman, Gene 159
Norris, John 11
Norris, Walter 240
Norvo, Red 74
Nottingham, Jimmy 38

Oliver, Sy 40
Ore, John 282
Otis, Johnny 133, 134
Outcalt, Chips 114
Owens, Jimmy 248

Page, Walter 38
Palmer, Earl 146, 148
Parker, Charlie 'Bird' '
  Yardbird' 25, 41, 51, 60, 61,
  67, 74, 91, 112, 145, 150, 170,
  209, 214, 282, 288,
Parrish, Avery 147
Parrott, Nicki 232
Patitucci, John 232
Patrick, Pat 250
Payne, Don 161
Payne, Sonny 52
Payton, Nicholas 223
Peagler, Curtis 141

Pedersen, Niels-Henning
  Ørsted 187
Peplowski, Ken 291
Pepper, Art 159–161
Perkins, Bill 157, 162
Perkins, Bob 35
Perry, Ray 38, 60
Person, Houston Jr. 184–193
Peterson, Oscar 49
Petit, Buddy 14
Petties, Leon 149
Pettiford, Oscar 84
Phillips, Barre 161
Phillips, Reuben 49, 85
Phillips, Sonny 190
Picou, Alphonse 179
Pierce, Nat 87, 104
Pierson, Eddie 14, 110
Pine, Courtney 175
Piron, A.J. 14
Pizzarelli, Bucky 146
Poindexter, Pony 132
Polcer, Ed 195, 198, 202, 205,
  206
Pope, Lee 27
Porcelli, Bobby 217
Porello, Rick 46
Porter, Bob, 191
Porter, Gene 149
Porter, Jake 87
Porter, Roy 131
Poston, Ken 157
Potter, Chris 256
Powell, Benny 100, 107–125,
  131, 305
Powell, Bud 26
Powell, Ian 7, 46
Powell, Mel 74
Powell, Seldon 52, 85
Price, Leontyne 293
Priester, Julian 51, 150
Prine, Bill 300
Pring, Bobby 222
Prior, Richard 257
Pruit, Ben 240
Puente, Tito 250
Pugh, Jim 301
Pullen, Don 250
Prysock, Red 141
Purnell, Theodore 13

Rader, Don 53, 166
Raglin, Junior 140
Reagan, Ronald 158

Red, Sonny 169
Redford, Robert 276
Redman, Don 25, 238
Reeves, Dianne 177
Rehak, Frank 169
Reid, Doris 226
Reid, Rufus 225–233
Reingold, Harry 64–66
Reinhart, Randy 207
René, Googie
René, Kid 13, 14
René, Leon 134
Rhodes, George 46, 51
Rich, Buddy 201, 220
Richard, Florida 127
Richard, Renald 129, 148
Richardson, Jerome 49, 132,
  286, 301
Rickenberg, Dave 224
Riddle, Nelson 152
Riley, Herlin 300
Riley, Herman 103, 144–154,
  305
Roach, Max 85, 129, 141
Robertson, Lester 159
Robey, Don 148
Robinson, Ikey 55
Robinson, Jim 14
Robinson, Prince 247
Robinson, Scott 222
Robinson, Spike 156
Rollins, Sonny 151, 224, 250,
  251, 257
Rongetti, Nick 63
Ross, Annie 280, 288
Rotondi, Jim 223, 285
Royal, Marshal 100, 101, 171,
  270
Rubin, Stan 198, 199
Rubottom, Doris 23
Ruiz, Hilton 249
Russell, Pee Wee 67, 69, 209
Russell, Snookums 23
Rutherford, Rudy 34
Ryan, Jimmy 202, 204, 209, 271
Ryan, Peter 305

Sanborn, David 256
Sanders, Pharoah 243
Sater, Fred 108, 305
Satterwhite, Harvey 140
Saunders, Red 50–52, 55
Sauter, Eddie 163
Sayles, Emanuel 13

Schaap, Phil 274
Schull, Tad 207
Schoenberg, Loren 221, 222, 301
Scott, Little Jimmy 138
Scott, Rhoda 127
Scott, Ronnie 8, 124, 125, 235, 236
Sebesky, Don 166, 301
Seeger, Pete 28
Segal, Joe 229
Severin, Chris 177
Shank, Bud 157, 160, 165
Shapiro, Dave 205
Sharpe, C. 283, 285
Shavers, Charlie 23, 64, 66, 67
Shaw, Artie 61, 159
Shaw, Arvell 206
Shaw, Jaleel 256
Sheils, Prince 244
Sheldon, Jack 100, 102, 130
Shines, Johnny 138
Short, Bobby 221, 222
Shorter, Wayne 247
Silver, Horace 189, 211
Simpkins, Andy 102, 229
Simmonds, Jim 23
Sims, Zoot 91, 146
Sinatra, Frank 75, 134
Skeat, Len 280
Slater, Chester 27
Slaughter, James 51
Small, Ernie 161, 163
Smalls, Clifton 'Cliff' 49
Smith, Bessie 146
Smith, Bill 161
Smith, Fletcher 26
Smith, Jimmy 145, 152, 154
Smith, Johnny 'Hammond' 189
Smith, Keely 157
Smith, Keith 205, 206
Smith, Leo 246
Smith, Mamie 20
Smith, Mauricio 250
Smith, Smitty 286
Smith, Sonelius 242
Smith, Stuff 57
Smith, 'Willie the Lion' 35, 41
Solomon, Clifford 131, 145
Spann, Les 148
Spencer, Victor 14
Sproles, Victor 287
Stamm, Marvin 215, 223
Staton, Dakota 192

Stephens, Stanley 177
Stephenson, Ernie 'Mix' 140
Staples, Mavis 291
Stevens, Leo 189
Stewart, Rex 104
Stewart, Sandy 71
Stewart, Slam 60
Still, William Grant 249, 258
Stitt, Sonny 91, 151
Strassburg, Jimmy 217
Stringer, Al 229
Stroman, Scott 226
Stubblefield, John 8, 234–263, 305
Stuckey, Jack 223
Sudhalter, Richard 68
Suggs, Milton 248, 249
Sullivan, Joe 63
Suonsari, Klaus 223
Swanson, Chris 216

Tabackin, Lew 204, 220, 301
Tabard, Dutchie 23
Tapscott, Horace 248
Tate, Buddy 38
Tate, Frank 195, 223
Tate, Grady 301
Tatum, Art 25, 57, 64, 141, 178, 209, 288,
Taylor, Billy 209
Taylor, Johnny 242
Taylor, Tubs 23
Teagarden, Jack 69
Teasley, Pops 141
Tedeschi, Simon 276
Temperley, Joe 222
Terry, Clark 38, 41, 49, 292–296, 305
Thigpen, Ben 49
Thigpen, Ed 49
Thomas, Herbie 21–23
Thomas, Joe 41, 116
Thomas, Kid 15, 16
Thomas, Millard 28
Thomas, Worthia 15
Thompson, Emery aka Umar Sharif 112, 148
Thompson, Johnny 47, 49
Threadgill, Henry 244, 246, 247
Thrower, Ruby 25
Tibbs, Harvey 207
Tinney, Al 30
Titone, Bill 295

Tolliver, Charles 248
Tompkins, Ross 101
Toots, Hartley 23
Tormé, Mel 161, 295
Totah, Nobby 218
Towles, Nat 83
Trice, Clarence 49
Tristano, Lennie 283
Trowers, Robert 138
Trujillo, Bill 162
Turner, Big Joe 272, 275
Turner, Danny 297, 298
Turner, Tina 229
Turney, Norris 140, 141, 221
Turrentine, Stanley 233, 257, 258
Turrentine, Tommy 253
Tyner, McCoy 235, 241, 280

Vacchiano, William 216
Vaché, Warren 202, 273, 275, 278, 280
Valente, Caterina 85, 297
Valentine, Kid Thomas 154
Vandross, Luther 261
Vaughan, Mathew 23, 46
Vaughan, Sarah 102, 269, 274, 293
Veal, Reginald 177
Venture, Charlie 117
Verteuil, Ed De 26
Vick, Harold 257
Victor, Valmar 125
Villepique, Paul 161
Vinson, Eddie 'Cleanhead' 20, 23, 26, 27, 43

Wadley, Spirey 34
Waits, Tom 187
Wald, Ted 283
Waldo, Terry 291
Wallace, Harold 37
Waller, Fats 238, 270
Walrath, Jack 254
Walter, Little 245
Walton, Cedar 163, 189
Wanzo, Mel 141, 142
Ware, Eugene 13
Ware, Wilbur 246
Warren, Earle 38
Warwick, Carl 'Bama' 23
Warwick, Dionne 189
Watson, Bobby 247
Watson, James 37, 189

Watson, John 35
Washington, Dinah 27, 51, 130, 133
Washington, Jack 38
Washington, Leon 50, 55
Washington, Peter 232
Waters, Ethel 190
Waters, Muddy 245
Watkins, Julius 248
Watson, Bobby 247
Watson, James 37
Watson, Jimmy 189
Watson, John 305
Watts, Noble 83
Webb, Chick 29
Webster, Ben 64, 70
Weedon, Paul 142
Wein, George 16
Weinstock, Bob 191
Weiss, Myron 30
Wells, Dicky 38, 110
Wells, Henry 25
Wellstood, Dick 271, 272, 274
Wendholt, Scott 223
Wess, Frank 221
Weston, Randy 108, 109, 254
Whigham, Jiggs 217
White, Chip 187
Whiteman, Paul 40
Whiteman, Wilberforce 40
Whitfield, Scott 207
Whittemore, Jack 257
Wichard, Al 'Cake' 131
Wiggins, Gerald 101
Wilber, Bob 206
Wilburn, Yorke 239, 240
Wilcox, Edwin 41
Willette, 'Baby Face' 244
Williams, Clarence 28
Williams, Cootie 20, 26, 30, 301
Williams, Floyd 'Horsecollar' 25
Williams, Franc 29, 52
Williams, Freddy
Williams, Howard 213, 220
Williams, Joe 54, 204, 257
Williams, Mary Lou 237, 248, 249
Williams, Stanley 147, 154
Willis, Larry 259
Wilson, Gerald 31–44, 49, 87, 221
Wilson, Jack 51

Wilson, Jackie 240
Wilson, Joe 35, 257
Wilson, John 272
Wilson, Nancy 33, 257, 269
Wilson, Robert 51
Wilson, Teddy 34
Winding, Kai 47
Wofford, Mike 273
Wolf, Howlin' 245, 246
Wonder, Stevie 238
Wood, C. 241
Woodman, Britt 100, 255, 301
Woods, Chris 295
Woods, Phil 71, 217
Woodyard, Sam 214
Workman, Reggie 223
Worth, Bobby 280
Wright, Leo 132, 163, 189
Wright, O.V. 242
Wright, Raeburn 294

Yanow, Scott 173
Yeager, Bobby 141
Yerbury, Professor 22
Yonkers, Vernon 83
Young, Bob 162
Young, Charles 188
Young, Gilbert 14
Young, Larry 250
Young, Lester 60, 69, 75, 83, 104, 131, 145, 186, 235, 247
Young, Snooky 39, 40, 49, 53, 97, 221
Young, Trummy 35, 62, 110

Zentner, Si 164, 215
Zigman, Eliott 218